The Chansons of Orlando di Lasso and Their Protestant Listeners

Eastman Studies in Music

Ralph P. Locke, Senior Editor
Eastman School of Music

(ISSN 1071–9989)

The Chansons of Orlando di Lasso and Their Protestant Listeners

Music, Piety, and Print in Sixteenth-Century France

Richard Freedman

University of Rochester Press

First published 2001
by the University of Rochester Press

The University of Rochester Press is an imprint of Boydell & Brewer, Inc.
668 Mt. Hope Avenue, Rochester, NY 14620, USA
and of Boydell & Brewer, Ltd.
P.O. Box 9, Woodbridge, Suffolk IP12 3DF, UK

ISBN 1–58046–075–5
ISSN 1071–9989

Library of Congress Cataloging-in-Publication Data
Freedman, Richard.
The chansons of Orlando di Lasso and their Protestant listeners : music, piety,
and print in sixteenth-century France / Richard Freedman.
p. cm. — (Eastman studies in music, ISSN 1071-9989 ; 15)
Includes bibliographical references (p.) and index.
ISBN 1-58046-075-5 (alk. paper)
1. Lasso, Orlando di, 1532–1594. Chansons.   2. Polyphonic chansons—16th
century—Texts.   3. Music—Religious aspects—Protestantism.
4. Protestantism—France—History—16th century.   5. Music printing—
France—16th century.
I. Title.   II. Series.

ML410.L3 F74 2000
782.4'3'092—dc21

00-059945

British Library Cataloguing-in-Publication Data
A catalogue record for this book is
available from the British Library

Designed and typeset by Isis-1 Corporation
Printed in the United States of America
This publication is printed on acid-free paper

Contents

Illustrations

Tables

Musical Examples

Preface

First Words

How did music touch sixteenth-century listeners? And what role did printed books of music play in shaping such meanings? This book attempts to give a partial answer to these related questions by examining the French chansons of Orlando di Lasso. Lasso's chansons were among the most widely circulated and beloved musical works of sixteenth-century Europe. But for one particular community of listeners these songs were at once inspiring and troublesome. French Protestants were frank in their recognition of the power of these tones to inspire them, even to draw the soul itself from the body. They were equally convinced, however, that Lasso's literary choices were utterly incompatible with their own moral and spiritual sensibilities. For some of these Huguenot listeners, printed books became the means by which Lasso's music might be "corrected," even as it had been the means by which Lasso the composer had been promoted in France, and elsewhere, too. But before turning to the story of why and how the Huguenots sought to transform Lasso's music through print, we should pause to consider a series of contexts and interpretive stances (of the sixteenth and twentieth centuries) that will frame this project.

Spiritual Sounds and Spiritual Texts

For Jean de Léry, sixteenth-century Calvinist missionary to coastal Brazil, the songs, ceremonies, and myths of the local Tupinamba culture were at once fascinating and troubling. In the late 1550s, when he was clandestine witness to the religious ceremonies of their shamanistic clan, the Caraïbes, Léry was deeply moved by what he called the "measured harmony" of the assembled ceremonial voices. "Whenever I remember it," he wrote some two decades later in his 1578 narrative of the journey, "my heart trembles; it seems their voices are still in my ears." Léry's native interpreter provided the French traveler with only a schematic outline of the songs he heard. They were, he reports, laments for departed ancestors, prayers for a promised afterlife, and the story of an ancient deluge in which the Tupinamba's ancestors alone took refuge from rising waters in the highest trees. "This last point," Léry confides in us, "which is the closest they come to the Holy Scriptures, I have heard them reiterate several times since. And, indeed, it is likely that from father to son they have heard something of the universal flood that occurred in the time of Noah. In keeping with the habit of men, which is always to corrupt the truth and turn it into falsehood, they have

added this fable. Being altogether deprived of writing, it is hard for them to retain things in their purity."[1]

Léry's narrative is thus not simply reportage of his travels in the New World. It is instead an attempt to confront the emotional power of his encounters with the unanticipated human diversity. Here Léry sensed divine order but also was reminded of his own belief in the efficacy of the written word as a means of preserving the authority of Scripture. As I hope to demonstrate, many of these same concerns are also at work in the Huguenot reception of French secular music of the sixteenth century, above all in the remarkable efforts undertaken to rewrite the chansons of Orlando di Lasso for pious listeners. The Lasso chansons, as any student of the sixteenth-century chanson will acknowledge, dominate the secular anthologies brought out by firms such as Le Roy et Ballard in Paris and Pierre Phalèse in Louvain. During the 1570s the French royal printer Le Roy collaborated directly with Lasso in issuing retrospective sets such as the *Mellange d'Orlande* of 1570 and *Les meslanges d'Orlande* of 1576 (see Figure 7.1), which brought together in a single set of partbooks the bulk of the composer's French secular music that had appeared in print to that time.[2]

Perhaps less well known, however, is the fact that the chansons of Lasso also figured quite prominently among the sacred parodies of secular songs issued by Protestant printers during the 1560s and 1570s. Scholars have not given much credence to these collections, in which some of Lasso's profane lyrics have been changed to convey spiritual meanings, presumably because the changes were not Lasso's own and thus tell us little about his own intentions. Devotional paraphrases of the sort found in Thomas Vautrollier's *Recueil du mellange d'Orlande* (London, 1570; see Figure 1.4), in Jean Pasquier's *Mellange d'Orlande de Lassus* (La Rochelle, 1575 and 1576; see Figure 1.3), or in Simon Goulart's *Thrésor de musique d'Orlande* ([Geneva], 1576, 1582, and 1594; see Figure 1.2) are self-consciously moralizing in their approach to Lasso's poetic texts.[3] The prefaces that accompany these collections, moreover, make plain a number of key assumptions about the special expressive power of his music.[4] The Protestant *contrafacta* of the Lasso chansons, as we shall discover, reveal much about how one community of musicians found a powerful spiritual essence in the sound of those pieces and how they sought to bind that essence to appropriate poetic texts. For these editors, and for their largely Protestant audience also, the "divins accords" of Lasso's privileged idiom—like the ancient songs of Léry's Tupinamba shamans—could be a suitable musical goal only if they were enlisted in the expression of an equally suitable written text. By examining the Lasso chansons and their appropriation by Huguenot editors, the present study explores how one group of Renaissance listeners encountered his music and discovered in it a mirror of their own spiritual sensibilities. My principal aim, in short, is to transfer Léry's experience of song and his concern for the Word to the chansons of Lasso as heard by Léry's fellow Protestants.

Lasso, Texts, and Tones

The subject of Lasso the man and Lasso the composer has spawned an immense scholarly legacy, much of it fascinated with the patent logocentrism of his finest works, especially with the power of those works to embody religious sensibilities. Commentaries on his settings of the *Penitential Psalms* by the sixteenth-century humanist and Munich court physician Samuel Quickelberg have long served as a touchstone for such explorations of Lasso's sacred music. In this body of works, the musical representation of the texts at hand brings their semantic and affective valences (in Quickelberg's words) "almost alive before the eyes."[5] During the early years of the seventeenth century the Rostock schoolmaster Joachim Burmeister likewise celebrated the vivid representational powers of Lasso's sacred music.[6] But no less important for Burmeister were the ways in which polyphonic musical gestures found in Lasso's works (and in others by masters of the later sixteenth century) enacted the conventional figures of classical rhetoric. Indeed, Burmeister's rhetorical exegesis of Lasso's motet "In me transierunt" is often cited as the first published example of an abstract "analysis" of a musical composition.[7]

More recently, David Crook suggests that certain of Lasso's compositions can be understood as expressions of Catholic piety and of Counter-Reformation concerns about the spiritual power of polyphonic music. At the center of Crook's argument are Lasso's Magnificats and the secular polyphony upon which several of them were based. The text of the Magnificat, he notes, is written in the voice of Mary, whose words were characterized by St. Peter Canisius (a Jesuit writer who served as a kind of spiritual advisor to the Munich court during the 1570s) as the verbal expression of a "purest soul": for this reason St. Peter valorized the Magnificats as paradigms of spiritual song. In Crook's view, Lasso's appropriation of madrigals, chansons (including some of his own), and instrumental music as the compositional basis of polyphonic settings of this Latin canticle constitutes an elevation of his source material (in which those borrowed tones were redirected towards a spiritual purpose).[8] We might also add that Lasso's approach clothes Mary's pious song in familiar garb.

At first glance this all seems very distant from the Huguenot *contrafacta* of Lasso's chansons. But the *contrafacta* and the "imitation" Magnificats share a number of common elements. Both of these repertories trope old sounds with new texts. They also both replace an "original" set of intentions with new ones presumed to meet the expectations of some particular audience. What is more, each of these appropriations attempts to discover spiritual meanings in familiar tones, allowing Lasso's music to "speak" in new ways. Finally, both the imitation Magnificats and the *contrafacta* of secular chansons provide a means of enacting private pieties through the shared hearing and performance of musical works. All of this serves to remind us that "sounds" per se—even sounds carefully crafted to the sense and structure of the words they originally set—could move between realms of experience normally thought of as distinct. We are reminded, too, of the ways in which the logocentrism that French Protestant listeners brought to this music differs perhaps not so greatly from the concerns of other Renaissance audiences.

Contrafacta as a Set of Interpretive Problems

Considered from the standpoint of Romantic aesthetic sensibilities, the very idea of a *contrafactum* seems absurd. "Our Western tradition," observes Umberto Eco, "forces us to take 'work' in the sense of a personal production which may well vary in the ways it can be received but which always maintains a coherent identity of its own and which displays the personal imprint that makes it a specific, vital, and significant act of communication."[9] At the very least the results of such radical postcompositional substitution of new words for old in the context of a musical work challenges many basic assumptions about the aesthetic unity of a work of art and about what we presume to be the authorial intentions it embodies. At worst, the makers of such *contrafacta* risk justifying a kind of theft on the grounds of the utility of the result. Like pious Robin Hoods, Pasquier, Goulart, and their consociates claim for their edited versions of the Lasso's chansons a meaning more authentic than that of the composer himself, inasmuch as their new texts redirect the emotional valences of his music to a higher moral purpose than did the original lyrics.

Lasso certainly did not intend or even authorize the new texts attached to his music by his Protestant editors. To the contrary, from what we know of his special authorial privilege over the publication of his music in France, there is good reason to think that he would have objected to these publications as an infringement upon his right of intellectual property alone. But elaborate troping of the sort encountered in the Lasso *contrafacta,* which plays upon text-tone relationships at work in the original chansons, offers important clues about the private meanings that one small group of Renaissance listeners sought to attach to those compositions. Of course we cannot know in any direct way exactly what Huguenot listeners heard when they sang Lasso's chansons, any more than we can hope to recover Lasso's original intentions for his works. Our aim in this context should not be to discover some singular, authentic, or rarefied "meaning" for these chansons. Instead, we should try to articulate some of the processes by which such works can be heard and felt in different ways, and how these multiple hearings are in some respects contingent upon the mental habits, emotional sensibilities, and even spiritual attitudes of the listeners who confront these tones. This is less an objective accounting of *what* was heard by some group of Renaissance listeners than an exploration of *how* they understood the music they encountered.[10]

The Plan of This Study

I begin by examining the place of music in Calvinist thought, ideas that help to set the *contrafacta* books against a backdrop of Renaissance approaches to music and personal piety. I next turn to the story of how Protestant printers (notably those active in Lyons and Geneva) issued books of what might loosely be called the Huguenot "chansonnier": that diverse repertory of popular *timbres, chansons spirituelles, chansons historiques,* and *contrafacta* of polyphonic chansons in collections intended for use by Huguenot musicians. These repertories, like the books of *contrafacta* based on Lasso's chansons, were of course not destined for congregational singing but were instead envisaged as domestic forms of spiritual expression. Indeed, the prefaces, dedications, and other liminary materials from the books of Lasso's "revised" chansons offer a particularly clear picture of why Protestant editors were drawn to this composer's music, and the sorts of listeners for whom the "purified" chansons were so spiritually effective. Many of the themes expressed in the *contrafacta* texts assembled here echo those found in the small but significant body of devotional writings that emerged in France during the 1560s and 1570s, a period of profound religious and cultural tensions between Catholics and Protestants in that kingdom. This devotional literature, as I argue in subsequent chapters of my book, can serve as a frame through which we can attempt to "listen along" with the Huguenot audiences who encountered these chansons.

With all of these contexts in mind, the second through sixth chapters of my study turn to the chansons themselves. Here I begin with a survey of Lasso's poetic choices for his chansons, and what his musical responses to these texts reveal about his relationship to the chanson tradition of the sixteenth century. The principal method of these middle chapters is to use the correspondence and divergence among rival *contrafacta* texts as a means of discovering what sorts of musical gestures Protestant listeners found significant in Lasso's chansons. In all of this I attend to details of the works themselves, and how one and the same musical gesture might serve (or fail to serve) a different text among the various "versions" of the chanson. My own critical explorations of these pieces, therefore, are readings of other readings, and as such are often comparative, using the rival "purified" chansons as ways of understanding how different readers and listeners heard the sounds that accompany these "already interpreted" texts. In so doing, I consider overall patterns of musical form, rhythmic and melodic gestures, polyphonic texture, and cadential or tonal structures as they variously articulate, represent, or give rhetorical and emotional force to the form, language, and ideas presented in the literary texts at hand.

Not all *contrafacta,* it seems, are equally successful in making use of the significant gestures and ideas that typify Lasso's text setting. Some *contrafacta* are simply a series of missed opportunities. But others do a surprisingly good job of crafting new words to suit these musical moments. A few actually find significance in musical ideas that had no great importance when heard in the context of the original poems. Here I proceed according to thematic groups, picking and choosing what I consider to be works representative of the sorts of spiritual concerns at hand in the *contrafacta* repertory as a whole: works taken over into the spiritual chansonniers with little or no change; revisions of poems by Ronsard; and texts that offer advice or admonish the listener. The transformation of lyrical love poetry into a spiritual register, I have found, is especially rich in musical possibilities. Here, for instance, we find simple statements of fidelity of a sort that figure in countless French chansons of the first half of the sixteenth century. These themes of service apparently meshed seamlessly with the relationship between believer and deity. Still other *contrafacta* give poetic expression to personal prayer. Like the ardent love poetry they revise, these texts are lyrical, first-person contemplations of the self, albeit ones that do not regard the conditions of love, but instead meditate on the emotional effects of moral transgressions and the hopes of salvation. Slipping between secular and spiritual registers, the music that accompanies these chansons often serves to emphasize, to express, and to enact in sound the very sorts of conditions described in the poems, making these works particularly apt embodiments of the devotional ideals of Protestant listeners.

I next turn to the musical organization of the books of *contrafacta* devoted to Lasso's chansons. Here I show how these volumes were not random collections of spiritualized chansons, but that they were collections directly modeled on the great Lasso chansonniers issued by the Parisian firm of Le Roy et Ballard. I explore in particular Le Roy et Ballard's great Lasso collection, the *Mellange d'Orlande* of 1570, and its expanded republication, *Les meslanges d'Orlande* of 1576. In these and other books devoted exclusively to Lasso's music, we find clear evidence of the increasing sensibility of Le Roy (and no doubt Lasso, who actively collaborated with his editor during this period) to the modal organization of these volumes. I also argue that Simon Goulart's revision of this modal plan can be understood as an attempt to use modal ordering (although not the individual modes) as way of preparing readers for the spiritual sensibilities that Goulart uncovers among the chansons. The increasing comprehensiveness of the Le

Roy–Lasso compilations, in sum, bears witness to Lasso's recognition of the importance of the press as a means of creative control. But in the hands of Protestant editors like Goulart, that same medium became a means to correct what they understood to be the spiritual failings of Lasso's chansons as a whole. By imposing a systematic musical plan upon the entire repertory, I argue, Goulart's printed "treasury" can quite literally become a place where old sounds are invested with new meanings.

The final chapter turns our attention to questions of authorship, piracy, and printed books. Here I trace the special circumstances that surrounded Lasso's collaboration with the official French music printer Le Roy, above all the remarkable authorial privilege that Lasso was granted by the French king to control the publication of his works. Viewed in the context of this authorial control and official approval of the chansons found in *Les meslanges d'Orlande* and the other great Lasso–Le Roy chansonniers, these volumes, I suggest, are not just the musical models of the Protestant *contrafacta* books, they are the ideological counterparts of those volumes. Each attempts to shape—for different communities of readers—particular versions of the composer's musical production.

Acknowledgments

This study could not have been completed without the help and understanding of friends and colleagues. To the Provost's office and the Whitehead Faculty Development Fund of Haverford College I owe many thanks for funds that gave me time to write (during 1992–93 and again in 1996–97) and that helped buy microfilms and other important materials for my work. Wolfson College at Oxford University kindly played host to me during my 1992–93 sabbatical, during which time my first thoughts on the *contrafacta* began to develop. Margaret Bent, Bonnie Blackburn, Jeffrey Dean, Leofranc Holford-Strevens, John Milsom, and Rob Wegman were the ideal circle of friends for the airing of this and other work in progress. To Ignace Bossuyt and other conveners of the International Musicological Society colloquium *Orlandus Lassus and his Time* I also owe thanks for including my first paper on the *contrafacta* books, and for engendering the sort of scholarly exchange that kept the project going. Henri Vanhulst (Brussels) and Bernhold Schmid (Munich) were particularly welcoming of these new thoughts and generous with their own ideas. Colleagues at the *Music as Heard* conference convened at Princeton in 1997 by Rob Wegman provided a wonderfully rich range of contexts for my developing ideas. Librarians in Oxford, London, Paris, La Rochelle, Geneva, Regensburg, and Munich kindly fielded requests for information, books, and microfilms. Portions of the Preface and Chapter 6 appeared in my essay, "The Lassus Chansons and Their Protestant Listeners of the Late Sixteenth Century,"

The Musical Quarterly 82 (1998): 564–85. I am grateful to Oxford University Press for permission to reprint this material here.

Back in Haverford a number of colleagues and students helped to keep my thoughts in continuous development. Marcel Gutwirth corrected and improved my translations. The Work in Progress group (especially Paul Smith, David Dawson, Jim Krippner-Martinez, and Laurie Hart) forced me to articulate my musical thoughts in a broader context of ideas about printing and piety. Students in *The Renaissance Text and Its Musical Readers* patiently listened to parts of the work in progress, and some of their seminar papers have shaped my own thoughts on individual pieces explored in the book. I am especially grateful to Michelle Mazzocco, Lauren Theodore, and Nemesio Valle III for sharing their work with me, and for allowing me to draw upon it here. Jason Gersh read the final text of the book, and offered many useful suggestions.

I owe particular thanks to Jeanice Brooks, David Crook, Susan Jackson, Patrick Macey, Jessie Ann Owens, and Harold Powers. Lawrence Bernstein and Kate van Orden gave detailed reports at subsequent stages of the project. I am especially grateful for the time they took to improve my work. Ralph Locke, senior editor of the Eastman Studies in Music, and Louise Goldberg, managing editor of the University of Rochester Press, were likewise invaluable at every stage of this work.

Funds to defray the costs of producing musical examples (deftly typeset by Hyunjung Choi) were provided through the generous assistance of the Manfred Bukofzer Publication Endowment Fund of the American Musicological Society.

Last, though certainly not least, is my debt to my family, who endured for months while a sometimes absent, often distracted son/husband/father toiled to answer the ultimate question: "Is he done yet?"

Editorial Principles

The musical examples and poetic texts have been transcribed from original sources and edited according to a number of basic principles. In the musical transcriptions I have reduced all note values by one half, and of course both added bar lines and arranged the individual parts in score format. Flat and sharp signs appearing on the staff itself are found in the original sources. Those appearing above the staff in the modern transcriptions are implied by contrapuntal contexts—in order to avoid forbidden intervals with other signed alterations, or in order to create complete cadences. Ligatures have been marked above the notes they connect, and serve to confirm text underlay by preventing a change of syllable.

The musical readings are those of the 1570 and 1576 editions of Le Roy et Ballard's *Les meslanges d'Orlande*. "D'amours me va" comes from the *Chanson nouvelles* of 1571. The musical readings found here agree in all details (rhythms, pitches, flat and natural signs, ligatures) with the extant partbooks of the various *contrafacta* sets prepared by Vautrollier, Pasquier, and Goulart. I have otherwise made no critical comparisons of the Le Roy *Les meslanges d'Orlande* volumes with other printed editions of the individual Lasso chansons.

In the literary texts, the interchangable letters i/j and u/v have been standardized in accordance with modern spellings. I have added the *cedilla* to distinguish the soft from the hard c, and have in some places added the acute accent to distinguish the accented from the mute e. I have also regularized (according to a majority rule) minor orthographic variation among the various voice parts of individual chansons. In cases where the reading of a poetic text in Le Roy's edition departs significantly in wording or orthography from standard literary sources of texts by Marot and Ronsard, I have offered the Le Roy readings and explained such departures in the accompanying notes in the body of the text.

Le Roy et Ballard's typesetters, as well as the typesetters who worked for Vautrollier, Pasquier, and Goulart, seem to have been especially keen to coordinate texts with the musical notation to which they are to be sung (see Figures 6.1, 6.2, and 6.3). Phrases, individual words, and at times even individual syllables are neatly aligned to reflect beginnings and ends of phrases, as well as appropriate places for the repetition of lines, parts of lines, and individual words. I have realized such text repetitions, whether indicated with written out text or with item marks ("ii"), without further designation in the modern editions. In some cases individual words or groups of them were abbreviated with conventional signs, which I have also expanded without special remarks. The original prints use capital letters at the start of each poetic line. I have retained this practice (though not in the

case of text repetitions), and have lightly punctuated the texts with com-
mas between lines and between repetitions of lines or parts of lines.

Of course in the original *contrafacta* sets the new texts appear beneath
each of the voice parts. In my modern editions, however, the texts of the
contrafacta appear only beneath the Bassus part, aligned with the musical
notes of this voice part. The reader will in some cases need to infer the
exact placement of *contrafacta* texts relative to the upper voices, but since
the original texts may already be found there, this should not be too difficult. By laying the texts out in this way I have sought to conserve space and
make the examples as uncluttered as possible, but still allow readers to
compare directly the Protestant readings of the chansons with the original
versions of these works. In any event my underlay for the spiritual versions
of the chansons is based upon the surviving partbooks from the various
sets of *contrafacta*: the Tenor partbook from Pasquier's book of four-voice
chansons; the Tenor and Superius partbooks from his set of five-voice chansons; and the Contratenor of the 1594 edition of Goulart's *Le thrésor de
musique d'Orlande*. The alignment of text and musical notation is very
clear in these books (with clear indication of text repetition and syllabifica-
tion), and leaves little doubt as to the intent of the Protestant editors with
respect to the other voice parts.

Abbreviations

Boetticher Lasso:
Wolfgang Boetticher, *Orlando di Lasso und seine Zeit, 1532–1594*, rev. ed., 2 vols. (Wilhelmshaven: Florian Noetzel, 1998).

Chansons nouvelles:
Orlando di Lasso, *Livre de chansons nouvelles à cinc parties, avec deux dialogues: à huict* (Paris: Adrian Le Roy et Robert Ballard, 1571).

Lasso Chansons:
Orlando di Lasso, *Chansons from the Atelier of Le Roy and Ballard*, ed. Jane Bernstein, 4 vols., The Sixteenth-Century Chanson, 11–14 (New York: Garland, 1987).

Lasso Werke:
Orlando di Lasso, *Sämtliche Werke*, ed. F. X. Haberl and A. Sandberger, rev. ed., edited by Hörst Leuchtmann, 21 vols. (Leipzig, 1894; reprint, Leipzig and Wiesbaden: Breitkopf und Härtel, 1968–1990). [The chansons appear in vols. 12, 14, and 16.]

Les meslanges d'Orlande:
Orlando di Lasso, *Les meslanges d'Orlande de Lassus, contenantz plusieurs chansons à III, V, VI, VIII, X parties: reveuz par luy, et augmentez* (Paris: Adrian Le Roy et Robert Ballard, 1576).

Le thrésor de musique d'Orlande [1582]:
Orlando di Lasso, *Le thrésor de musique d'Orlande de Lassus . . . contenant ses chansons françoises, italiennes, et latines, à quatre, cinq et six parties: augmenté de plus de la moitié en ceste seconde edition* ([Geneva]: [S. Goulart], 1582).

Le thrésor de musique d'Orlande [1594]:
Orlando di Lasso, *Le thresor de musique d'Orlande de Lassus . . . contenant ses chansons françoises, italiennes, et latines, à quatre, cinq, et six parties: reveu et corrigé diligemment en ceste troisieme edition* ([Cologny]: [Paul Marceau], 1594).

Mellange d'Orlande 1575:
Orlando di Lasso, *Mellange d'Orlande de Lassus, contenant plusieurs chansons, à quatre parties, desquelles la lettre profane a esté changée en spirituelle* (La Rochelle: Haultin, 1575).

Mellange d'Orlande 1576:
  Orlando di Lasso, *Mellange d'Orlande de Lassus, contenant plusieurs chansons, à cinq, et huit parties, desquelles la lettre profane a este changée en spirituelle* (La Rochelle: Haultin, 1576).

Mellange d'Orlande:
  Orlando di Lasso, *Mellange d'Orlande de Lassus, contenant plusieurs chansons, tant en vers latin qu'en ryme françoyse, à quatre, cinq, six, huit dix parties* (Paris: Adrian Le Roy et Robert Ballard, 1570).

Recueil du mellange d'Orlande:
  Orlando di Lasso, *Recueil du mellange d'Orlande de Lassus, contenant plusieurs chansons tant en vers latins qu'en ryme françoyse, à quatre, et cinq parties* (London: Thomas Vautrollier, 1570).

RISM-A
  Répertoire international des sources musicales. International Inventory of Musical Sources. Serie A: Einzeldrucke vor 1800, 11 vols. (Kassel: Bärenreiter, 1971–79).

Thrésor de musique d'Orlande:
  Orlando di Lasso, *Thrésor de musique d'Orlande de Lassus, contenant ses chansons à quatre, cinq, et six parties* ([Geneva]: [S. Goulart], 1576).

Chapter 1

Music, Piety, and Printing in Sixteenth-Century France

Printing and Piety among the Huguenots

It seems no coincidence that the Lasso *contrafacta* books were issued in centers closely associated with the Protestant book trade at the very height of the social upheavals that marked the French wars of religion. Faced at first with oppression and later with obliteration, during the 1560s and 1570s the Huguenot minority had sought refuge in provincial cities like Lyons and La Rochelle, or emigrated to Calvin's Geneva, and England.[1] Families active in the print trades (as well as other literate artisans) had from the outset of the French Reformation been attracted to the Huguenot cause in disproportionate numbers, with the result that these same urban centers were also focal points of the Protestant press.[2] During the second half of the sixteenth century, the great printing firms of La Rochelle, Lyons, and Geneva issued an overwhelming number of books for use by Protestant readers: French Bibles, Psalters, sermons, commentaries on sacred texts, as well as poetry, political pamphlets, and placards. Indeed, the books of *contrafacta* of the Lasso chansons were prepared by printers and editors known as much for their literary and theological imprints as for their musical ones. The expatriate Huguenot Thomas Vautrollier, for instance, is best remembered for his publications of the writings of Calvin, not for his book of Lasso *contrafacta* (see Figure 1.4) or his work with William Byrd.[3] Goulart (see Figure 1.1) edited quite a few music prints: in addition to the Lasso *contrafacta* books he also prepared editions of Lasso's motets,[4] and *contrafacta* of chansons by Toulouse composers Anthoine de Bertrand and Guillaume Boni.[5] But he was also an editor of everything from Seneca to Montaigne in versions prepared for Calvinist readership.[6] Lastly, in the Protestant stronghold of La Rochelle on the western coast of France, the Haultin press offered Protestant readers an impressive range of texts.[7] Thanks to his extensive clandestine contacts with colleagues in Lyons, Geneva, and elsewhere, Haultin afforded readers ready access to the latest offerings of other Protestant presses. Thus in addition to Haultin's own editions of *chansons spirituelles* (see Figure 1.5),[8] books of Lasso's motets,[9] and of course the *contrafacta* of the Lasso chansons (see Figures 1.3 and

6.2), readers in La Rochelle could obtain political discourse, Biblical exegesis and commentary, anthologies of poetry, and other books printed in
Lyons, Geneva, and elsewhere. Here, for instance, we find Goulart's important chronicle of recent persecutions of fellow Protestants in France, as
well as his important edition of *La Sepmaine,* the creation week commentary by the humanist poet Guillaume Saluste du Bartas.

Clearly the Huguenots were a community of readers acutely aware of
the power of the printed word as a weapon in the battle for spiritual and
political authority. It should thus come of little surprise that the volumes
devoted to the spiritual "purification" of the Lasso chansons are not merely
compilations of edited songs, but books in which the current selection—
and even sequence—of songs depends significantly upon still other printed
books of music. In troping the "livres de Paris," (as Goulart calls them)
Protestant editors recognized both that their readers would have been aware
of the existence of the original books and that they would have understood
the need for the appropriation of form as well as of content. Indeed, Huguenot printers and book sellers had long colluded to circumvent the attempts by parliamentary and royal authorities at censorship and commercial control that were the mainstay of the French book privilege system
during the sixteenth century. Books that appropriated other books were
simply standard practice in the Protestant book trade of the day.[10] As we
have noted, Haultin's editions of Lasso borrow heavily from Parisian imprints, while Goulart's editions of chansons by Lasso and other composers
either conveniently neglect to mention a place of publication and printer,
or offer a fictitious one instead.[11]

The Lasso *Contrafacta* Books and Their Audiences

Simon Goulart (see Figure 1.1) played an important role in the editorial
work on literatures related to his *contrafacta* of the Lasso chansons. Plainly
his Genevan audiences would have been only too familiar with the cultural, religious, and political crises given voice in the redacted versions of
these chansons. "For some time now," he wrote to his dedicatee, Philippe
de Pas, in the preface to the first edition (see Figure 1.2) of his *Thrésor de
musique d'Orlande* of 1576,

> I have heard that you wanted me to present to you this volume of the chansons
> of Orlande de Lassus, so altered that one may sing them or play them upon
> instruments without soiling the mouths or offending Christian ears. Since you
> exhorted me to put my hand to it, I take your wish as my command. As I allowed
> my imagination to take hold, I changed in several of these chansons that which
> appeared to me detestable. This undertaking remained shrouded on account of
> the terrible events we have seen of late.[12]

Figure 1.1. Portrait of Simon Goulart, from an engraving of the mid-seventeenth century. Reproduced by permission of the Bibliothèque publique et universitaire, Geneva.

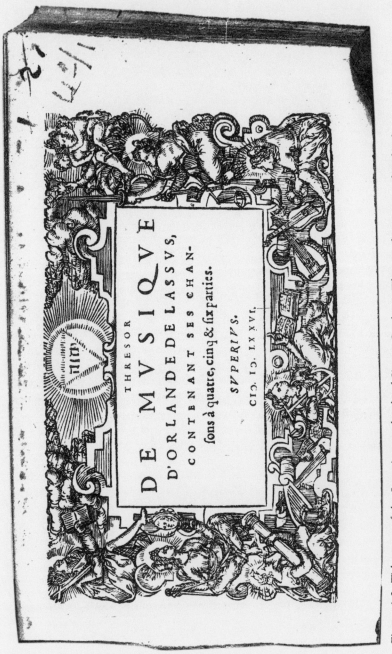

Figure 1.2. Title page of the Superius partbook of Simon Goulart's *Thrésor de musique d'Orlande 1575* (Geneva, 1576). Reproduced by permission of the Bayerische Staatsbibliothek, Munich.

Jean Pasquier likewise reminded his readers in La Rochelle of the difficult circumstances that motivated his editorial enterprise, offering music that might "give some refreshment to poor Christian souls that seem transformed by so many afflictions that press upon us from all sides." "After retiring to this place," he wrote in the preface to his first book of Lasso *contrafacta,*

> in order to save myself from the miseries and calamities of this most difficult and dangerous age, for fear that I would not be found wasted or useless in the church of God, I decided to make music my calling, offering to my brothers the benefit of the little talent that the Lord imbued in me, in order to put it to good use.[13]

Pasquier himself unfortunately remains mostly an enigma, for aside from the *contrafacta* volumes (see Figures 1.3 and 1.5) little is known about the man or his career.[14] Of Pasquier's immediate audience we can be a little more certain: Jean addressed his books of Lasso *contrafacta* to Catherine de Parthenay[15] and François de la Noüe,[16] members of two families with illustrious reputations as protectors of Huguenot causes and of the arts. "You did me this honor," he wrote to the latter patron, "of asking me to come make music in your house, in order (by this means) to help you to chase away care and sadness that these civil wars have brought you."[17] It thus seems likely that the "spiritualized" music offered here was heard in domestic circumstances rather than as part of any congregational worship.

In addition, liminary poems from the editions likewise mention a half-dozen women whom Pasquier calls his students ("disciples"). These include Marie Blanc,[18] Judith Mage,[19] Jaquette Rolland,[20] Susanne Poussart,[21] Elizabeth de la Forest,[22] and Esther Boisseau.[23] Several of these women were members of important Protestant families with long traditions of literacy and interest in the literary arts.[24] Indeed, among several of the *contrafacta* in Pasquier's (and Goulart's) book are texts that speak directly to women (the reworkings of Marot's "Fleur de quinze ans," for instance) or speak from a feminine perspective (as in the revisions of "Quand mon mari"). Such poems echo an extensive tradition of Calvinist writing on the proper roles that women play in domestic life, the sorts of spiritual attitudes they ought to espouse, and biblical women as *exempla.*[25] As it happens, among the Lasso *contrafacta* by Pasquier and also by Goulart are texts that touch not only on the proper conduct of women, but on the primacy of sacred texts, and above all on the proper conduct of the self.

The readership of Thomas Vautrollier's *Recueil du mellange d'Orlande* (see Figure 1.4) is in some respects still more difficult to measure than either Pasquier's or Goulart's prints, which seem to have been conceived rather narrowly for the needs of Protestant audiences. Vautrollier himself was part of the important Huguenot community that settled in England

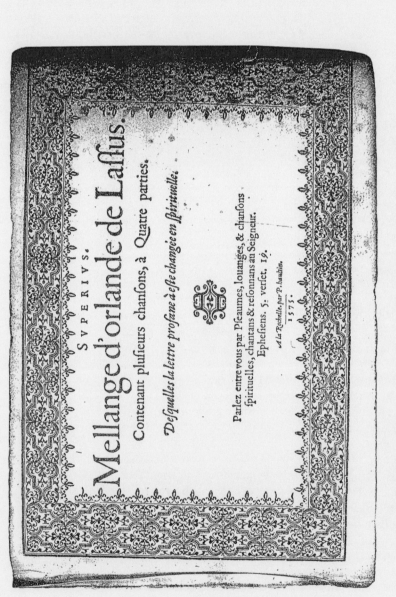

Figure 1.3. Title page from the Superius partbook of Jean Pasquier's *Mellange d'Orlande 1575* (La Rochelle, 1575). Reproduced by permission of the Governing Body of Christ Church, Oxford.

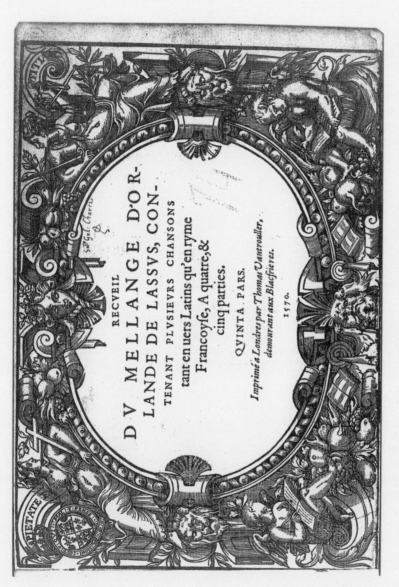

Figure 1.4. Title page from the Quintus partbook of Thomas Vautrollier's *Recueil du mellange d'Orlande* (London, 1570). Reproduced by permission of the Bodleian Library, Oxford.

following the start of the violent persecution of Protestants in France. Originally from the paper-making center of Troyes, he had served for a time as a bookseller for the Antwerp publishing firm of Plantin before undertaking publications of his own in London (and later in Scotland). Many of his nonmusical imprints were of Reformation texts. It would seem logical, then, that the French preface of the *Recueil du mellange d'Orlande* was aimed to appeal to a Huguenot readership in England.

On the other hand, we must also note that Vautrollier's dedicatee, the Count of Arundel, was a member of a family with a long history of Catholic sympathies in Protestant England. In this sense, and in Vautrollier's repeated praise for the tolerance of the English queen, we can suppose that the urge to make Lasso's music more spiritual was one that transcended the seemingly wide gulf that separated Protestants and Catholics. Indeed, Joseph Kerman once observed that Vautrollier's *contrafacta* "were neutral enough to dedicate to his Catholic patron," censoring some of the more ribald language of Lasso's chosen lyrics ("joined with serious texts and removed from all impurity" is the editor's claim),[26] while simultaneously avoiding overtly Protestant positions. We should note, too, that in addition to containing fewer pieces than either Pasquier's or Goulart's books Vautrollier's print also offers a greater proportion of the pieces that it does contain without any change to the lyrics at all.[27] This careful skirting of sectarian divisions, Kerman suggests, may be why Vautrollier seems to have "hidden" Lasso's four-voice setting of the Calvinist hymn tune "Du fonds de ma pensée" (it is the only piece in the print that did not also appear in the original *Mellange d'Orlande* issued by Le Roy in 1570) among the five-voice pieces of the *Recueil du mellange d'Orlande*.[28]

The Aims and Assumptions of the Lasso *Contrafacta* Books

Above all else, the editors of the books of *contrafacta* were fascinated by the inherent power they found in Lasso's music. They recognized in his compositional voice a means to draw the soul itself out of the body and into some ideal spiritual plane. "For my part," Goulart confesses, "I have found in music, and especially in [that] of Orlande, powerful remedies for various injuries to the soul. . . . Who has not a soul touched and sweetly drawn forth from the body by the melodious concord of such beautiful music as that of Orlande?"[29] Vautrollier, too, freely admitted that in music—and especially in that of Lasso—he felt a powerful force that served to "ravish" the soul of the listener. In some important ways, then, Vautrollier's and Goulart's remarks about music and its influence over the spirit echo comments that appear in the writings of their Catholic contemporaries, including Pierre de Ronsard and Pontus de Tyard, who embraced Neoplatonic ideas (expressed most plainly in the Greek writer's *Phaedo* and in *Timaeus*) about the immortality of the soul and its affinities with harmony.[30]

Despite their sectarian differences, all of these writers were fascinated by the seemingly unmediated access that music afforded to the spirit. And like their Catholic contemporaries, Huguenot editors seem to have invested in music (again with Plato's encouragement) the power to restore human society itself. Vautrollier, for instance, alludes to the metaphysical harmony that exists among the various parts of a well-ruled state (such as that of his adopted England) whose workings compare favorably to the concordant union of polyphonic parts in a motet ("despite the differences," he observes, "among them they make no discord at all").[31] Such speculation about the parallels between musical and social harmony recall, of course, Plato's famous views from *Republic* on the connection between ideal aesthetic and political forms. Vautrollier even goes so far as to imagine what Plato might have thought of Lasso's exemplary music. Indeed, it was the hope that Lasso's chansons could serve to sustain social harmony that seemed in this instance to have prompted in Vautrollier the urge to print these works in the first place, albeit in a form that gave them distance from "all impurity" by linking them to appropriate texts.

We should also recall that the ascription to music of such metaphysical effects as the transport of the soul and the restoration of human society had long been a subtext of Calvinist thought on song and spirituality. Already in the first printed edition of the Genevan Psalter (in 1543), Calvin wrote of music "that it has a secret and almost incredible power to move our hearts in one way or another."[32] Yet along with this recognition of the spiritual potential of music came a simultaneous concern about its sensuous effects and how to control them. For Calvin, the solution was to be found not by discriminating the effects of one sound from another, but instead by making the potentially salutary effects of music upon the listener dependent on the kinds of verbal texts to which it was bound, for in this way he hoped "to moderate the use of music to make it serve all that is of good repute. . . ."[33]

This same assumption underpins the Huguenot approach to Lasso's music. Indeed, the concern about appropriate texts takes on special significance for the Lasso chanson repertory, since in his works, as editors of the *contrafacta* books readily acknowledge, the alliance between text and tone is particularly acute: Orlande designed "according to the words," Goulart wrote in the preface to his *Thrésor de musique d'Orlande* of 1576, "in which respect he is excellent (as he is an all aspects of this liberal science) beyond all musicians of our era."[34] Addressing the first of his Lasso chanson volumes to Catherine de Parthenay, Pasquier likewise gives eloquent testimony both to the esteem with which Lasso's compositions were held among members of this new church and to the ideal alliance between what he called "l'harmonie de la voix" and "l'affection de la parolle":

> I thought that I might do my Christian duty by purging these very graceful and
> pleasant chords of such evils and filth with which they have been soiled. I instead
> returned them to their true and natural subject, namely to sing of the power,
> sagacity, and goodness of the Eternal. Having therefore solicited several of my
> friends and borrowed from them some *cantiques* of similar subject, in place of
> these lewd and vain reveries, I accommodated these verses to the music. Notice
> the extent to which the harmony of the voice corresponds to the affection of the
> word, as much as it is able.[35]

Above all, the avowed purpose of these new versions was thus the restoration of music in general (an art whose true purpose was the glorification of
the divine and the relief of human sorrow) and in particular of the "divins
accords d'Orlande," which Pasquier has snatched back from profanity "like
precious stones from a vile mud-pit."[36] Goulart, too, articulates a similar
stance as justification for his editorial intervention in Lasso's works: "In
removing several or many of these words and accommodating them (as
well as it has been possible for me) to the Music," he explains, "I rendered
these chansons for the most part honest and Christian. . . ."[37] This same
moralizing tone, in which the persuasive effects of music upon its listeners
are permitted only so long as they are tied to an appropriately devotional
text, of course, enjoyed long circulation in Calvinist writings on music,
language, and spirituality.

Already by the middle years of the sixteenth century a number of Protestant composers (most importantly Claude Goudimel and Loys Bourgeois)
took careful steps to create a musical repertory of Psalm harmonizations
(using the new French translations of those texts by Theodore de Bèze and
Clément Marot) suitable for domestic devotion among adherents of the
new faith.[38] The use of contrapuntal music in congregational worship was
never fully embraced by the Calvinist theocracy in Geneva, but the background of Calvinist thought on music and its proper spiritual effects on
performers and listeners certainly informed musical practice and even music pedagogy among Protestant musicians. In *Le droict chemin de musique*
(1550), for instance, Loys Bourgeois bitterly complained of the salacious-
ness of the secular music of his day, preferring instead "choses sainctes et
divines," meaning in this case a Psalm or spiritual song.[39] At the heart of
this approach to music, then, were strong convictions about the primacy of
the written word in general and sacred texts in particular: Bourgeois's method
book calls for the abandonment of the old didactic *gamme,* by which he
means the Guidonian hand, in favor of studying music "en papier aussi
bien que les autres sciences." In this respect the "droict chemin" of
Bourgeois's title designates both a proper pedagogical tool (affirming the
authority of a written text over an unwritten *aide mémoire*) and a correct
spiritual goal (reclaiming music as an expression of personal piety rather
than a form of entertainment). For Bourgeois and doubtless for the editors

of the Lasso *contrafacta* books as well, music was a maker of moral fiber rather than a manifestation of worldly civility.

Ironically Bourgeois himself was the object of some of the very efforts to control music that he himself promoted. Having arrived in Geneva in the middle years of the 1540s to succeed Guillaume Franc as *maître de chant* for the Huguenot refuge, Bourgeois began to play an active role in the publication of Psalm tunes and modest Psalm harmonizations. At first he collaborated with the Beringen brothers in Lyons, who were apparently more experienced than any printer in Geneva with the problems of setting music in type. But by 1551 Bourgeois supervised the publication in Geneva of a monophonic Psalter (the *Pseaumes octantetrois*) expanded to include French translations of Psalms newly versified by Bèze at Calvin's request. Bourgeois also took the opportunity to make a few small changes in a dozen of the tunes that had been inadvertently corrupted in the earlier Lyonnais imprints of the monophonic Psalter. His *Avertissement* alerted readers to the changes and why they were necessary. Surprisingly, the print was not well received by the Genevan Council, who promptly had Bourgeois arrested (and briefly imprisoned) for what they took to be unauthorized alterations that Bourgeois had made to official melodies and because his *Avertissement* cited conciliar approval when none had been granted. Apparently only the intervention of Calvin himself saved Bourgeois from censure. Clearly Genevan authorities were keen to control the musical press, and to control the sounds that such texts helped to prescribe.[40]

The Psalms, of course, held special political importance for Protestants, and became a means of public solidarity as well as congregational worship. Barbara Diefendorf, for instance, has recently shown how Psalm tunes were sung in the streets even as Huguenots were persecuted by the intolerant.[41] Political chansons, poems that recounted important events or skirmishes, and that lambasted enemies of the Protestant cause, form another subgenre of French texts that circulated among Huguenot audiences during the middle years of the sixteenth century.[42]

Spiritual *contrafacta* of popular chanson tunes (or *timbres*) form another important element in the Protestant musical repertory. This practice can in some respects be seen as a specifically Huguenot expression of popular musical piety, much in the same way that the French *noël* and Italian *lauda* served for other communities of believers drawn from the ranks of the urban populace.[43] In the middle years of the sixteenth century there also appeared a growing printed repertory of *chansons spirituelles*, poems on religious themes that were crafted in expectation of being set to music. The most famous example of this genre of Protestant song, Guillaume Guéroult's "Susanne un jour," as it happens, leads us directly into the complex publication history that characterizes the Protestant press, and also into one of the musical traditions that figure among the Lasso chansons. Guéroult's chanson first appeared set to music in Didier Lupi Second's *Pre-*

mier livre de chansons spirituelles, issued in Lyons by the Beringens in 1548.[44] Many of the chansons there are accompanied by rubrics identifying an intended significance for the literary texts, suggesting that Protestant readers understood chanson lyrics as adopting a kind of musical or poetic persona. "Susanne un jour" is here identified as "Complainte de Susanne estant à tort condamnée à mort." Other pieces are described as "Chansons plainctive du Chrestien persecuté par son ennemy" or "Chanson spirituelle de l'âme chrestienne, où elle récite le contentement qu'elle trouve en l'amour de son espoux Jesus Christ."

The Tenor of Lupi's chanson was subsequently used in some two dozen polyphonic compositions and arrangements, including one by Lasso.[45] Perhaps less well known, however, is the fact that Lupi's *Premier livre* was itself reprinted (in Lyons and in Paris) and extensively "mined" for musical material that figured in other books of *chansons spirituelles* or secular chansons edited to make them accord with spiritual sensibilities.[46] Music from Lupi's book, for instance, was appropriated for Le Roy et Ballard's *Tiers livre de chansons spirituelles* of 1553. Pieces from his 1548 print also figured in two collections: Simon du Bosc's and Guillaume Guéroult's *Tiers livre où sont contenues plusieurs chansons . . . desquelles avons changé la verbe lubrique en lettre spirituelle et chrestienne* (Geneva, 1555) and in Jean Pasquier's *Premier [-Second] livre des cantiques et chansons spirituelles à quatre parties en quatre volumes, recueillies de plusieurs excellens musiciens* (La Rochelle, 1578).[47] Throughout this repertory, as Jacques Pineaux has amply demonstrated, Protestant poets reveal abiding concern, not merely to correct what might be understood as inappropriate texts, but to do so with a minimum of violence to the rhyme scheme, syntax, and even sound of these lyrics. Theirs was preeminently an enterprise of *imitatio,* as much at work here in the "reprise" of secular models as it was the central mode of countless emulations of sacred texts, especially the Psalms.[48]

The Texts of the *Contrafacta* and the Language of Huguenot Devotional Poetry

The books of *contrafacta* based on Lasso's chansons, in short, join a well-established tradition of converting secular music for spiritual purposes. Of course in this case Huguenot editors assumed the task of reforming the poetry of polyphonic chansons by a composer whose music was particularly beloved precisely on account of its subtle treatment of literary texts. As we will discover, the job of crafting new words to chansons already built around complex narrative and lyrical poetry was often not so simple. The Lasso *contrafacta,* like the original texts they trope, dwell in a variety of voices and themes. Some of the poems chosen by Lasso were apparently seen as entirely compatible with the sensibilities of Protestant readers and listeners, for they were reprinted in the *contrafacta* books without editorial change. Many others, of course, were changed in small or substantial ways. Poetry by Ronsard and by some of Ronsard's contemporaries, for instance, was carefully edited to suppress humanistic references to classical themes doubtless viewed by Huguenot theologians as patently un-Christian. Some texts, too, with their frequent use of the interrogative, assonance, and syntactic interruption or juxtaposition, share an affinity with the animated preaching style of Calvinist ministers. (We would do well to recall that Goulart, and probably Pasquier, too, counted themselves among the ranks of such spiritual orators.) Above all, such "sermon-poems" (as Terence Cave characterizes them) condemn the vanity of everyday concerns, the impermanence of human endeavors, and the abiding importance of sacred texts.[49]

In revising some of Lasso's chansons, the Protestant editors have translated the sentiments of lyrical love poetry into a spiritual register with surprising directness. Some of these are simple statements of fidelity not unlike those figuring in countless French chansons of the first half of the sixteenth century. Such themes apparently meshed seamlessly with the relationship between believer and Deity. Finally, still other *contrafacta* give poetic expression to personal prayer and reflection. Like the ardent love poetry they revise, these texts are lyrical, first-person contemplations of the self, albeit ones that contemplate the emotional effects of moral transgressions and the hopes of salvation. At times these two modalities of self-examination are combined, with language typical of a whole range of Calvinist meditative poetry. These sorts of texts, in Terence Cave's view, stress "the sharp antithesis between the humiliation of the sinner and the glory of God."[50] Slipping between secular and spiritual registers, the music that accompanies these chansons often serves to emphasize, to express, and to enact the very sorts of conditions described in the poems, making these works particularly apt embodiments of the devotional ideals of Protestant listeners.

The French Protestant church, of course, lacked elaborate penitential traditions centered on the lives of the saints or Jesus similar to those actively promoted in Catholic circles during the sixteenth century. But already in the French translation of Calvin's *Institution de la religion chrestienne* of 1541 we find a budding recognition by that Protestant theologian of how meditative texts might serve "as an incitement to emotion."[51] Similar concern for the affective qualities of language is voiced in other Calvinist prose of the sixteenth century, including the *Chrestiennes méditations sur huict Pseaumes,* a series of reflections issued in 1582 by Bèze. A similar volume, the *Méditations chrestiennes sur quatre Pseaumes du Prophète David* by Philippe de Mornay (Geneva, 1591) included Simon

Goulart's French translation of Savonarola's famous contemplation of "Miserere mei deus" (Psalm 51).[52]

All of this material, according to Terence Cave, aims to direct the emotional intensity of language to the needs of affective prayer. In his view, the shared concern for the persuasive power of language at work in these meditations and in vernacular literature on religious themes brought about something of a *rapprochement* between the needs of devotional practice and literary expression.[53] For poetry, he argues, the first great expression of this convergence comes in a collection issued in Geneva in 1574, the *Poèmes chrestiennes de B. Montméja et autres divers auteurs,* in which Montméja, Bèze, and Goulart (among others) rework the processes of devotion and meditative reflection in verse. Indeed, Goulart was one of the central figures in the development of this sort of literature, working not only as an editor of the Lasso chansonniers and several other similar music books, but also on a wide range of related projects, such as his own book of prose meditations on death and dying, the *Quarante tableaux de la mort* of 1601.[54]

Throughout this devotional literature we find a number of central concerns, chief among them being the identification of sin or moral transgression with physical ailment or death, a recognition of the cleansing power of lamentation (thus likewise of tears and of sighs), and finally an appeal to divine grace or mercy. These ideas are neatly embodied in the images and conditions circumscribed in many of the *contrafacta* for the Lasso chansons, which repeatedly repudiate past sins ("péchés") or the vanities of daily life and the sufferings of illness, death, and misfortune ("mort," and "malheur") they have caused. Moved to sighs ("souspirs"), heartfelt cries ("mon coeur gemissant") other expressions of emotion, the poetic persona of many of these poems appeals to divine clemency ("grace divine") and affirms the power of Scripture ("sainte Escrite") as the means to find release from spiritual suffering. What is more, the editors of the *contrafacta* books seem to have taken considerable effort to join these devotional themes to some of the most striking and affective moments of the Lasso chansons.

Perhaps not surprisingly, the sorts of poems provided by Goulart (and Pasquier, too) in their books of chanson *contrafacta* frequently rely on the same literary devices and themes that dominated their independent poetry. But the editors of these books were doing more than merely purging secular chansons of repugnant language and ideas—they were instead attempting to enlist the power of musical expression in the service of a contemplative ideal. The "new" chansons, like the prose meditations of Goulart's *Quarante tableaux de la mort,* inscribe and invoke affective qualities of a sort sought in devotional practice, often with an intensity and immediacy that verbal language could not easily manage. And like an oral sermon, music becomes a public (and often collective) medium with a manifestly private effect: performance and listening are here a means to a shared spiritual experience.

Reformed Spaces, Reformed Songs

Catharine Randall has recently shown how the Calvinist appropriation of Catholic public and sacred places can be understood as an attempt to infuse preexisting external forms with new spiritual content. "The Calvinist ideology," she writes of the great reformer's encounter with the old Episcopal seat of Geneva, "was to redetermine space by occupying it."[55] Protestants gave new meaning to Catholic churches in part by altering the interiors of such ritual spaces—above all by removing what they took to be distracting ornaments and representational artworks. But no less important, in Randall's view, was the role played by texts—maps, illustrations, and inscriptions on buildings themselves—that constitute "forms of verbal inhabiting" and give new meaning to existing structures.[56] Calvinist theologians and architects linked the experience of faith and space by any of a number of verbal figures and visual images. For the purposes of our study of the *contrafacta,* perhaps the most important of these themes is the idea of interiority. Grottos, hidden paths, and secret gardens, in Randall's view, serve in this literature as sites that mark out protected, private, spiritual spaces for a religious minority threatened by persecution and isolated by dispersal. These "inside" places have a significance that goes beyond surface appearances. The Huguenot architect Bernard de Palissy, for instance, wrote in his *Recepte véritable* of 1562—published at the outset of the first wave of religious war in France—that in order to conceptualize his ideal garden "I enter into myself, to delve into the secrets of my heart, and to enter into my conscience, to learn what there is within me."[57] Such interior spaces, in short, can provide paths to inner spiritual realms.

Neither buildings nor civic plans, of course, move through time in the way that music and other performing arts do. But the Protestant habit of retexting Catholic spaces offers some striking analogies with the sorts of strategies encountered in the Calvinist *contrafacta* of the Lasso chansons, and even with the imagery of the *contrafacta* books themselves. Here, as in the case of architectural schemes, we have a set of ready-made forms—in this case Lasso's chansons—which become "inhabited" with new meanings thanks to the agency of textual inscription. It thus seems hardly coincidental that so many of the adaptations of Lasso's chosen lyrics self-consciously concern themselves with "interiors" of various kinds, and with their spiritual valences. In the Huguenot revision of "En un lieu," for instance, sacred texts ("Ta parolle, O Dieu") serve as the only reliable guiding light "in a place" where little can been seen ("En un lieu ou l'on ne void goutte," reads the first line). Sacred texts, according to the Protestant editors of these songs, have an illuminative power that can save the speaker from "Satan and the flesh," which threaten to engulf this dark moral space. The idea of a spiritual "place" also rests behind Simon Goulart's adaptation of "Si du mahleur." In his version of this text the speaker worries over his abandonment by a deity that seems to have withdrawn: "to be forgotten, O Lord, through your absence. Absent I die, and then in your presence all at once my soul is ravished." The space implied here is of course not a physical but a metaphysical one—the "life" of the believer depending on the relative proximity of the soul to the Divine.

As we will discover, when Lasso's chansons are transformed by such texts, they can become musical vessels whereby spiritual feelings are heard and shared by listeners. Like the grottos, caves, and contained spaces that figure in the Calvinist view of buildings and cities, these songs make room for the expression of attitudes central to Huguenot piety. But we can also view the books of *contrafacta* themselves as "containers" that make room for the articulation of spiritual frames of mind. The title page of Jean Pasquier's *Premier livre des cantiques et chansons spirituelles* (issued in 1578, a few short years after his books based on the Lasso chansons) features an engraving that shows God (through the agency of time) retrieving Truth from the darkness of a craggy cave (see Figure 1.5). The emblem vividly recalls the iconography of Calvinist spiritual spaces, but in a very direct sense relates to the chansons contained in the book that this image adorns, for through the agency of Pasquier's new texts "hidden" spiritual truths will emerge from the music itself. A similar effect is suggested by the title page of Goulart's *Thrésor de musique d'Orlande* which features an engraving of the divine name (in Hebrew characters) blazing from the empty space that dominates its center (see Figure 1.2). This emblem, unlike the one on Pasquier's book, needs no caption, since it is its own text. But like the image on Pasquier's book of chansons spirituelles, this engraving alerts the reader to the spiritual essence that this book finds in the sounds hidden within its covers. Books such as these thus may have worked in much the same way as the Protestant "Cabinet," a private collection of emblematic objects that are brought together with the aim of conveying the viewer towards spiritual self-understanding. Catharine Randall characterizes the "Cabinet" as "a preparatory site for the reception of Scripture . . . or of the Word in a scripturally conforming sense."[58] That Goulart should have chosen to entitle his book of Lasso chansons a "thrésor" (literally a "treasury" in the sense of a place where precious objects are kept) hardly seems coincidental. His publication is not simply a collection (conveyed, perhaps, by the word "Mélange") but a repository where new spiritual meanings are prepared and inscribed.

All of this brings us back to the very condition that motivated the publication of the Lasso *contrafacta* in the first instance. Here was a community that was faced with persecution and even physical annihilation during the 1560s and 1570s. Just as many of these believers were obligated to seek refuge in places like London, La Rochelle, or Geneva, and to inscribe spiritual meanings in their new physical surroundings, they also sought spiritual refuge in the metaphorical "spaces" of Lasso's chansons. These works,

Figure 1.5. Title page from the Contratenor partbook of Jean Pasquier's *Premier livre des cantiques et chansons spirituelles* (La Rochelle, 1578). Reproduced by permission of the Bodleian Library, Oxford.

as we have suggested, were held in great esteem precisely for their power to touch the soul and to move the emotions. Although the Calvinists approached such effects with caution, they were in this instance appropriated as powerful vehicles for the representation of spiritual conditions. The work of this transformation moved forward principally through the power of the printed page to shape how readers encountered this music.

Chapter 2

The Chansons and Their Listeners

Lasso's Poetic Choices

Lasso's chansons embrace a remarkable variety of literary and musical traditions. His earliest published works, perhaps not surprisingly, draw on epigrams from a poetic stock encountered in chansons by earlier composers such as Claudin de Sermisy and Clemens non Papa. Many of these texts—typically arranged in four- or eight-line stanzas of decasyllabic verse—circulated in printed anthologies of poetry that appeared before 1550.[1] Among his chansons are settings of verse by Clément Marot, onetime royal favorite and subsequently translator of the Psalms in versions widely used in the Huguenot community. (Marot himself sympathized with the Protestant cause.) His secular poetry circulated widely in the middle years of the sixteenth century, and was frequently set to music by composers such as Claudin and Clément Janequin. Lasso, too, set Marot's lyrics, poems that range in subject matter from the sufferings and joys of love to narrative verse that recounts the exploits and speech of figures drawn from popular culture. Not a few of these lyrics, as it happens, also turn up in the Huguenot *contrafacta* books, often in surpising ways: Marot's "Fleur de quinze ans," in which a would-be lover offers a young woman dubious advice on love, was converted by Pasquier and Goulart into a lesson about good behavior. Perhaps more surprisingly, Marot's tale of a drunken abbot, "Monsieur l'Abbé," was carried over into the Lasso *contrafacta* books without change, where it doubtless found sympathy among the often anticlerical Protestant readers of these books.[2]

Lasso also had a preference for old-fashioned *rondeaux* and other refrain forms, albeit in musical settings that radically rework or even ignore some of the important formal conventions of such texts. In this respect he is not unique, of course, inasmuch as these sorts of poems were frequently handled in this way by Crequillon and other Northern composers of the mid-sixteenth century (and earlier, also).[3] Lasso, however, like a number of his contemporaries, borrowed from other polyphonic settings of the texts he chose—his setting of "Ce faux amour" seems to have been modeled on one by Clément Janequin, while his treatments of "Toutes les nuitz" and

"Quand me souvient" owe something to settings of this poem by Thomas Crequillon.[4] Of course some of Lasso's chansons themselves served as models for composers of the later years of the sixteenth century. Lasso's setting of Guillaume Guéroult's paradigmatic *chanson spirituelle* of feminine chastity and endurance, "Susanne un jour" (itself drawing upon the Tenor part of Didier Lupi's setting of this text), was widely reworked by vocal and instrumental composers well into the seventeenth century.[5]

New poetic fashions, too, can be found among his chanson texts, as in the case of poems by Joachim Du Bellay, Remy Belleau, and Pierre de Ronsard. Collectively these writers revisited Greek and Roman poetry, borrowing extensively from their formal and metrical vocabulary as a means of renovating current literary practice. Theoretical manifestos by these poets—notably Du Bellay's *Deffense et illustration de la langue françoise* (1549) and Ronsard's *Abrégé de l'art poétique françoys* (1565)—valorized the ancient ideals of a union between poetry and music, and the power of solo song. Some of Ronsard's French contemporaries attempted to give musical voice to these ideals, or at least to find ways for current polyphonic practice to participate in the enterprise envisaged by the so-called Pléiade poets. In a now famous musical *Supplément* to Ronsard's sonnet cycle, *Les Amours,* published by Nicholas Du Chemin in 1552, French composers such as Claude Goudimel and Pierre Certon offered a number of basic models for performing Ronsard's lyrics. Pléiade poetics and literary ideals were actively cultivated in late-sixteenth-century France, especially among musicians like Anthoine de Bertrand, Guillaume Boni, Pierre Clereau, and others as well. [6] In contrast to the clear formal presentation of strophic songs and schematic approaches to setting sonnets heard in their music, Lasso preferred rather open, discursive forms and complex contrapuntal textures. His setting of Du Bellay's sonnet, "La nuict froide et sombre," is a good case in point, for it brings together the ardent literary concerns of the Pléiade with Lasso's obvious interest in the representational conventions of the contemporary Italian madrigal.

Kate van Orden has suggested that we should sense in all of this a manifest self-consciousness on Lasso's part about the past, a marked historicism "projected through musical and poetic imitations" remarkable for their independence from other canonical sources preferred by composers of mid-sixteenth-century France.[7] It may be too hopeful to think that Lasso's chanson production was undertaken from its outset (as early as 1555) as a kind of "historicizing" enterprise, although clearly *Les meslanges d'Orlande* of 1570 and 1576 cast a retrospective gaze over his output in ways also encountered in other "Meslanges" of the later sixteenth century—notably Le Roy et Ballard's famous *Livre de meslanges* of 1560 (revised in 1572 as the *Mellange de chansons*), and in the various *Meslanges* books brought out on behalf of Pierre Certon, Claude Le Jeune, and others.[8] The books of Protestant *contrafacta* assume something of this same quality of "retrospection," but we should nevertheless also remember the patent variety at hand in the Lasso chansons, and understand the varied responses it engendered.

Editorial Assent among the *Contrafacta*

Despite the often grand claims of the title pages of the *contrafacta* books about the single-mindedness with which the profane poetry of Lasso's chansons has been reformed for use by pious Huguenots, not all of the works presented in these anthologies have been subjected to the same degree of censorship or correction. Nearly half of the thirty-eight chansons included in Thomas Vautrollier's *Recueil du mellange d'Orlande* were printed there without change. Two five-voice pieces by Philippe de Monte that were included in Goulart's book of 1576, his printer admits with some embarrassment, were likewise never censored before having been set in type.[9] And even among those Lasso chansons that were reviewed prior to typesetting are several in which the texts remain just as they were in the original Parisian prints, for in these the editor apparently found no moral fault. (Goulart's printer also acknowledges the apparent oversight as intentional: "Et si en plusieurs la lettre est demeurée telle qu'elle est es livres de Paris, cela est procédé de la volonté du correcteur, qui ne s'est voulu ingerer de ragencer ce qui est passable." See Appendix A for the full text and translation.) The editors (and, in turn, readers) of the *contrafacta* volumes, in short, well recognized the literary (and moral) variety latent in Lasso's chosen texts, lyrics whose suitability for Protestant readers evidently depended upon the subject and language at hand.

"La nuict froide et sombre"

Among the works which Goulart printed without change, for instance, is one of the most celebrated of all of Lasso's chansons: his rhapsodic setting of du Bellay's "La Nuict froide et sombre." It would be risky to interpret too much from editorial silence, of course, but given the character of Goulart's other *contrafacta* and the literary themes of some of his own sonnets, too, we might venture to guess that this poem, with its abiding respect for the fullness of creation and the inevitable succession of night and day, accorded well with some central themes of the literatures of devotion, echoing, among other things, the despair and hope of the Evening and Morning meditations.[10]

Example 2.1a. Lasso, "La nuict froide et sombre," mm. 1–18.

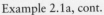

Example 2.1a, cont.

Example 2.1b. Lasso, "La nuict froide et sombre," mm. 26–34.

La nuict froide et sombre
Couvrant d'obscure ombre
La terre et les cieux
Aussi doux que miel
Fait couler du ciel
Le sommeil aux yeux.

Puis le jour suivant[11]
Au labeur duisant
Sa lueur expose;
Et d'un tein[12] divers
Ce grand univers
Tapisse et compose.

Translation:
The cold and somber night covering with its obscure shadows the earth and
the skies, as sweet as honey, brings flowing from the heavens sleep to the eyes.
Day then ensues, its light suited to labor, sending forth its glow and in hues
diverse this great universe weaves and composes.

Lasso's approach to this and some of the other Pléiade poems he set is in
many ways remarkable from the standpoint of traditions of chanson composition in France. Indeed, this work, with its through-composed succession of melodic and contrapuntal gestures crafted to the sense and meaning
of individual words and lines, seems more like what we would expect of a
mid-sixteenth-century madrigal or motet than a French chanson. (See Exs.
2.1a and 2.1b.) In the first lines of text, for instance, Lasso uses a series of
stark and slow-moving sonorities to evoke the sobriety of approaching night
(see measures 1–4). Elsewhere extreme contrasts of register (low, then high)
map out in sound the vast space between earth and the heavens (measures
7–10), while the neat isolation of the "soft" B flat at "doux" (in measure
11) between the "hard" B natural and G sharp (in measures 10 and 13)
suggest an intensity "as sweet as honey." A long chain of drooping suspensions (in measures 15–18) mimic the effect of sleep upon the eyes, while
closing allusions to the creative, compositional powers of day itself find
apt musical representation in a long, contrapuntal web that spins out the
last lines of the chanson (measures 26–34).

"Monsieur l'Abbé"

Lasso's setting of Marot's "Monsieur l'Abbé" was also taken over into the
Protestant chansonniers unchanged, but for reasons very different from the
ones at work in "La nuict froide et sombre." "Monsieur l'Abbé" recounts
in narrative verse the tale of an errant Catholic cleric that must have been
well suited to the broader political and theological outlook of the Huguenot movement in its struggle against what its members saw as the inherent

corruption of the established church. As we will discover in the next chapter, this sort of carnivalesque narrative verse figures prominently among Lasso's chansons.

> *Marot's Original Poem As Printed by Le Roy et Ballard:*[13]
> Monsieur l'Abé et monsieur son varlet
> Sont fais égaux tous deux comme de cire,
> L'un est grand fol, l'autre petit follet;
> L'un veut railler, l'autre gaudir et rire;
> L'un boit du bon, l'autre ne boit du pire;
>
> Mais un debat au soir entre eux s'esmeut,
> Car maistre Abé tout la nuict ne veut
> Estre sans vin que sans secours ne meure
> Et son varlet jamais dormir ne peut
> Tandis qu'au pot une goutte en demeure.

> *Translation:*
> Monsieur Abbot and his valet are as alike to each other as wax: One is a big fool, the other a small one; one wants to jest, the other laughs and plays; One drinks well, the other doesn't drink badly.
> But a quarrel arises between them in the evening, because Master Abbot doesn't want to be long deprived of wine, lest he perish unsuccored. And his valet cannot get a wink of sleep as long as a single drop is still in the jar.

Anticlerical propaganda had long been a component of the large repertory of *timbres* and other monophonic *contrafacta* promoted by Calvinist thinkers as a means of securing solidarity among Huguenots, a kind of political protest song to complement the sacred Psalter. Perhaps it was this political significance that prompted Pasquier to give "Monsieur l'Abbé" pride of *last* place in his book of four-voice *contrafacta*.[14] Perhaps no less significant is the fact that one of the few collections of purified chansons intended for Catholic audiences, the *Premier livre des chansons à quatre et cincq parties . . . de nouveau plus correctement que cy devant imprimées et emendées* (Louvain: Pierre Phalèse, 1570), treats this text in an entirely different manner, replacing the errant "Abbé" with a "Maistre Robbin."[15] These rival appropriations of Lasso's chanson are striking, and should serve as a warning (as Horst Leuchtmann wisely advises) against the temptation to view Lasso himself as having been allied exclusively with the cultural program of the Counter Reformation.[16] The challenge, we should recall, is not to delineate Lasso's personal stance in relation to the theological or cultural debates that raged between Protestants and Catholics during the sixteenth century, but rather to discover the means by which one audience or another sought to enlist his music in the service of what for them was a broader aim.

How the Huguenots Heard: Worldly Texts and Spiritual Sounds

The patent variety of Lasso's poetic choices and musical responses, in short, should serve as a warning against simple judgments about the *contrafacta* as "purified" chansons. At times there seems to have been something of a consensus on the part of the makers of the *contrafacta* about what seemed right or wrong about some poem. But such unanimity is surprisingly rare, and instead the process of textual reform was, in the case of Lasso chansons, often extraordinarily complex. At the very least Pasquier and Goulart charged themselves with the elimination of offensive language, or suggestions of eroticism, with the explicit condemnation of vain or superficial pursuits, and with the promotion of self-examination and enduring faith in God. All of this had to be undertaken in the context of musical settings that were themselves often carefully attuned to the formal, syntactic, and thematic nuances of the original texts Lasso chose to set.

Simon Goulart was especially sensitive to the sorts of musical embodiments of verbal forms and ideas just encountered. In "Ce faux amour," for example, Lasso was careful to make his musical gestures attend to syntactic units of meaning rather than the formal divisions of rhyme and prosody, enjambing successive lines of verse when the sentence structure seemed to call for it. Well aware of this kind of alliance between text and tone, Goulart used it ably in the service of his own devotional poetry. In reworking the texts for "Bon jour mon coeur" and "En un lieu," Goulart builds upon Lasso's formal structure, in which melodic and harmonic material from the outset of each chanson was recalled near its close, apparently in an effort to mirror the verbal return at work in his chosen poems. For Goulart, the musical recapitulations heard in these chansons are not used to support poetic form (there is no literal return in the poetry) but instead become a way of involving the listener in a process of recollection and *metaphorical* return (to the Divine, in this case) that is proposed in the new text. Thanks to Goulart's poems, in short, the musical recapitulation here becomes a means for us to mime the very attitudes proposed by the *contrafactum*.

Lasso had a talent for setting important words with apt musical gestures. His musical reading of "La nuict froide et sombre" may owe a measure of its longevity in part to its rampantly "semiotic" approach to the visual imagery at hand in this text. Many of Lasso's chansons share (albeit with a more subtle touch) this concern for the power of music to represent in tones the visual, aural, or symbolic attributes of individual words. Lasso's Huguenot redactors seem to have been well aware of this aspect of his art. In "D'amours me va tout au rebours" (see Exs. 4.3a and 4.3b), Lasso's canon by inversion serves as an apt musical representation of the metaphorical "reversal" ("au rebours") announced in the first (and last) lines of the poem. In his setting of Ronsard's "Ren moy mon coeur" (see Ex. 6.2), to cite another example, Lasso used registral contrast of melodic gestures to suggest the striking juxtaposition of life and death, and of the emotional tensions of a poetic persona poised between these two states. Elsewhere among the Lasso chansons, "Ce faux amour" (see Ex. 3.1) and its spiritual transformations use tonal juxtapositions of B flats, F sharps, and C sharps as means of intensifying the emotional cries and exclamations at work in those poems, engendering a kind of musical parlance that imitates speech itself. In the hands of Goulart and Pasquier, as we shall see, the urgency of these musical and verbal correspondences are converted into expressions of spiritual ecstacies and the affective utterances they prompt. Listening, in the case of these chansons, becomes a means to recreate the extremes of pious devotion.

It has also been suggested that Lasso's disposition of tonal gestures can be seen as a kind of sounding representation of verbal ideas. In an important series of writings on the subject, Bernhard Meier has argued that for composers of the sixteenth century the eight traditional modal categories constituted a clear set of tonal scripts to be confirmed or thwarted in accordance with the expressive needs of a particular text, much in the way that a composer of the eighteenth or nineteenth century might use an unexpected succession of harmonies to support a striking dramatic, rhetorical, or emotional moment in song or opera.[17] Nowhere, in Meier's view, is this possibility better articulated than in the works of Lasso, for whom irregular cadential formulas and unexpected positions for cadences within a given musical mode could serve as a means of text presentation. Indeed, we need look no further than his cycle of *Penitential Psalms* for ample evidence of this technique: irregular or faulty cadences frequently mark allusions to evil, error, or transgression, while cadences in unusual positions mark off notions of failings, opposition, and otherness.[18] In an intriguing study of the relationship between modality and the musical representation of literary texts, Jean-Pierre Ouvrard, too, heard special correspondence between gestures associated with the Deuterus/Phrygian modes (that pair nominally based around the tone E) and expressions of pathos in verbal texts.[19] According to Ouvrard's research, sixteenth-century musicians heard the characteristic cadence of these modes, in which the lowest voice part descended by semitone, as eliciting pathos or suffering. As it happens such cadences were not confined to the so-called Phrygian modes, but were occasionally adopted in other contexts, as well, often (in Ouvrard's experience) in conjunction with texts expressing sentiments of suffering or lamentation.

We may readily hear some of these same devices in the Lasso chansons, and in their reworkings by Huguenot editors. According to Meier, for instance, the unusual variety of tonal positions for cadences in Lasso's setting of "Quand me souvient" (see Ex. 5.2) can be understood as a representation of the remembered sadness that dominates this *complainte*. In this piece we encounter regular cadential progression (in measures 5 and 6); a

Phrygian cadence (in measure 22); and an evaded cadence, in which the Bassus moves upwards to thwart the closure implied by the other parts (in m. 25). The self-consciousness with which Lasso seems to have deployed these unusual gestures mirrors the self-conscious poetic persona of the speaker, who in the fictive world of the poem examines his own situation and responds with an affective "helas." For Pasquier and Goulart, this mode of introspection—and the musical gestures that give it voice—are easily converted into expressions of devotional practice.[20] In "Si du mahleur" (see Ex. 5.3), to cite another example, Meier reads a sudden "mi" cadence to E and a thwarted one to C (both in the context of a piece nominally centered around G as a transposed version of Mode 2) as illustrations of how the "foreignness" of certain cadential positions to a given musical mode enact a kind of distancing that suits well the central theme of this poem, in which the poetic persona fears being forgotten "by too long absence." The Protestant *contrafacta* of this piece appropriate this poetic stance—and the musical gestures that support it—in ways that enact in sound precisely the process of reflection and affective prayer envisioned by their spiritual program.[21] Related conjunctions of unusual cadences or "mi"-cadences with important affective moments in literary texts also appear in Lasso's setting of Ronsard's "Ren moy mon coeur," (see Ex. 6.2) in both his four- and five-voice settings of "Ardant amour" (see Exs. 3.2 and 3.3), in "Toutes les nuitz" (see Ex. 5.1), and in "Mon coeur se recommande à vous" (see Ex. 4.1).

In crafting his music to the formal, syntactic, and semantic details of his chosen texts, Lasso created chansons with special power to move his listeners. For the Huguenot editors who attempted to reform these lyrics, then, the central challenge was to craft a spiritual text that could be convincingly intensified by Lasso's musical gestures. The critical exploration presented in the following chapters are thus readings of other readings, and as such are often comparative, using the differences among "purified" versions of the same chansons as ways of understanding how spiritual listeners heard the sounds that accompany these "already interpreted" texts. Our explorations will also attempt to show how the Huguenot encounter with Lasso's music was shaped by the attitudes and practices of religious devotion.

Chapter 3

Courtly Love and Its Spiritual Tropes

The continuing literary influence of the *amour courtois* of the later Middle Ages upon the love lyrics of Renaissance France is heard profoundly in Lasso's chansons, and in their appropriation by Protestant listeners. Whether or not the highly conventional codes articulated in the various writings on courtly love originated with any social reality in medieval Aquitaine or Provence, they exerted a profound influence over literary expression well into the sixteenth century and beyond. Themes of the *amour courtois* are readable in such diverse works as the chansons of Guillaume de Machaut, the Laura sonnets of Petrarch, and in Dante's Beatrice from the *La divina commedia*. At heart, this poetry builds its erotic, social, and religious sensibilities from a number of basic conceits, among them love as a kind of faithful service; love as a physical illness to which the beloved alone holds the cure; and the beloved as an idealized or unattainable vision. Perhaps the most famous chanson from the first half of the sixteenth century, Claudin de Sermisy's setting of Clément Marot's "Tant que vivray," recalls some of this language, describing the ideal beauty of the beloved, and characterizing love itself as a form of service: "While I am in my prime I will serve the mighty god of love. . . . For a long time he left me languishing, but afterwards he made me rejoice, for now I have the love of a shapely beauty."[1]

A number of the texts chosen by Lasso rely on ideas very similar to those found in Marot's poem. Perhaps more important for our purposes is the surprising ease with which the rhetoric of courtly love, with its repeated expressions of distance and longing, were enlisted in the expression of a specifically spiritual yearing, often with only minor changes to individual poems. "Je l'ayme bien" can serve as a good case in point. In changing but a single word in the refrain of this modest stanza, the poet's devotion is directed by Pasquier and Goulart alike towards the divine rather than an indeterminate beloved: "Je l'ayme bien et l'aymeray" becomes "J'aime mon Dieu et l'aymeray." The rest of the poem remains unchanged, apparently compatible with the program of religious devotion heard in other Huguenot *contrafacta*.[2]

"Du corps absent"

"Du corps absent" provides a particularly focused example of this sort of transformation. In the original poem, the speaker offers the beloved a disembodied heart as token of an enduring loyalty sustained by hope alone. For the Protestant editors, the heart symbolizes the spirit or soul, which thanks to focused intent is sustained by mere faith (itself an important element in Calvinist teachings). We might also observe the aptness of Pasquier's substitution of "captif" for "absent" in the first line of his *contrafactum*. In a literal sense it recalls Protestant concerns about the body and its hold over the human spirit. "Du corps captif," thanks in part to Lasso's musical setting, echoes some of the visual imagery employed in Calvinist writings about "inner" spaces as locations of hidden, spiritual truths. This is just the sort of imagery found on the title page of Jean Pasquier's own edition of the *Premier livre des cantiques et chansons spirituelles* of 1578 (not to be confused with his editions of Lasso's chansons) which depicts a figure of truth emblematically liberated from a grotto where she had been confined (see Figure 1.5).[3]

Poem as set by Lasso:
Du corps absent le coeur je te presente
Qui loyaument sans fin te servira
Et en tous lieux comme ton serf ira
Vivant d'espoir se nourrissant d'attente.

Translation:
A heart I offer you from its body removed that shall serve you loyally and evermore. And will go everywhere as your attendant, living on hope, feeding on expectation.

Pasquier:
Du cors captif l'esprit je te presente
Qui libre O Dieu tousjours te servira
Et constamment tes louanges dira
Vivant de foy, et se paissant d'attente.

Translation:
A spirit captive in its body I offer you, who once freed, O God, will serve you forever and speak your praises constantly, living on faith, feeding on expectation.

Goulart:
Du corps absent le coeur je te presente
Qui loiaument, O Dieu, te servira
Et sous tes loix, comme ton serf ira
Vivant de Foi, se nourissant d'attente.

Translation:
A heart I offer you from its body removed that shall serve you loyally and evermore. And, under your laws, as your slave will go everywhere, living on hope, feeding on expectation.

"Ce faux amour"

In "Ce faux amour" the speaker calls out to the beloved as the only source of solace for the intense pain of love's sharp arrows. This poetic imagery borrows heavily from the language of battle ("alarme, alarme, sus à l'assaut"), and perhaps not surprisingly, Lasso's setting of this poem, with its rhythmic animation and coordinated homorhythmic writing, strongly recalls the descriptive battle pieces of Clément Janequin, which use similar musical idioms to represent the energy and sounds of warfare.[4]

Poem as set by Lasso:
> Ce faux amour d'arc et de fléches s'arme,
> Et prend son feu pour me livrer l'assaut,
> Il me contraint crier alarme, alarme,
> Sus à l'assaut! resister il luy faut.
> Las! il me brule, o que son feu est chault!
> Au feu, Au feu, secourez moy madame,
> Misericorde! autre je ne reclame.
> Vous me pouvez rendre victorieux
> Et remporter ce grand honneur sans blame
> D'avoir vaincu celuy qui vainct les dieux.

Translation:
> This false love armed with bow and arrows, takes aim to make assault on me, he compels me to cry "alarm, alarm to battle." Resist I must. Alas! I burn, oh, but his fire is hot. "Fire, fire, help me madame, for pity's sake!" I can say no more. You can grant me victory, and earn without incurring blame the great honor of having vanquished him who vanquishes the gods.

Goulart:
> Ce faux Satan de ma vanité s'arme,
> Voila son feu pour me livrer l'assaut:
> Il me contraint crier alarme, alarme:
> Sus à l'assaut, reisiter il lui faut.
> Las, il me brusle! Ô Dieu, voi ce feu chaud.
> Au feu, au feu, donne secours à l'âme.
> Misericorde: autre je ne reclame,
> Toi seul me peux rendre victorieux,
> Que j'aye donc ce grand honneur sans blame
> D'avoir vaincu l'ennemi furieux.

Translation:
> This false Satan taking arms from my vanity—behold his fire that assails me. I am compelled to cry "alarm, alarm, to battle." Resist I must. Alas, I burn, O God, see his hot fire. "Fire, fire, send help for my soul. Take pity": I can say no more." You alone can grant me victory. Let me then have the great honor, without incurring blame, of having vanquished the furious enemy.

Example 3.1. Lasso, "Ce faux amour," mm. 1–25.

Example 3.1, cont.

Example 3.1, cont.

Lasso's chanson articulates the complex syntactic design organizing this poem. The *enjambements* that link the third and the fourth verses (and likewise the fifth and sixth) receive ellided musical lines that underscore the grammatical sense of those passages rather than their end rhymes (see Ex. 3.1, measures 9–10 and 17–18). Perhaps more importantly, Lasso also attends to the frequent expression of suffering and calls for help heard here: the exclamation "Las" in the fifth line, for instance, is marked by a sudden shift to a sonority built on B flat (measure 14), while "Misericorde" in line 7 is musically embodied in pathetic and slowly moving sonorities that include F sharp and C sharp (see measures 21–24). The various cries of "alarm," "to battle" "fire," already repeated in the poem, are repeated still further thanks to the polyphonic patter and hockets of Lasso's composition.

The Protestant *contrafacta* of "Ce faux amour" take care to preserve the various imitations of speech and the syntactic subtleties of the original poem in ways that make good use of Lasso's vivid musical setting of it. In Pasquier's and Vautrollier's verses, Cupid is replaced by a Christian enemy—"Satan," also brandishing fire—and God replaces the mistress as a source of aid.[5] Goulart also opens his *contrafactum* with an allusion to the devil, but in a characteristically introspective twist, his "Satan" is a poetic personification of an internal demon, a projection of vain sensibilities from which divine power alone offers defense. Here Goulart has used the expressive agency of Lasso's chansons to enact in tones a battle against one's own forbidden bodily impulses.

"Ardant amour"

The various Protestant adaptations of the eight-line poem "Ardant amour" also offer compelling evidence about how the burning desire of courtly love could be displaced to a spiritual register, and how music might serve as a means to support the sensibilities those registers share. This chanson makes a particularly good example of this process, because Lasso himself composed two different settings of the same text (one for four voices, the other for five voices).[6] These two settings differ in some important ways, and the *contrafacta* accommodate themselves to these tones with differing degrees of success. The poem deals principally with a lover's desire to confess his love, a desire balanced by fear of rejection and anxiety that such feelings will not be well received. The first half describes the speaker's situation up to the point of this narration, while the second half suggests what will happen if God fails to make the beloved understand these inner desires "without having to say." Within this broad progress, each couplet represents a coherent poetic idea, resulting in a series of parallel oppositions circling around the contradictory conditions of declaration and silence: "love wants me to confess, but fear of rejection prevents me;" and "torment will continue, unless God helps the beloved to understand without the speaker having to speak openly."

> *Poem as set by Lasso:*
> Ardant amour souvent me fait instance
> De declairer mon coeur ouvertement
> Mais du refus la si grande doutance
> Ne me le veut permettre nullement.
> Dont à jamais souffriray le tourment
> Qu'amour craintif donne aux siens pour martire,
> Si Dieu ne fait pour mon alegement
> Qu'elle entende mon vouloir sans le dire.

Translation:
> Burning love often demands that I declare openly my heart. But the great fear of being turned down will no wise permit me to do so. On account of which I will forever suffer the torment that timid love inflicts upon its own for martyrdom. If God for my relief will not make her hear my wish without my having to say it.

Lasso attended carefully to these formal and rhetorical divisions in his four-voice setting of this poem (see Ex. 3.2).[7] The same music, for instance, is used for each of the first two couplets, with a convincing cadence reserved only for the second line in each pair (see measures 1–11 and 12–22). This repetition thus serves to emphasize the rhyme scheme while juxtaposing the contradictory "desire—impediment" relationship circumscribed by those couplets. The second half of the poem follows a similar plan, but with greater flexibility: here the enjambed pairs of lines (5 and 6; 7 and 8) are joined musically, with strong cadences reserved for the second line of each couplet. The effect helps Lasso to accommodate his music to some of the rather complex syntax at work here. In measures 38–40, for instance, the Contratenor line begins line 8 before the Superius reaches the last phrase of line 7 ("pour mon allegement") a verbal idea that is somewhat parenthetical to the main business of lines 7 and 8. The musical *enjambement,* by isolating that phrase within a broader gesture, helps to bring out the overall sense of the statement that embraces both verses. Other gestures, too, serve to capture the longing that rests behind this chanson: in measures 9 through 11, for instance, a melodic sweep on the word "ouvertement" literally "opens" the music to a cadence on D (measure 11—the suddenly silent Bassus part only underscores the contingent quality of this gesture), a tonal space that contrasts nicely with the G cadence that otherwise begins and ends the composition. Lasso's disposition of vocal forces and his judicious use of text repetition, in contrast, give voice to the frustration that for the poetic speaker impedes the open confession of love: the second part of line 4, "ne me le veut permettre" is repeated by the Bassus and Contratenor parts alone (measures 15–21), suggesting a kind of musical impediment to the progress of the rest of the voices. Similarly the phrase "dont à jamais" is declaimed first by the upper three voices and then repeated for all four parts, seemingly defying the very suffering to which the speaker's condition binds him (measures 22–23). Finally (and perhaps most interesting of all) the repetition of the last line of the poem, itself a well-worn convention of chanson composition, creates something of an ironic twist of the meaning of the text (which is the desire to communicate without explicit statement). In a sense, the musical gesture enacts the declaration that the poet has so long desired but has not been able to say in so many words.

The emotional stance of this poem aligns with a long tradition of lyrical expression in which confessions of love are advanced amid fears about

Example 3.2. Lasso, "Ardant amour," mm. 1–51 [the four-voice setting].

Example 3.2, cont.

Example 3.2, cont.

Example 3.2, cont.

Example 3.2, cont.

Example 3.2, cont.

desire itself. Poised between ardent longings and self-reproach for the origins of such desires, such poems are in many ways already Christian in their semiotics, for they articulate a stoic endurance of torment worthy of a martyr combined with fervent appeal for a saving intervention. As such, "Ardant amour" was largely compatible with the devotional attitudes articulated by many of the other *contrafacta* offered by Goulart and Pasquier. Both editors preserved large parts of the poem, but they also made different changes, and these differences offer important clues about how they understood the poem and Lasso's own treatment of it. Goulart's *contrafactum,* for instance, follows very closely the rhyme scheme, syntactic structure, and the rhetoric of the model poem. The same conflict between a desire to reveal inner emotion (in this case, "firm faith") and the thwarting of this desire (here by "bold sin") is also at hand in his *contrafactum.* Goulart seems to have been keen to preserve some of the key musical moments in Lasso's chanson—the previously described periodic structure and the word repetitions all fit nicely with the sense and design of the Genevan writer's language.

> *Goulart's Contrafactum for the four-voice setting:*
> La ferme foi souvent me fait instance
> De descouvrir mon coeur, ouvertement.
> Mais mon péché audacieux s'avance
> Et ne le veut permettre nullement.
> En danger suis de souffrir le tourment
> Que ce tyran donne aux siens pour martyre:
> Si Dieu ne veut, pour mon allegement
> Entendre, helas! mon desir sans le dire.

> *Translation:*
> Firm faith often makes entreaty to openly reveal my heart. But my bold sin comes forth and will nowise at all permit me to do so. I am in danger of suffering the torment that this tyrant gives to his own for martyrdom: If God for my relief will not hear, alas!, my wish without my having to say it.

Pasquier takes a characteristically individual approach to the poem and to the chanson. In general he preserves far less of the original secular text than did Goulart, and his poem uses a different voice and traverses a different emotional trajectory than those texts. The "ardent amour" of Pasquier's poem belongs to Jesus, not the speaker, and as such this poem confines itself to a narrative of his life and the proposed significance of his martyrdom for humanity, all culminating in an admonishment for Christians to love and to remember his words. Pasquier's is clearly the voice of a preacher, in strong contrast to the deeply personal piety articulated by Goulart's poem.

> *Pasquier's Contrafactum for both settings:*[8]
> Ardent amour fit Dieu du ciel descendre
> Pour se monstrer à tous ouvertment
> Quand il daigna ta chair o homme prendre
> Et endurer en elle durement
> Pour tes pechez de la croix le tourment:
> Par quoy amour ja plus ne te martire,
> Car il ne veut pour tel bien payement
> Sinon d'amour, et que gardes son dire.

> *Translation:*
> Burning love made God descend from the heavens to show himself openly to all, when he deigned, o man, to take on your flesh and therein endure harshly, for your sins, the torment of the cross: Whereby love can no longer torment you. For he wants no reward for such a boon except love, and that you hold to his teaching.

At times Pasquier's poem finds only grudging support in Lasso's music. The close syntactic connection between lines 4 and 5, for instance, does not work particularly well with the strong cadence that separates these lines in the chanson (measure 22). As a result, the music serves two conjoined ideas (Jesus' endurance; the sins of humanity) absolutely essential to Pasquier's own message. On the other hand, his poem makes some new and very effective use of the music for line 8 (measures 42–43). Here Pasquier's reference ("sinon d'amour") back to the opening words of the poem "ardent amour") mirrors the musical connection between the cadences for lines 2 and 4 (measures 10–11 and 20–22) and the present context.

Lasso's five-voice setting of "Ardant amour" shares some gestures with the four-voice version just considered (see Ex. 3.3).[9] Yet it departs from that composition in other ways, too. Like many other five-voice chansons, the piece is somewhat more motet-like in its imitative textures than compositions for four voices, and as such there is more overlap between successive lines of the text. The clear reinforcement of the syntactic and rhetorical relationship between the opening couplets heard in the four-voice piece is thus less obvious here, despite the fact that Lasso again uses the same music for each of these pairs of lines (see measures 1–13 and 13–24). This blurring of structural distinctions is heard elsewhere in the five-voice setting also. There is, in general, much more repetition of text in this composition than in the other version of the piece. Once again "dont à jamais" is singled out for exceptional treatment, being repeated three times, each more homorhythmic than the preceding, all culminating with insistent, simultaneous declamation (measures 26–27 and 29–30). A bit of tonal allegory may rest behind the gesture that underscores line 7: here the speaker's hope for divine intervention to relieve suffering is metaphorically (and aurally) played out in a rapid sweep of motion through E, A, D, and finally a relieved cadence on G (see measures 37–43). Even more than in the previous setting, Lasso uses the conventional peroration of the densely textured five-voice genre as pretext for expanding, repeating, and even dramatizing the last line of text, spending some seventeen measures saying in music what the poet has not even been able to say once.

Pasquier's reuse of the same *contrafactum* for the five-voice version of "Ardant amour" as for the four-voice setting of this text might at first seem a hopeless enterprise, for already in that context the new words and old music made only passing agreement. The narrative of Jesus' life and the admonition to remember his teachings, however, works tolerably well. (Was Pasquier's text in fact crafted with this setting in mind rather than the four-voice piece?) In this case his asymmetrical division of the poem, in which lines 4 and 5 were linked as a single syntactic unit, seems less a liability in the context of the rather continuous vocal fabric. On the other hand, the strong cadence at the end of the seventh line of the poem (measure 43) articulates a division that does not exist in Pasquier's poem. The multiple

Example 3.3. Lasso, "Ardant amour," mm. 1–60 [the five-voice setting].

Example 3.3, cont.

Example 3.3, cont.

Example 3.3, cont.

Example 3.3, cont.

Example 3.3, cont.

repetitions of the final line of text, although no longer giving voice to sentiments "unsaid," could nevertheless be understood to embody the increasingly urgent wish by a sermonizing narrator to have listeners "hold to his teaching."

Goulart chose to write a new text for the five-voice chanson, one that follows the same overall plan as the original one (enjambed couplets, clear division of the poem into two complementary halves) but differs in the details of its emotional language. For this speaker, opposing poles (good and evil) of moral ardor burn within his psyche, a torment that will continue unless divine force intervenes to squelch the temptation of sin. Responding to the greater turbulence of Lasso's music for the five-voice setting, Goulart here chose vivid and even powerful metaphors ("m'enflame," "danger," "deschire") as well as preserving some ("tourment," "martyre") from the original poem.

Goulart's Contrafactum for the five-voice setting:
Divin amour qui eschauffe mon ame
Donne à mon coeur un vrai contentement.
Mais mon peché d'un autre feu m'enflamme
Et l'autre feu estaint ouvertement.
En danger suis de souffrir le tourment
Dont ce tyran ses esclaves deschire,
Si Dieu ne fait pour mon allegement
Mourir ce feu qui tousjours me martyre.

Translation:
Divine love which enflames my soul gives my heart a true contentment. But my sin fires me with a different flame and staunches the other fire openly. I am in danger of suffering the torment by which this tyrant tears apart his slaves, if God will not, for my relief destroy this fire which martyrs me forever.

The repetition that Lasso built into line 5 works well to highlight the speaker's cry "en danger suis" (see measures 26–27 and 29–30). The reiteration of the second half of line 6 accents the vivid depiction there of the rending of those enslaved to sin. This in turn leads to the rapid tonal motion and consequent emotional relief that comes with the hope for divine intervention described in the next line of text (measures 34–43). The latter line, in fact, was carried over without change from the original version of the poem, showing once again how careful Goulart seems to have been to convert the chansons to his needs rather than to replace outright the emotional valences they engender.

Among Lasso's chansons we have encountered works that echo a long tradition of lyrics informed by the *amour courtois*. These poems, in which the conditions of love are idealized as a form of service and as a form of almost stoic endurance, were readily spiritualized by Protestant editors. For Medieval readers steeped in Latin lyrics, the intense veneration of a distant beloved found in many of these texts could already be understood to carry Marian overtones. For Protestant editors such as Pasquier and Goulart, texts such as "Ce faux amour" and "Ardant amour" provided a ready means of transforming the stereotypical love longing of such texts into the spiritual vocabulary of Calvinist thought. Here it is the divine alone that offers relief from the physical sufferings of moral transgression. Enacted in sound through the agency of Lasso's music, this intense struggle between physical form and spiritual longing is not just something to be read in the poetic texts, but something to be heard, even felt as a physical sensation by those who sang and heard these chansons. The listeners themselves became, in short, sites where the profound effects of music were enlisted in the spiritual program of Huguenot belief.

Chapter 4

The Poetry of Marot, the Carnivalesque, and the Preacher's Voice

The writings and literary career of Clément Marot must have presented an especially challenging prospect for Huguenot editors. The poet was himself an early sympathizer to the Protestant cause. He collaborated with Théodore de Bèze in the project to translate the Psalms and other biblical writings into French. During the 1530s he resided at the Ferrarese court of Renée de France, who was herself an important ally of Protestant thinkers from France.[1] This same court, we should also note, was at the time home to Anne de Parthenay (herself a member of Renée's household), grandmother of Catherine de Parthenay, the Huguenot patron to whom the first volume of Jean Pasquier's *Mellange d'Orlande* was dedicated in 1575 (see chapter 1, above). Marot's name, in short, resonated deeply with the entire sweep of Huguenot literary expression.

"Mon coeur se recommande"

Among Marot's lyrical poems—including those set to music by Lasso—we find literary themes that must have alternately moved and shocked Protestant readers. Some, in recalling the unrequited love of the *amour courtois,* were converted with surprising ease to the constraints of Huguenot piety. The Protestant adaptations of Marot's "Mon coeur se recommande à vous" can serve as a good example of this process. Marot's lyrics hinged on a literary commonplace of unrequited love stretching back at least to Ockeghem's "Ma bouche rit": a suffering heart seeks sympathy while a vindictive mouth denounces the conditions of separation from the beloved. But whereas in the original poem the poet's "voice" can only curse ("ne faict maintenant que maudire"), in the *contrafacta* it instead offers praise in the form of melodious song ("fai dire ton los en chant melodieux"). Lasso's music serves to amplify ideas expressed in the original text in various ways, some of which are converted to a spiritual register in the Protestant reworkings of the lyrics. Vautrollier, Pasquier, and Goulart each retain, for instance, the affective language that dominates the second line of this poem, in which the poetic persona reveals a heart "all full of weariness and suffering." These sentiments are aptly embodied in the descending lines, syncopations, and multiple suspensions heard in Lasso's chanson.[2] Thanks to its multiple repetitions of text fragments and use of contrasting vocal choirs, the concluding section of Lasso's chanson also works surprisingly well with the sense of the spiritual texts, recognizing the new-found musicality ("en chant melodieux") at work in the poem (see Ex. 4.1, measures 31–42).[3]

Marot's poem as set by Lasso:
> Mon coeur se recommande à vous
> Tout plain d'ennuy et de martire,
> Au moins en despit des jaloux
> Faites qu'à-dieu vous puisse dire.
> Ma bouche qui vous souloit rire
> Et comter propos gratieux
> Ne faict maintenant que maudire
> Ceux qui m'ont banny de vos yeux.

Translation:
> My heart commends itself to you all full of weariness and suffering. In despite of jealousy give me leave at least to say my farewell. My mouth, which used to laugh with you and bandy sweet sayings, now only curses those who have banished me from your fair eyes.

Pasquier and Vautrollier:
> Mon coeur se rend a toy seigneur,
> Tout plein d'ennuy et de martyre
> Helas! car j'ai de ta faveur
> Trop abusé, donc je souspire.
> Ma bouche qui se souloit rire
> Et conter propos vicieux[4]
> Ne fera desormais que dire
> Ton los, en chant melodieux.

Translation:
> My heart gives itself to you, Lord, all full of weariness and suffering. Alas! for I much abused your favor, of which I now sigh. My mouth, which used to laugh and speak words of malice, can now only speak your praises in melodious song.

Goulart:
> Mon coeur se rend a toy seigneur,
> Tout plein d'ennuy et de martyre
> Helas! car j'ai de ta faveur
> Trop abusé, donc je souspire.
> Ma bouche n'oseroit plus rire,
> Ni compter propos gracieux.
> Ouvre la donc, et lui fai dire
> Ton los en chant melodieux.

Translation:

My heart gives itself to you, Lord, all full of weariness and suffering. Alas! for I much abused your favor, of which I now sigh. My mouth can no longer laugh, nor bandy sweet words. Open it then, and make it speak your praises in melodious song.

Other poems by Marot, however, dwell in an expressive landscape very different from that just encountered. Here in place of the idealized, distant, and almost spiritual love that dominates the codes of the courtly mode, we find behavior that enacts precisely those physical behaviors that such lyrics eschew: frank sexuality, abandoned chastity, and drunken abandon. What is more, the characters who inhabit this space are drawn from a cast unlikely to be part of the courtly world itself, including peasant lovers, ill-suited couples, and errant clergy who behave in ways more risible than poignant.

Much current critical thought on this kind of poetry stems from the insights offered in Mikhail Bakhtin's *Rabelais and His World,* which understands such ribald verse (like the famously grotesque stories of Rabelais's *Gargantua and Pantagruel*) as originating with popular fairs or carnivals but serving in the context of literary culture some rather different ends. According to this view, whether or not a poem like Marot's "Monsieur l'Abbé" (the story of a drunken priest) relates the antics of any "real" clergy is less important than the recognizing how an anticlerical poem could serve to question ecclesiastical authority, and other forms of authority, too. As we have observed, this way of thinking helps to explain why Calvinist editors took Lasso's setting of "Monsieur l'Abbé" over into their chansonniers without change, for their audiences would have recognized in this Abbot's behavior a recurring criticism leveled by Protestant ministers at what they saw as the hypocrisy of a spiritually irresponsible Catholic clergy.[5]

Such poetry can also be understood as a means of self-fashioning for members of courtly or bourgeois society itself. As Kate van Orden has recently argued, when these popular themes are appropriated in a literary context they can be seen as a mirror image of elite identities, an inverted and distant realm in which common folk take part in the kinds of physical love, broken vows of chastity, and drunken abandon specifically excluded from the *amour courtois.*[6] The speaker of Marot's "Mon coeur se recommande à vous," for instance, could hardly be imagined to take part in the riotous physicality of the same poet's "Martin menoit son porceau au marché," in which a pair of copulating peasants are nearly dragged off by their precious pig, which has been tied to the woman's leg in order to prevent its accidental escape.[7] Through such poetry, van Orden contends, the nobility defined itself through representations of what (in theory, at least) it decidedly was *not.* Such negative examples could even be understood as a place where repressed desires were played out at a safe distance.

Example 4.1. Lasso, "Mon coeur se recommande," mm. 31–42.

Example 4.1, cont.

"Fleur de quinze ans"

One technique that Vautrollier, Pasquier, and Goulart used in reforming this carnivalesque poetry was to frame licentious behavior as a negative example. This is the approach taken in the case of Marot's "Fleur de quinze ans." The original poem offers advice of a rather dubious nature to a young woman, tracing the steps of seduction from glance to kiss to touch, and finally to something that the poetic persona refrains from saying but would rather demonstrate. Not surprisingly, the poem required heavy editing by Goulart and Pasquier, who transformed this seductive entreaty into a warning against vain pleasure.[8] Just as interesting as the correction itself, however, are the ways in which the redacted texts align with the musical gestures

Example 4.2a. Lasso, "Fleur de quinze ans," mm. 1–8.

Example 4.2b. Lasso, "Fleur de quinze ans," mm. 11–25.

Example 4.2b, cont.

Lasso crafted for the original poem. His setting, like Marot's lyric, unfolds as a sequence of somewhat independent musical gestures corresponding to the rhetorical gestures of the text: a long declamatory line and clear cadence mark off the opening two lines of the poem, with their introductory announcement of "five main points" of advice for the young listener (see Exs. 4.2a and 4.2b; measures 1–7). Lines 3 and 4, which offer the first few pieces of erotic wisdom, are marked by a sudden shift to triple mensuration (measures 7ff), and line 5, which describes how touch follows quickly on from the kiss with its increasingly rapid rhythmic movement and melodic patter song, captures the sense of that line of text. All of this rhythmic energy suddenly ceases, however, at the rhetorical question "qui est"—for here a suitably embarrassed series of musical stutters cast as alternating duos and tense silences (see measures 19–20) ultimately give way to the paired imitative duets setting the epigrammatic close of the poem (measures 20–33).

Marot's poem as set by Lasso:[10]

> Fleur de quinze ans si Dieu vous sauve et gard'
> J'ay en amour trouvé cinq poins exprès:
> Premierement il y a le regard,
> Puis le devis et le baiser apres,
> L'atouchement suit le baiser de pres,
> Et tous ceux le tendent au dernier point
> Qui est—qui est?—Je ne le diray point,
> Mais s'il vois plait en ma chambre vous rendre,
> Je me mettray volontiers en pourpoint
> Voire tout nud pour le vous faire apprendre.

Translation:

> Flower of fifteen (may God preserve and keep you) I have found in love these five main points: First comes the glance. It is followed by talk and then by the kiss. Kissing yields to caressing without delay. And all the above brings us to the last point, which is—which is—I won't say exactly. But if you'd like to come to my chamber I'll be more than happy in my doublet or even better in the nude to teach you.

Pasquier:

> Fleur de quinze ans Dieu vous conserve et gard',
> J'ay quelques poins à vous monstrer expres,
> C'est que n'ayez effronté regard,
> Soyez donc humble et honneste en apres,
> L'honnesteté la vertu suit de pres
> Qui vous fera hair le vain plaisir
> D'amour, d'amour, et l'effrené desir,
> Dont est tousjours la jeunesse suivie,
> Sur tout de Dieu la crainte faut choisir,
> Pour vous mener en l'éternelle vie.

Translation:

> Flower of fifteen God preserve you and keep you. I have several main things to tell you: Do not give impudent looks, be humble and honest, too; Virtue will follow honesty close on, and will make you hate the vain pleasure of love, of love, and unbounded desire, youth's constant sequel. Choose above all to fear God to ensure for yourself eternal life.

Marot's poem, with its explicit air of seduction, apparently offended a fair number of sixteenth-century readers and listeners, Calvinist and Catholic alike. Vautrollier omitted the chanson from his edition of the "purified" Lasso chansons altogether. Pasquier and Goulart each retained Marot's basic conceit, in which a speaker offers advice to a young woman. Here, however, the message is moralizing rather than erotic: avoid improper glances, flee from the vanity of temporary, physical pleasure. Taking a cue from the Protestant *contrafacta*, perhaps, reprints of Le Roy et Ballard's *Les meslanges d'Orlande* and Pierre Phalèse's *Fleur de chansons* of 1592 likewise replace Marot's original poem with Goulart's *contrafactum*.[9]

We should also note a remarkable coincidence between the fictive space of the *contrafactum* and the audience envisaged by one of the books that contains it. One of Pasquier's Lasso chansonniers, after all, was dedicated to a woman and included introductory poems that addressed his female pupils. In this respect the advice heard in the chanson acquires two sets of listeners: one in the text and the other among the auditors of the chanson itself.[11] It is perhaps fitting, therefore, that the signal moment of reversal in the original poem, where the stream of dubious advice at last refrains from saying what the speaker prefers to demonstrate ("Qui est—qui est?") here in the context of the *contrafacta* poems, the musical phrase enjambs lines 6 and 7 ("You should hate the vain pleasure/*Of love*"). As heard in the chanson, we pause for repetition (thanks in some measure to a dramatic rift in the rhythmic and contrapuntal texture of Lasso's chanson) in a way that might be understood to question or to subvert "amour" rather than to promote it. Was this just an accident or was it part of a considered plan on the part of Pasquier and Goulart to direct the meaning away from the original poetic context of Lasso's gesture?[12]

"Quand mon mari"

Like the adaptations of "Fleur de quinze ans," still other *contrafacta* rework carnivalesque lyrics in ways designed to reflect the social and moral norms of Calvinist communities. "Quand mon mari," to cite but a single example of such adaptations, was originally the lament of a "mal mariée" young wife physically abused by her old husband. The scenario was recast by Pasquier as a testimonial to the happiness that comes with marital devotion and domestic tranquility, albeit one that preserves the phonetic qualities of the original rhyme, and much of the original syntax, too. Goulart in turn adapted Pasquier's *contrafactum* of this chanson as a tale of marital fidelity, but in so doing suppressed the first-person voice of the woman, preferring instead simply to describe the happy household in third-person narration. The adaptations make no special acknowledgment of the animated rhythmic profile of Lasso's musical setting of this text, with its short melodic quips (prompted perhaps by the short eight-syllable lines) and its largely perfunctory homorhythmic textures. But as in the case of "Fleur de quinze ans" we might guess that this adaptation was intended first and foremost as a way to inculcate female complacency and obedience even if the lively music might seem to work against those goals.[13]

Poem as set by Lasso:
    Quand mon mary vient de dehors,
    Ma rente est d'estre batue,
    Il prend la cuillier du pot
    A la teste il me la rue.
    J'ay grand peur qu'il ne me tue,
    C'est un faux villain jaloux,
    C'est un villain rioteux grommeleux:
    Je suis jeune et il est vieux.

Translation:
    When my husband comes home, beating is my portion and lot; he grabs the
    spoon from the pot and hits me on the head with it. I am so afraid that he
    will kill me; He is a false, jealous villain; He is a villainous, ill-tempered,
    grumbler. I am young and he is old.

Pasquier:
    Quand mon mari s'en va dehors
    Troter ne vay en la rue
    Mais à la besongne alors,
    Menagere je me rue.
    S'il revient de la charrue
    Acueil luy fay gracieux
    Il n'est vilain grommeleur ni facheux
    Bien que sois jeune et luy vieux.

Translation:
    When my husband goes out, I don't rush out to the street but instead stay at
    my housework. If he returns from the plough I make him right welcome. He's
    neither an evil complainer nor false. Even though I am young and he is old.

Goulart:
    Quand l'homme honneste va dehors,
    Sa femme n'est par la rue.
    Ains à la besongne alors
    Mesnagere elle se rue.
    S'il revient ell'le salue,
    Et fait acueil gracieux.
    Il n'est vilain, rioteux, grommeleux
    S'elle est jeune, et s'il est vieux.

Translation:
    When the good man goes out, his wife isn't out on the street. Into house-
    work, rather, she throws herself. If he returns she greets him and welcomes
    him graciously. He's not a villainous, ill-tempered, grumbler, though she is
    young and he is old.

"D'amours me va"

Another enduring theme of the Protestant *contrafacta* dwells on the vanity of the contemporary world, which is itself seen as a carnivalesque inversion of the pious life. This is richly demonstrated in Goulart's adaptation of Marot's "D'amours me va." The original poem describes a lover "reversed" by the trials of an unfufilled relationship, culminating in the chiastic syntax of the last couplet, " In love, with me all goes topsy-turvy. All topsy-turvy goes love with me."[14]

Marot's poem as set by Lasso:
> D'Amours me va tout au rebours,
> Ja ne fault que de cela mente,
> I'ay refus en lieu de secours;
> M'amie rit et je lamente.
> C'est la cause pourquoy je chante:
> D'Amours me va tout au rebours,
> Tout au rebours me va d'amours.

Translation:
> In love, with me all goes topsy-turvy. By no means do I lie. Rejection is my lot, instead of succor. My beloved laughs and I lament. That is the reason I sing: "In love, with me all goes topsy-turvy. All topsy-turvy goes love with me."

Goulart:
> Le monde va tout à rebours:
> Si verité vient, il lamente:
> Du Seigneur il fuit le secours
> De vanités il se contente
> C'est la cause pourquoy je chante,
> Le monde va tout à rebours,
> Le monde va tout à rebours.

Translation:
> The world goes all topsy-turvy: If truth presents itself, the world laments. The Lord's helping hand it flees. With vanities it is content. That is the reason I sing: "The world goes all topsy-turvy, the world goes all topsy-turvy."

Taking the chiastic reversal embraced by the last two verses of the poem as his cue, Lasso crafts a five-voice setting in which the Tenor part is a canonic inversion of the Quintus, which it follows at the interval of a *breve* (see Exs. 4.3a and 4.3b). In so doing the composer offers a symbolic manifestation of the amorous "reversal" described in the poem, while simultaneously avoiding the temptation to represent or to connote the laughter

Example 4.3a. Lasso, "D'amours me va," mm. 1–8.

and lamentation of Marot's poetic persona and the speaker's beloved. What is more, the canonic design, with its extended musical process of statement and immediate inverted imitation, also anticipates the final line, which is a reprise of the first.[15] The frequent pauses, motivic entries, and careful alignment of text and tone in the concluding section of the piece highlight the "circular" syntax and reversal at hand in the final pair of verses. By the time Lasso is finished, the listener hardly knows whether "d'amours" is the start of this pair of lines or the end. In so doing, Lasso points out the problem of closure inherent in Marot's poem, and of course the problem of closure inherent in all musical canons of this kind—they each hinge on a process that is simple to begin but tricky to conclude. The ending of Goulart's poem is less rich than Marot's original in this respect, for the fifth line of his text is simply repeated as the sixth, without the syntactic "inversion."

Example 4.3b. Lasso, "D'amours me va," mm. 22–34.

Example 4.3b, cont.

But the simple refrain (now the reader can hardly miss the parallel with the first verse) does serve to emphasize the "inverted" moral landscape that Calvinist writers saw in the contemporaneous social world of the late sixteenth century: a world in which vanity took pride of place over sacred truths. In this respect Lasso's canonic procedure serves well as a symbolic representation of one of the enduring commonplaces of the *contrafacta* and of the devotional literature from which they derive.

"Qui dort icy?"

Goulart's and Pasquier's revisions of Marot's "Qui dort icy?" likewise reveal their abiding interest in the *vanitas* theme. Marot's poem was first published (in the *Adolescence clémentine* of 1533) with a rubric identifying it as a contemplation of a statue of a sleeping Venus ("De la statue de Venus endormye"). This emblem serves for Marot as a rhetorical point of departure, posing and answering his own questions about the classical goddess of Love.[16]

> *Poem by Marot as set by Lasso:*
> Qui dort icy? Le faut il demander?
> Venus y dort, qui vous peut commander,
> Ne l'esveillez, elle ne vous nuira:
> Si l'esveillez, croyez qu'elle ouvrira
> Ses deux beaux yeux, pour les vostres bander.

> *Translation:*
> Who sleeps here? Must you ask? Venus sleeps here, who may command you. Let her sleep and she will do you no harm; but if you wake her, know that she will open her two fair eyes, in order to blindfold yours.

Lasso's musical approach to this poem does well to underscore both its rhetoric stance and the theme of "awakening" (see Exs. 4.4a and 4.4b).[17] The reciprocal questions of the first line of poetry, "Who sleeps here? Must you ask?," for instance, are musically juxtaposed by two contrasting choirs of voices, the first high, the second low (see measures 1–5), in a gesture that stresses the exchange as well as the rhyme and verse structure of the *cinquain* in which it figures (the division corresponds, after all, to the conventional "four plus six" division of decasyllabic verse). The slow-moving full choir that follows these contrasting pairs nicely represents the repose of the response: "Venus sleeps here" (measures 5–8). The music for the last two lines of the setting likewise underscores the poetic structure and the ideas it expresses: Lasso ignores the syntactic *enjambement* of lines four and five (" . . .that she will open/Her two fair eyes . . ."), preferring instead to pause rather strikingly at the end of the fourth line with a gesture that aptly represents the moment of awakening with a bold shift to a sonority that introduces the first B natural in the piece (see measure 15). The music for the fifth line of text, too, offers fitting representation of the ideas contained there: more paired choirs for Venus's now open eyes in the first hemistich, and a long series of overlapping imitative lines that enact the "blindfolding" of the viewer's eyes (see measures 16–28).

The revision of poems on antique themes seems to have been something of a special genre in the Protestant devotional literature. According to Terence Cave, the appeal was twofold, offering an opportunity to suppress references to pagan deities on one hand while stressing the impermanence of human endeavors—evidenced by the decay of classical civilization—on the other.[18] The condemnation of vanity and the impermanence of human endeavors, he also notes, figure in a genre of what he calls "sermon-poems" that address a fictive readership through the use of dialogue, or take an accusative stance towards some imagined listener. Cave presumes an affinity between such poems, with their frequent use of interrogative, assonance, and syntactic interruption or juxtaposition, and the animated, public preaching style of Calvinist ministers (we would do well to recall that Goulart, and probably Pasquier, too, counted themselves among the ranks of such spiritual orators).[19] The Protestant adaptations of Marot's "Qui dort icy" exemplify this trend nicely.

Jean Pasquier's *contrafactum,* for instance, retains the questions of Marot's opening line, and in general accords well with the musical gestures that Lasso used to set it. But instead of cautioning the listener to step lightly around the pagan goddess of love, the new poem warns him or her against the vice of laziness. In so doing the last two lines of text obliterate Lasso's play upon "awakening" and "blindfolding" in the original:

Example 4.4a. Lasso, "Qui dort icy?" mm. 1–10.

Example 4.4b. Lasso, "Qui dort icy?" mm. 14–23.

Pasquier:

Qui dort ici? Le faut il demander?
Un paresseux a qui tant commander
Le somne on voit, que pauvreté viendra,
Tandis qu'au lit en dormant se tiendra,
Si mieux ne veut sa paresse amander.

Translation:

Who sleeps here? Must you ask? A lazy one, so commanded by sleep, as you see, that poverty will follow, as long as he keeps to his bed, if he will not his sloth amend.

Goulart's *contrafactum,* too, opens with similar—though more rhetorical—questions, and continues with a warning of moral danger, but reveals an altogether more subtle sense of Marot's language and of Lasso's musical setting. Here, for instance, the opening question is not "Who sleeps *here*?" but "Who sleeps in *us*?"—a change that involves the speaker and reader alike in a process of moral self-examination much more immediate than Pasquier's finger-pointing at a bad example.

Goulart:

Qui dort en nous? Le fault il demander?
La vanité, qui ne peut s'amender.
Ne l'esveillez, elle ne vous nuira.
Si l'esveillez, croyez qu'elle ouvrira
Ses deux faux yeux pour les vostres bander.

Translation:

Who sleeps in us? Must you ask? Vanity, which cannot mend its ways. Don't wake her, and she'll do you no harm. If you wake her, know that she will open her two false eyes in order to blindfold yours.

Goulart's response to his opening query is similarly subtle in its transformation of the original lyrics, for the sleeping danger is not Venus, but "Vanité." It is thus with good effect that the assonant similarity of *Venus* and *vanity* are recalled in the slow-moving full choir setting this line of the poem. Likewise Goulart retains the verb "ouvrira" at the conclusion of the fourth line of poetry, which in the original setting was so neatly joined to striking tonal gestures. So, too, Goulart's description of the false eyes of vanity ("faux" bearing a convenient assonance with the former "beaux"), finds sympathetic gestures in Lasso's music. Here as in the original poem the contrasting vocal duos represent that dangerous pair (a bit of *Augenmusik* if ever there was), while the elaborate melismas and syncopation of the final hemistich suggest the "blindfolding" that will result if Venus/Vanity stirs. Preferring local adjustment of the text to a thorough revision like Pasquier's, Goulart's poem takes surprisingly good advantage of Lasso's musical treatment of the final two lines of the chanson. Joined with the most effective moments of Lasso's chansons, Goulart's *contrafactum* becomes an equally effective means of prompting self-examination of the sort he plainly thinks will guard against the vanity that lurks not in the world at large but within his readers.

"En un lieu"

As we have seen, Pasquier's (and Goulart's) adaptations of "Qui dort icy," like other sermonizing devotional literature, condemn the profound *vanitas* of much external human activity, advocating instead a pious inner sensibility alone as a worthy pursuit. Believers apparently sought this knowledge not through direct proof, but rather through the ongoing process of textual interpretation. It should thus not be so surprising that the importance of sacred texts—and in turn the processes of exegesis through which they become manifest—are themselves thematized in some of the *contrafacta*. In his reworking of "En un lieu,"[20] for instance, Pasquier uses a chanson about a candle in a dark cave as a vehicle for an important affirmation of the illuminative power of sacred texts: "keep before and behind you God's word and give it ear," his poem advises. Goulart similarly uses the figure of a saving light at the edge of a dark cave as a metaphorical projection of the internal struggle between physical temptation and spiritual enlightenment: "For whether I go forward or back Satan and the flesh I fear. . . .Your Word, O God, which I heed, will always be my light."

Poem as set by Lasso:
 En un lieu ou l'on ne void goutte,
 Je n'iray jamais sans lumiere,
 Car tant devant comme derriere
 On en a bien souvent la goutte.
 Puis que du pertuis je me doute,
 Chandelle ne me sera chere.
 En un lieu ou l'on ne void goutte,
 Je n'iray jamais sans lumiere.

Translation:
 In a place where one can see not a whit, I never go without a light, for, front and back, it often gives you the gout. As I can't be sure of the door, I'll not hold candle too dear. In a place where one can't see a bit, I will never go without a light.

Pasquier:
 En un lieu ou l'on voit goutte
 S'il ne faut aller sans lumiere,
 Ayes devant toy et derriere
 De Dieu la parole et l'ecoute:

Si l'as avec toy n'ayes doute,
Droit iras en toute maniere.
En un lieu ou l'on ne voit goutte
Il ne faut aller sans lumiere.

Translation:

In a place where one can see not a whit one must never go without a light.
Keep before and behind you God's word and give it ear: If you have it with
you have no fear—you will go straight in every way. In a place where one
can't see a whit must never go without light.

Goulart:

En ce monde où l'on ne voit goute,
Je n'iray jamais sans lumiere,
Car marchant avant ou arriere
Satan et ma chair je redoute.
Puis que du malheur je me doute
Chandelle ne me sera chere:
Ta Parolle, O Dieu, que j'escoute,
Me sera tousjours pour lumiere.

Translation:

In this world where one can see not a whit I will never venture without a
light. For whether I go forward or back Satan and the flesh I fear. Since I
fear mishap I'll not hold a candle too dear: Your Word, O God, which I
heed, will always be my light.

Lasso's musical treatment of this *huitain* adapts itself well to each of
these *contrafacta,* albeit for different reasons (see Exs. 4.5a and 4.5b).[21]
The chanson opens with a passage in triple mensuration, which, thanks to
a 16th-century notational convention, could be written entirely in a series
of "empty" semi-breves that signified in graphical forms the void described
in the text itself. This same musical device returns at line 7 of the original
poem, which recapitulates the opening pair of lines from this poem (see
measures 28–30). Pasquier's text uses the same refrain structure, and largely
the same language for the opening (and closing) pair of lines. As such it
builds upon Lasso's musical refrain, which strengthens the metaphorical
meaning Pasquier attaches to the void and the "light" that disperses it.

Goulart's chanson provides a subtle twist on its model: the opening couplet of his *contrafactum* retains the darkness/lamp imagery nicely symbol-
ized by the musical notation. But in other respects his text is quite different
from Pasquier's: whereas the poetic persona of the latter chanson recounted
second- and third-person advice about sacred texts and moral dangers,
Goulart's *contrafactum* is cast in the first person ("Satan and the flesh I
fear"). Perhaps more important, the last two lines of Goulart's poem are
not the same as the first. Instead the speaker pledges God to hear (and thus

Example 4.5a. Lasso, "En un lieu," mm. 1–10.

Example 4.5b. Lasso, "En un lieu," mm. 25–37.

Example 4.5b, cont.

attend to) the Word as an eternal lamp: "Ta Parolle, O Dieu, que j'escoute, Me sera tousjours pour lumiere." It hardly seems coincidental that this allusion to aural comprehension and obedience comes at the same moment that marks the return of the musical gesture from the opening of the chanson (measures 28–30). Thanks to Lasso's chanson, in short, Goulart's text does more than advise a particular fidelity to the Word. Instead it actively involves its performers and listeners in a process of recollection analogous to the process of rehearing proposed by the *contrafactum* itself.

"De tout mon coeur"

The importance of sacred texts is similarly emphasized in the spiritual revisions of "De tout mon coeur," particularly Goulart's *contrafactum,* which makes apt use of a refrain design at work in the musical setting to emphasize the central point of his lesson. The original poem (anonymous, but sharing language and themes with verse from Marot's pen) is built around one of the most enduring commonplaces of Renaissance love lyrics, in which the beloved is compared to a single flower prized above all others. This theme is set out clearly already in the first line of the poem, which also returns as the sixth and final verse. Lasso once again designs a musical setting that recognizes this poetic refrain (see Exs. 4.6a, 4.6b, and 4.6c—compare measures 1ff. with measures 41ff.).[22] Indeed, his approach to the chanson stresses the formal elements of rhyme and of the customary division of ten-syllable lines into two hemistichs of four and six syllables, which he often repeats as small poetic and melodic units. In some of his other chansons Lasso took particular care to reflect poetic syntax with musical gestures that followed the sense rather than the form or prosody of the verse. But the syntactic *enjambement* of the third and fourth verses in this

Example 4.6a. Lasso, "De tout mon coeur," mm. 1–9.

Example 4.6b. Lasso, "De tout mon coeur," mm. 17–31.

Example 4.6b, cont.

chanson receive no such musical attention (see measure 25). On the contrary, Meier has suggested that Lasso's musical reading of this text relies in
part upon his recognition of the power of modal organization to serve as a
means of expressing particular words, such as the phrase "Qu'elle procede/
En bonté et valeur" (see the Superius, measures 17–24), which receives
motives emphasizing the "G to B flat" melodic repercussion that Meier
sees as a hallmark of Mode 1 (in this case transposed from its usual position on D to G). In so doing, Meier argues, Lasso equates the "goodness"
of the flower described in the poem with a propriety of modal polyphony:
"Something taken for granted is here recognized by the listener as something unusual and is understood as a musical metaphor for it."[23]

Example 4.6c. Lasso, "De tout mon coeur," mm. 41–51.

Example 4.6c, cont.

Poem as set by Lasso:
>De tout mon coeur j'ayme la Marguerite
>Et di pour vray combien qu'elle est petite
>Qu'elle precede en bonté, et valeur
>Beauté, couleur toute autre plaisant' fleur:
>Parquoy sur tout (qui voudra s'en dépite.)
>De tout mon coeur j'ayme la Marguerite.

Translation:
>With all my heart I love the daisy, and say truly that, however tiny, she exceeds in goodness and worth, beauty, and color all other flowers. That is why above all (resent it if you will): With all my heart I love the daisy.

Pasquier and Vautrollier:[24]
>De tout mon coeur j'aime la marguerite,
>Qui est (O Dieu) en ta loy sainte escrite
>Car elle excede en bonté et valeur
>Tous les thresors de l'humaine grandeur.
>Soit donc qu'aucun s'en courrouce ou despite,
>De tout mon coeur j'aime la marguerite.

Translation:
>With all my heart I love the daisy, which is (oh God) in your holy law inscribed, for it exceeds in goodness and worth all the treasures of human grandeur. So be it then that any be wroth or vexed, with all my heart I love the daisy.

Goulart:
>De tout mon coeur j'aime ceste Parole,
>Qui est, O Dieu, ta gracieuse escole,
>Elle precede en bonté et valeur

Tous les thresors de l'humaine grandeur.
Par quoi sur tout (qui voudra s'en affole),
De tout mon coeur j'aime ceste Parole.

Translation:
With all my heart I love this Word, which is, oh God, your gracious teaching. It exceeds in goodness and worth all the treasures of human grandeur, on account of which above all (let who will be maddened); with all my heart I love this Word.

Vautrollier and Pasquier provide the same *contrafactum* text, a poem that retains the wording of the original first (and last) line, and also preserves the original rhyme scheme (aabbaa). There is nothing in this new poem, in short, that runs counter to the largely formal approach to the poem taken by Lasso. The parenthetical, aphoristic cry to the divine in the second verse, for instance, is neatly confined to the first hemistich of that line, and as such aligns neatly with Lasso's division of that verse into two musical ideas. For Pasquier and Vautrollier the flower of the opening line is scripture itself, which exceeds all the vanities of human endeavors.

Goulart's text, like the one offered by Pasquier and Vautrollier, retains the same overall pattern of rhyme as in the original. And he, too, prizes sacred texts above mortal vanities. But in some other respects he departs from the model. The primacy of the Word, for instance, is introduced in the very first line, with the result that the reference to the metaphorical flower of the original verse and of the previous *contrafactum* is entirely suppressed. Goulart's poem, by transferring concern for the Word to the first (and last) line thus uses the plagal ending of the chanson to better advantage than the Pasquier-Vautrollier chanson, making a virtue of the musical gesture that in their *contrafactum* (and in Lasso's original) seems poetically unjustified. Drawing devotional significance from a musical gesture that had no such importance in the original, the technique of refrain and reinterpretation recalls the procedure at work in Goulart's *contrafactum* of "En un lieu."

The poetry of Clément Marot, as we have seen, was frequently set to music by Lasso, and, in turn, revised by Protestant editors such as Pasquier and Goulart. These lyrics embrace a wide range of literary themes, notably echoes of the poetry of the old *amour courtois* and its inverted double, the landscape of the carnivalesque love. In converting some of Marot's most worldly poetry—and anonymous verse that speaks in similar ways—into moralizing messages, the editors of the Lasso *contrafacta* books effect a radical transformation of a set of literary codes patently at odds with their own world views. When joined with Lasso's music, these new poems become songs that attempt not so much to "represent" moral viewpoints, but rather a means by which listeners could enter into a process of reflection, recollection, and change that mirrored the spiritual processes proposed in the poems themselves. Through these songs the preacher's voice and Lasso's voice become one and the same.

Chapter 5

Lasso's Chansons and the Spiritual Self

As we have just seen, some of the *contrafacta* of the Lasso chansons attempt to elevate carnivalesque language found in some of Clément Marot's poems. Still other spiritual revisions of secular verse use dialogue structures to preach about proper conduct and about the importance of sacred texts as moral signposts. Among these, Goulart's "Qui dort en nous?" points the way towards our next group of *contrafacta*, namely those that turn an inward gaze. But whereas "Qui dort en nous?" depended upon an interrogative strategy of admonition, the present set of chansons are instead lyrical, first person contemplations of the self. Transforming the conditions of love into the conditions of salvation, these texts echo an entire tradition of Calvinist devotional poetry, texts that in Terence Cave's view, stress "the sharp antithesis between the humiliation of the sinner and the glory of God."[1] Slipping between secular and spiritual registers, the music that accompanies these chansons often serves to emphasize, to express, and to enact in sound the very sorts of "inner" conditions described in the poems, making these works particularly apt embodiments of the devotional ideals of Protestant listeners.

"Toutes les nuitz"

An example of this can be seen in a refrain from a *rondeau sixain*, "Toutes les nuitz," and its adaptation by Pasquier and Goulart.[2] In this poem, the lonely and lovesick speaker dozes but does not rest, and kisses his pillow for solace.

> *Poem as set by Lasso:*
> Toutes les nuitz que sans vous je me couche,
> Pensant à vous ne fay que sommeiller
> Et en revant jusques au resveiller
> Incessament vous quiers parmi la couche
> Et bien souvent au lieu de vostre bouche
> En soupirant je baise l'oreiller
> Toutes les nuictz.

> *Translation:*
> Every night that I lie down without you, thinking of you I can only doze, and dreaming until I wake incessantly search for you in the bed. And very often in place of your mouth, sighing, I kiss the pillow—Every night.

Lasso's five-voice setting of this poem attends to several aspects of the literary text (see Ex. 5.1).[3] In line 2, for instance, the phrase "ne fay que sommeiller" ends with a weak cadence (measure 10) that nicely enacts the inconclusive condition of the dozing lover, who is caught between the continuity of wakefulness and the closure of sleep. In the third and fourth lines, in contrast, Lasso offers a single musical gesture that respects the syntactic *enjambement* of those poetic lines, and with a long series of cascading contrapuntal pairs simultaneously represents the "incessant search" described there (measures 10–20). The *enjambement* that links lines 5 and 6 is similarly recognized in the music, here with repeated pauses and sequential transpositions for the sighing mentioned in those lines (measures 27–30). Finally, this music is linked directly with the *rentrement*, (the customary half-line refrain found in some abbreviated *rondeaux*) which itself recalls the opening of the chanson (measures 34–37).

Thomas Vautrollier printed this chanson without change. But for Lasso's Calvinist editors on the Continent, the sighing lover and his pillow suggested a strong parallel with the tear-soaked bed mentioned in Psalm 6, and which, in commentaries by Marot, Bèze, and other prominent devotional writers, was taken as an emblem of extreme penitence: the tears were an outward sign of lamentation that cleansed the penitent of corruption.[4] Goulart and Pasquier alike thus offer a vignette in which an exemplary believer laments past sin by night and sings heartfelt praises to the Divine by day. These apparently habitual forms of spiritual expression—sighing, speaking, singing, crying—find fitting correspondence in Lasso's music for this chanson. In the *contrafacta*, for instance, the references to "chanter sons los" (Goulart) and "chanter de coeur" (Pasquier) in line 4 align nicely with the cascading musical gestures that supported "incessament vous quiers" in the original poem (measures 17–20). Likewise Pasquier and Goulart were each careful to retain the "sighing" of line 6 in a way that corresponds precisely with the imitation of that sound in Lasso's setting (measures 27–30).

Pasquier:
> Toutes les nuis que le Chrestien se couche
> Il doit à Dieu avant que sommeiller
> Crier mercy, et à son réveiller
> Chanter de coeur sa louange et de bouche
> Mesme de pleurs, quand son peché le touche,
> En souspirant baigner son oreiller
> Toutes les nuis.

Translation:
> Every night that the Christian lies down, before going to sleep he must cry out to God for mercy and upon waking sing with heart and mouth his praises. And with tears as well, when his sin pains him, in sighing bathe his pillow—every night.

Example 5.1. Lasso, "Toutes les nuitz," mm. 1–37.

Example 5.1, cont.

Example 5.1, cont.

Example 5.1, cont.

Goulart:
> Toutes les nuicts que le Chrestien se couche,
> Il doit à Dieu avant que sommeiller
> Crier merci, et puis au reveiller
> Chanter son los, et de coeur et de bouche
> Il fond en pleurs quand son peché le touche
> Et souspirant mouille son oreiller
> Toutes les nuits.

Translation:
> Every night that the Christian lies down, before going to sleep he must cry out to God for mercy, and upon waking sing his praises with heart and voice. He melts into tears when his sin pains him, and sighing bathes his pillow—every night.

"Quand me souvient"

"Quand me souvient" shares with "Toutes le nuitz" both a common formal procedure—the use of the *rentrement*—and a general thematic concern with lamentation and remembrance. And, as in the instance of the *contrafacta* for the chansons just examined, the *contrafacta* of "Quand me souvient" dwell in the rhetoric of retrospection and regret so nicely enacted by the formal device of the partial refrain. But this is also an unusual *rentrement,* for it consists of the *closing* words of the first line rather than the opening ones. In so doing, according to Frank Dobbins, Lasso may have been making a passing allusion to Crequillon's setting of the same poem, which features the same, special *rentrement.*[5] For Lasso, the appeal of Crequillon's approach may have been the way in which this peculiar *rentrement* could be made to seem an effective closing as well as a return to the beginning, for in the context of the last line of verse it neatly concludes the idea that prompts it. In the context of the last line, therefore, the *rentrement* emerges as the speech that remembrance has prompted: "of which night and day I must say, 'alas, sad fate.' "

Poem as set by Lasso:
> Quand me souvient de ma triste fortune
> Que j'ay perdu de mes yeux le soulas
> Plaindre m'y faut ma trop grand infortune
> Dont nuit et jour me convient dire, helas!
> Triste fortune.

Translation:
> When I think of my sad fate, that I have lost sight of solace, I must decry my too great misfortune, on account of which night and day I must say "alas, sad fate."

Pasquier:
> Le souvenir de ma vie passée
> Me cause ennuy et prive de soulas.
> O Dieu, par toy soit ma faute effacée,
> Qui bien souvent me fera dire, helas!
> Vie passée.

Translation:
> The remembrance of my past deeds gives me pain and takes away solace. O God, through you may my fault be wiped out, which will frequently make me say, "alas, passing life."

Goulart:
> Sentant l'effort, et la triste misere
> De mon peché qui me tient en ses laqs,
> Plaindre me veux à toi, mon Dieu, mon Pere,
> Et sans cesser nuict et jour dire, helas!
> Triste misere.

Translation:
> Feeling the strain, and the sad misery of my sin that holds me in its bonds, I must cry out to you, my God, my Father. And without pause night and day say "alas, sad misery."

Lasso's setting of this poem occupies an exceptionally low musical register, and dwells principally in a densely contrapuntal fabric that is saturated with frequent suspension figures, especially with semitonal inflections in the lowest sounding part of cadential designs. The conclusion of the fourth verse, with its incitement to speech itself, prompts a particularly striking juxtaposition of C sharp and B flat among the parts. These juxtapositions lead nicely into the long and similarly poignant coda, in which the *rentrement* is repeated and elaborated with melancholic effect (see Ex. 5.2, measures 19–30).[6] Indeed, Bernhard Meier sees in the large variety of tonal positions for cadences throughout this work an attempt by Lasso to represent in modal processes the prevailing affect of the remembered "sad fate" that is the subject of the poem. In this case a "mi" cadence to the tone A—a reasonably distant move in the context of Mode 4, in Meier's experience— here provides an expression of pain and misery: in measure 9 (at the words "Que j'ay perdu des mes yeux le *soulas*" and again in measure 22 (at the exclamation "dire, *helas*").[7] The self-consciousness with which Lasso seems to have deployed these unusual gestures, it might be added, mirrors the self-conscious reflections of the poet, who in the fictive world of the poem examines his own situation with a penetrating gaze that prompts the affective "helas" that Lasso so nicely enacted in sound.

For Huguenot listeners, the general mood of this regretful love lyric was

Example 5.2. Lasso, "Quand me souvient," mm. 1–30.

Example 5.2, cont.

Example 5.2, cont.

surprisingly close to the modes of retrospection and affective prayer at the heart of devotional sensibilities. Indeed, Thomas Vautrollier's *Recueil du mellange d'Orlande* of 1570 prints the chanson unchanged. Goulart and Pasquier each, in contrast, intervene in the text in ways that move the sounds even more explicitly to the modes of penitential practice. Goulart's rereading blames current sufferings on past transgressions, directs inarticulate cries of despair to God, and at last turns to speech itself, which also happens to be a recollection of the misery that began the poem in the first place. Pasquier's text likewise moves from remembrance to direct address and back again: the end-rhyme of his third line ("faute effacée") works particularly well with Lasso's musical gesture for this point in the poem, for its urge towards erasure and effacement finds clear correspondence in the avoided cadence that the composer employed here (see measures 16–17). Poised between the two memories of passing life, this evaded cadence serves nicely to support the important point made by Pasquier's verse, namely that it is only through Divine clemency that past faults may be forgiven.

"Si du malheur"

Lasso's setting of "Si du malheur" was first published only in 1573, and is, thus, possibly one of the newest chansons to be included the Le Roy et Ballard *Les meslanges d'Orlande* of 1576 and in Goulart's *Thrésor de musique d'Orlande*.[8] The poem recounts in striking language the afflictions suffered by a lover over the emptiness of separation and overwhelming joy that might come with reunion. Indeed, the entire eight-line poem hinges neatly upon the complementary ideas of absence and presence, which are doubly stressed (in both noun and adjective forms) in the fourth through sixth lines: "D'estre oublié par la trop longue *absence.*/*Absent* je meurs, et en vostre *presence*/*Present* aves de moy l'ame ravie." These repetitions serve, moreover, to complicate increasingly the syntax of the poem and to undermine the formal pattern of its rhyme scheme, culminating in the final line of verse, in which the two alternatives of absence and presence become the alternatives of death and life themselves:

Poem as set by Lasso:
  Si du malheur vous aviez cognoissance
  Dont ma vie est à rude mort contrainte
  Verriez à l'oeil ma perdurable crainte
  D'estre oublié par la trop longue absence.
  Absent je meurs, et en vostre presence
  Present aves de moy l'ame ravie,
  Helas! c'est bien par divine puissance
  Mourir aupres, et loing perdre la vie.

Translation:
> If you but knew the misfortune by which my life to cruel death is driven; you would readily see my unending fear: To be forgotten from too long an absence. Absent I die; and in your presence, you, present, have ravished the soul out of me. Alas! It is indeed by Divine power to die up close, and afar lose my life.

Goulart:
> De ce malheur tu as la cognoissance,
> Dont ma vie est à rude mort attainte
> Tu voids à l'oeil ma perdurable crainte
> D'estre oublié, ô Dieu, par ton absence.
> Absent je meurs, et puis en ta presence
> Soudain à toi je seu l'ame ravie.
> Helas, si tost n'apparoist la clemence,
> Je meurs pres toi, et loin je pers la vie.

Translation:
> You know of this misfortune by which my life has cruel death attained; you see before your eyes my endless fear to be forgotten, O Lord, through your absence. Absent I die, and then in your presence all at once my soul is ravished. Alas! If clemency does not come soon I die up close, and afar from you I lose my life.

Lasso's response to this poem retraces the emotional decline of the speaker and the formal dissolution of the neat agreement of rhyme and idea using a wide range of musical gestures—sudden changes in contrapuntal texture, varied melodic movement, and surprising harmonic effects (see Ex. 5.3).[9] Set in high clefs and rather high vocal tessitura, the overall registration of the chanson may itself have been understood as a representation of the extreme emotions revealed in the poem. At first, Lasso proceeds by joining each poetic verse to a single musical phrase, pausing briefly for the medial *caesura* after the fourth syllable of the line. The repetitive effect of this balanced approach to phrasing is nevertheless undercut by the varied cadences circumscribed by the first four rhymes, none of which pauses on the same central tone or voicing (see measures 5, 10, 14, and 19). But even this casual alignment of verse and tone quickly breaks down in the second half of the poem: *absence* and *absent* are here prolonged in a single sonority, a gesture that disguises the syntactic articulation and end rhyme that nominally divide them (measures 19–20). This same technique of elision through musical stasis recurs in the very next line, also, where *presence* and *present* are similarly passed over in a single sonority (measures 22–23). These gestures serve to highlight the word-play that links line 4 with 5 and 5 with 6, but they also afford Lasso the opportunity to fragment and to reassemble lines in simulation of the emotional turmoil of the final lines of text: strik-

Example 5.3. Lasso, "Si du malheur," mm. 1–37.

Example 5.3, cont.

Example 5.3, cont.

Example 5.3, cont.

ing silence separates "Absent je meurs" in line 5 from the remainder of that line (see measure 21), while silence again frames the poignant exclamation "Helas" at the outset of line 7 (measure 26). And the last line, itself repeated for emphasis, is divided into two distinct—and musically incompatible—gestures: brief silence and then low chords at "Mourir aupres" (measures 29–30), then a sweeping upward melodic leap, echoed in counterpoint that prolongs the sense of distance and finality implied by the text "et loing perdre la vie" (measures 30–33; these closely spaced contrapuntal patterns, it might be added, indirectly recall similar brief contrapuntal relationships that can be heard throughout the first half of the poem. See, for instance, the duos between Contratenor and Superius in measures 1–2; between Tenor and Bassus in measures 3–4; and similarly between same pairs of voice parts in measures 5–7.)

Meier sees in this work another example of how Lasso employed the contrast of normative and unusual positions of cadences within a given mode as a means of lending metaphorical support to the text at hand. For Meier this composition is nominally in Mode 2 (with a tonal center D and using high clefs), and as such the sudden "mi" cadence to E in measure 14 constitutes a radical departure from the norm that "frightens" the listener at "ma perdurable crainte."[10] Meier also considers this unexpected cadence and the thwarted one to C in measure 19 (the Tenor part drops out at the last moment) as illustrations of how the "foreignness" of certain cadential positions to a given mode enact a kind of distancing or removal also declared in the poem: "D'estre oublié par la trop longue absense." But there is more, for the same "avoided" cadence of measure 19 cedes to a sonority built around F that is in turn sustained into the beginning of the *next* line of poetry—and with good effect, as we have seen, since the two verses are joined by the verbal *chiasmus* of the repeated "absence."

Lasso, as we have just seen, used musical contrast and continuity to give voice to emotional qualities in "Si du malheur" not easily articulated by verse alone. Goulart's *contrafactum* of this chanson builds upon Lasso's musical reading of this text, adjusting its central themes—and the emotional urgency of its musical gestures—to ones already familiar in devotional poetry. For Goulart, the absence and presence mentioned in this poem are the absence and presence of the Divine itself ('D'estre oublié, ô Dieu, par ton absence./Absent je meurs, et puis en ta presence/Soudain à toi je sue l'ame ravie."). What is more, the rapid breakdown of the formal structure of the poem, so aptly emphasized in Lasso's music and culminating in the exclamatory "Helas" of the penultimate line of verse, enacts in sound precisely the process of reflection and affective prayer for clemency envisioned by Goulart's spiritual program. These same attitudes, as we have seen, are also at work in other *contrafacta*, which similarly build upon the musical means used to represent longing and to support the poetic recapitulations that frame those stances.

"Mes pas semez"

The Protestant adaptation of "Mes pas semez," like those of "Si du malheur," also transform ideas of despair into calls for Divine clemency. This curious, seven-line poem recounts the sufferings of its speaker in language that is at times Petrarchan in its allusions to "lonely places" and "watering eyes." Lasso's musical response to these lyrics is similarly striking, seemingly more consonant with the sorts of semantic representations heard in contemporaneous madrigals than in the chansons of the 1560s and 1570s (see Ex. 5.4).[11] The "scattered steps" of line 1, for instance, find apt correspondence in the wide melodic leaps of the vocal parts (measures 3–4), while thoughts "that make my eyes to water" are manifest in the melancholy juxtaposition of G sharp and B flat in the music for the third and fourth lines of text (measures 8–13). The repeated, echoing duos and ascending melodic lines that support line 5, finally, serve to realize and to represent the sort of habitual vocalizing implied by the poem ("the more I raise my voice") and emphasize the despair that dominates the remainder of the poem (measures 14–16).

Poem as set by Lasso:
> Mes pas semez et loings alez
> Par divers solitaires lieux
> Sont de pensers entremellez,
> Qui rendent humides mes yeux:
> Et tant plus j'ay ma voix haussée
> Tant moins je me sens exaucée
> Et si ne sçay quand j'auray mieux.

Translation:
> My scattered steps and distant goings by various lonely places are commingled with thoughts that make my eyes to water. And the more I raise my voice, the less I feel it heard and yet don't know when I will have it better.

Pasquier:
> Mes pas semez et loing et alez[12]
> Par divers solitaires lieux
> Furent de soin entremeslez
> Qui me firent pluvoir les yeux,
> Mais à Dieu j'ay ma voix haussée
> Et de luy ma voix exaucée.
> Croire me fait que j'auray mieux.

Translation:
> My errant steps and distant goings through various solitary places were commingled with care, which brought tears to my eyes. But to God I raised my voice, and His hearing my voice makes me believe that things will be better.

Example 5.4. Lasso, "Mes pas semez," mm. 1–17.

Example 5.4, cont.

Goulart:

> Mes pas, Seigneur, tant esgarez
> Par divers solitaires lieux
> Seront pour jamais asseurez
> Si tu jettes sur moy tes yeux.
> À toi seul j'ai ma voix haussée
> Aussi je la sens exaucée
> Et sçais tres-bien que j'aurai mieux.

Translation:

> My steps, Lord, so lost throughout various lonely places will be forever
> assured if only you cast your gaze upon me. To you alone I have raised my
> voice, and I feel answered, and know full well that things will be better.

Pasquier preserves much of the wording of the first four lines of this
text, and with them, the important ways in which Lasso's music evoked the

movements and feelings described there. The last three lines of the *contrafacta* similarly retain the idea of habitual speech. But in this case the result is quite different than before, since the speaker's thoughts are now raised up to God, who in attending to those prayers instills a sense of hopefulness in the conclusion of the poem. Goulart undertakes a similar transformation of the second half of the poem. The change also helps to point out a musical relationship that remained somewhat latent in the original settings, namely the way in which the music for the opening of the fifth line of text reworked the ascending melodic motives from the outset of the chanson (see measures 1–3 and 14–16). In the context of the original poem, this was simply a mildly strophic element that helped to mark off parallelism between the narration of past wanderings and that of past speech. Here in the *contrafacta*, the relationship is one of complementarity and reversal rather than parallelism, since the new prayers offer a specific promise of relief from the emotional trials of the errant (now spiritual) wanderings. And once again, Lasso's chanson emerges as the means to enact in sound recurring concerns about a believer's search for a divine presence in "solitary places."

"Chanter je veux"

Regrets over past transgressions, however, were not the only literary manifestation of devotional practices heard in the *contrafacta* of the Lasso chansons. No less important than songs like "Si du malheur" and "Mes pas semez" are songs celebrating Divine clemency and power, such as "Chanter je veux." In its original form this poem uses the theme of music itself as the vehicle for listing the attributes of a certain Catherine, who is compared to a divinely inspired *melos*:[13]

Poem as set by Lasso:
> Chanter je veux la gente damoiselle
> A qui le ciel tous ses tresors decelle
> Tous ses plus beaux et plus riches presens:
> Elle a l'esprit gentil,
> Elle a le sens rassis,
> Elle a bref tout ce que nature
> (Joint la beauté) mit donc en creature.
> Ne cessons donc de chanter Catherine,
> En exaltant la Musique divine.

Translation:
> I wish to sing of the fair maiden to whom heaven disclosed all its treasures, all its fairest and richest gifts: She has a gentle spirit, she has a steady manner, she has in short all that nature (besides beauty) put in its creations. Let us then never cease to sing [of] Catherine, in exalting divine music itself.

Lasso's response to this text is predictable: for him the allusions to music were simply an opportunity for melismatic melodies and frequent text repetitions that served to mark important themes in the poetry.[14] For the makers of the *contrafacta,* this chanson about song itself had clear resonance with a long convention of "singing" divine praises—above all through the biblical model of the Psalter. Indeed, as Barbara Diefendorf has shown, the public performance of Psalms served not just as a reflection of Protestant solidarity during the wars of religion, but a means of sustaining the community in those troubled times.[15] Thus we should not be surprised that in another of Simon Goulart's projects of musical reform, the Lasso chansons were joined to Bèze's French translations of the Psalms. Here Lasso's music for "Chanter je veux" is joined to "Chanter à Dieu une chanson nouvelle" (Psalm 96), a sacred text that doubtless served as the principal model for a considerable number of the *contrafacta* found in both Pasquier's *Mellange d'Orlande* and in Goulart's *Thrésor de musique d'Orlande.*[16]

In the *Thrésor de musique d'Orlande* Goulart transforms "Chanter je veux" into a "song" in praise of a faithful (and feminine) soul, which, endowed with the same patience and spiritual qualities formerly identified with the "Catherine" of the original text, is the ideal spouse for Jesus: "Chanter je veux l'heur de l'ame fidele . . .Aiant son Christ, son espoux amiable." Pasquier and Vautrollier pursue a similar, albeit more generalized conceit, in which the church and Jesus are personified as an amiable couple. Both *contrafacta,* in other words, use the theme of "poetry as song" to transfer spiritual affinities to a domestic context, and in so doing replace the sensibilities of buoyant love with the rhetoric of divine praise heard in the Psalms.

"Soyons joyeux"

Song as a celebration of divine bounty is also at work in the Protestant adaptations of Lasso's setting of a simple *quatrain* on a pastoral topic, "Soyons joyeux." In this poem, the first line of the verse returns as the fourth, and as such suggests a refrain form, perhaps of dance music:

Poem as set by Lasso:
    Soyons joyeux sur la plaisant' verdure,
    À ce beau may tant doux, tant fraiz et gay,
    Il resjouist tout coeur qui dueil endure,
    Soyons joyeux sur la plaisant' verdure.

Translation:
    Let us be joyous on the green, on this fair month of May so sweet, so fresh and gay. It revives all hearts that suffer sadness. Let us be joyous on the green.

Example 5.5a. Lasso, "Soyons joyeux," mm. 1–8.

Goulart:
Soyons joieux, sur la plaisant' verdure,
Chantons à Dieu tant doux et gracieux.
Il resjouit tout coeur qui dueil endure.
Soyons joieux, sur la plaisant" verdure.

Translation:
Let us be joyous on the green. Sing to God so sweet and gracious. He
revives completely a heart that suffers sadness. Let us be joyous on the
green.

Pasquier:
Soyons joieux, sur la belle verdure,
Chantons dehay un psalme beau et gay,
Pour alleger le mal qui tant nous dure.
Soyons joieux, sur la belle verdure.

Translation:
Let us be joyous on the green. Sing cheerily a Psalm fair and gay to lighten
the ill so long upon us. Let us be joyous on the green.

Pasquier and Goulart each retain the rhyme scheme and general character
of the text, but change the second verse, making explicit the musical theme
only hinted at in the original poem: "À ce beau may tant doux," with its
praise for the season of spring, becomes "chantons à Dieu tant doux"
(Goulart) or "chantons dehay un psalme," (Pasquier). Within the fictive
world of the *contrafacta*, these acts of prayer manifest in song serve to
relieve pain or efface the effects of past misfortune. The focus here is on the
affective states and the influence of prayer upon them.

Lasso's music for "Soyons joyeux" serves to underscore the structure
and meaning of the text and the *contrafacta* alike (see Ex. 5.5a, 5.5b, and
5.5c).[17] The imitative fabric, animated rhythms, and patter song of the
opening, for instance, are reworked as a kind of recapitulation in measures
24–34, in this case with much text repetition as well. The second verse is
set off as a homorhythmic section (measures 14–18), itself with individual
repetition of the two hemistichs. Goulart's *contrafactum* works particularly well with this division, since it serves to repeat "chantons à Dieu" as
a unit. In the third line of the poem, the close imitative entries for the first
hemistich of poetry help to amplify the restorative theme at work in the
text (and in the *contrafacta*, too, with their analogous emphasis of "resjouir"
and "alleger"). In the second hemistich of this phrase, multiple synco-
pes and suspensions inform a curious cadence that nicely suggests the
suffering mentioned in each of the texts (see measures 22–24 and 33–
34).

Example 5.5b. Lasso, "Soyons joyeux," mm. 13–18.

Example 5.5c. Lasso, "Soyons joyeux," mm. 21–35.

Example 5.5c, cont.

"O vin en vigne"

Goulart's "Bonté divine" similarly effects a transposition of a conventional secular genre, in this case a chanson in praise of wine (complete with nonsensical refrain), into a song in honor of divine providence ("Bonté divine").[18]

Poem as set by Lasso:
  O vin en vigne,
  Gentil joly vin en vigne,
  Vignon vigna vigne sur vigne,
  Et dehet, dehet, dehet
  Et gentil joly vin en vigne.
  O vin en grappe
  Gentil joly vin en grappe,
  Grapin grapa grappe sur grappe
  Et dehet, dehet, dehet
  Et gentil joly vin en grappe.

Translation:

O wine on the vine. Dear pretty wine on the vine and—oh joy—and dear pretty wine on the vine. O wine in the grape. Grapnel, grapple, grape on grape and—oh joy—and dear pretty wine in the grape.

Goulart:

Bonté divine, vien et monstre ta puissance
En m'ottroyant de mes pechez prompte delivrance
Gaiement je chanterai
Et publirai ta grand" clemence.

De toute ma misere as tu pas conoissance?
Monstre ta main, que soudainement elle s'avance.
Gaiement je chanterai
Qu'es maux tu es mon asseurance.

Translation:

Divine bounty, come and show your power in granting prompt deliverance from my sins. Gaily I'll sing of it and will proclaim your great clemency. Do you not know of all my misery? Show your hand, that on a sudden it come forward. Joyously I'll sing of it that in my woes you are my confidence.

In this complex array of *contrafacta* we have seen how Pasquier and Goulart bound the expressive power of Lasso's music to the language of self-examination, prayer, and celebration. With the aid of Lasso's richly nuanced musical idiom, the conditions expressed in the Huguenot revision of poems like "Si du malheur" and "Mes pas semez" seem to well up from an inner emotional space made more real than possible with words alone. This construction situates the believer in a desolate space that can only be filled by God. As such, *contrafacta* of chansons such as "Si du malheur" and "Mes pas semez" create in Lasso's chanson a musical representation of a kind of spiritual "place" that recalls the attempts by Calvinist thinkers to find religious experience in the seemingly "empty" surroundings of the Huguenot diaspora (see chapter 1, above). These "new" chansons slip with surprising ease from that private domain into the semi-public realm of musical performance, and from secular to spiritual registers. Thanks to Lasso's music, the songs make it possible for listeners to hear—and to share—attitudes that otherwise exist largely in a silent, personal space that is in some important ways beyond description in verbal language.

Chapter 6

The Spiritual Conversion of Ronsard's Poetry

The reform of poetry by writers closely associated with the Pléiade figures conspicuously in the second and third editions of Goulart's *Le thrésor de musique d'Orlande*. These books which make special efforts to offer *contrafacta* of the expanded edition of Le Roy et Ballard's *Les meslanges d'Orlande* of 1576. What is more, *Le thrésor de musique d'Orlande* also incorporates material from Lasso's otherwise autonomous *Chansons nouvelles* (issued by Le Roy et Ballard in 1571), a book itself remarkable for its high proportion of texts by Pléiade poets, notably Pierre de Ronsard. To be sure, among Goulart's other *contrafacta* projects are books devoted wholly or largely to the reform of texts by Ronsard, including chansonniers by Guillaume Boni and Anthoine de Bertrand (reprinted by Goulart in 1578) that were based wholly upon texts from Ronsard's famous cycle of love poems, *Les amours* (1552).[1] That the spiritualization of poetry by Pierre de Ronsard should occupy a prominent place in *Le thrésor de musique d'Orlande* and other books of *contrafacta* prepared by Goulart thus is not too surprising. Protestant editors in general viewed Ronsard's lyrics with an uneasy mixture of trepidation and contempt prompted by what they took to be his sympathy for the Catholic oligarchy, and the themes of sensualism and un-Christian humanism evident in his poetic output. The publication of Ronsard's own *Discours des misères de ce temps* (1562), a polemical response to Protestant critics, did not help to improve this climate.[2]

"Bon jour, mon coeur"

Contrafacta of Lasso's settings of poems by Ronsard afford a particularly rich set of examples of the issues at hand in this study. In these works we find striking relationships between Lasso's approach to these lyrics and the spiritual attitudes that shaped the Protestant reception of Ronsard and the aural experience of Lasso's music. These examples will also remind us of literary codes already encountered in our discussions of courtly and carnivalesque themes in Renaissance lyric, which Ronsard's own output revises in important ways. We will consider three of these chansons in some detail: his four-voice setting of "Bon jour, mon coeur"; a five-voice setting of a section of a sonnet, "Ren moy mon coeur"; and a five-voice setting of a strophe from one of the odes, "La terre les eaux va beuvant." The first of these pieces, which was initially published in 1564 and reprinted in nearly two dozen chansonniers of the late sixteenth and early seventeenth centuries, is certainly among the most celebrated of all of Lasso's chansons (see Ex. 6.1 and Figures 6.1, 6.2, and 6.3).[3]

Ronsard's poem as set by Lasso:
> Bon jour, mon coeur; bon jour, ma douce vie,
> Bon jour, mon oeil; bon jour, ma chere amie;
> Hé! bon jour, ma tourterelle,[4]
> Ma mignardise, bon jour,
> Mes delices, mon amour,
> Mon doux printemps, ma douce fleur nouvelle,
> Mon doux plaisir, ma douce colombelle,
> Mon passereau, ma gente tourterelle;
> Bon jour ma douce rebelle.

Translation:[5]
> Good day my heart, good day my sweet life. Good day my eye, good day my dear beloved. Ah! good day my turtledove, my loveliness, good day, my delight, my love, my sweet springtime, my sweet new flower, my sweet pleasure, my sweet little dove, my sparrow, my gentle turtledove, good day my gentle rebel.

Pasquier:
> Vive mon Dieu, a mon Seigneur soit gloire
> Avoir je veux ses faits en la memoire,
> Car il est ma forteresse,
> Il a esté mon sauveur
> Me presentant sa faveur
> En mes ennuis à luy seul je l'adresse
> C'est mon recours quand je suis en tristesse
> Au droit sentier mes pas conduit et dresse,
> Dont l'exalteray sans cesse.

Translation:
> Long live my God! Glory to my Lord, I want his deeds in my memory, for he is my fortress, he has been my savior, showing to me his favor. In my weariness I address to him alone, this is my only recourse when I am in sorrow. In the right path He straightens and directs my steps, wherefore I shall exalt him without end.

Goulart:
> Christ est mon Dieu, c'est mon heur et ma vie
> Il me conduit, me garde et vivifie.
> Tous les jours sa voix tant belle

Doucement vient retentir
En mon coeur, et fait sentir
Sa grand' bonté d'une force nouvelle,
O doux plaisir de l'ame à Dieu fidele.
O ferme bien de la vie immortelle
Leve à toi mon coeur rebelle.

Translation:

Christ is my God, my good fortune and my life. He leads me, watches over me and gives me life. Every day his voice so fair sweetly resounds in my heart, and makes his great bounty felt with a force renewed. O sweet pleasure of the soul faithful to God. O firm token of immortal life—raise unto thee my rebellious heart!

In this brief work, as in many of the master's lyrical chansons, there is a subtle union between text and tone, wherein the music, through its harmonies, phrasing, and rhythmic profile, represents in sound many of the syntactic, semantic, and affective qualities of the chosen poem. This chanson, like the text it sets, unfolds as a series of parallel statements. These repetitions add rhetorical urgency to the voice of the poetic persona: "Bon jour mon coeur, bon jour ma douce vie"; subsequently "Mon doux printemps, ma douce fleur nouvelle"; and finally returning to "Bon jour ma douce rebelle." Lasso doubtless recognized the musical potential of a text founded so firmly in the reiteration of a few ideas. Each line of the first couplet is set to the same large musical gesture. This phrase pauses briefly after an initial homorhythmic opening, acknowledging the pause (or caesura) that divides the first (four syllables) and second (six syllables) hemistichs of countless French lyrics of the sixteenth century. This division also helps to highlight the inner repetition of the greeting heard so often in this poem. Indeed, at the conclusion of the piece, Lasso even manages to rework this austere beginning, with its succession of plagal-sounding harmonies (measures 1–2), as a convincing close: at the second repetition of the final line of verse (see measures 28–31), the melody now rises up to D and then returns by step to the B that began the composition, here supported by harmonies that emphasize rather than avoid the suggestion of an authentic cadence.

The medial phrases of the chanson reflect the formal design and the subtle rhetoric of Ronsard's poem in still other ways. The second tercet, like the opening couplet, depends closely upon parallel turns of phrase ("Mon doux printems, ma douce fleur nouvelle") that at once recall the rhythmic profile of the initial verses (poetic caesura after the fourth syllable) and expand upon the attributes of the beloved. Originally figured as a kind of anatomical extension of the speaker ("coeur," "douce vie," "oeil," "chere amie"), here the beloved becomes elements in a pastoral landscape ("printemps," "fleur nouvelle," "colombelle," "passereau," "gente tourterelle"). Lasso responds to this rich imagery in ways that recall what

Example 6.1. Lasso, "Bon jour mon coeur," mm. 11–25.

Example 6.1, cont.

we have already heard in his treatment of du Bellay's "La nuict froide et sombre." In the sixth line of the poem ("sweet springtime," "sweet new flower" from measures 17–18) he moves quickly through *durum* harmonies, that is, those with a "hard" B natural, C sharp, or G sharp, all sounding to the modern ear like major triads built on the striking juxtaposition of G, A, and E. The ensuing line ("sweet pleasure," "sweet little dove" in measures 20–21) dwells principally upon sonorities that use the "soft" (or *mollum*) B flat. The eighth line, with its gently animated polyphony and patter song, seems an apt representation of the sounds of the lark and dove mentioned in the poem (measures 23–24). Still more subtle is the treatment Lasso affords the first tercet (starting "He! Bon jour"), where he underlines the syntactic interdependence of lines 4 and 5 by setting them as a single musical unit (measures 13–16). Here the syncopated accent at "Bon jour" in measure 13 (note also that it marks the melodic peak in this phrase

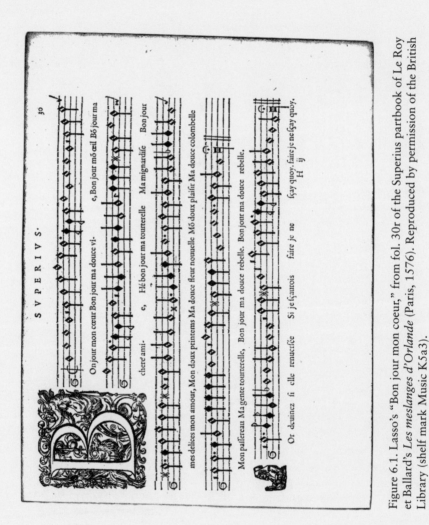

Figure 6.1. Lasso's "Bon jour mon coeur," from fol. 30r of the Superius partbook of Le Roy et Ballard's *Les meslanges d'Orlande* (Paris, 1576). Reproduced by permission of the British Library (shelf mark Music K5a3).

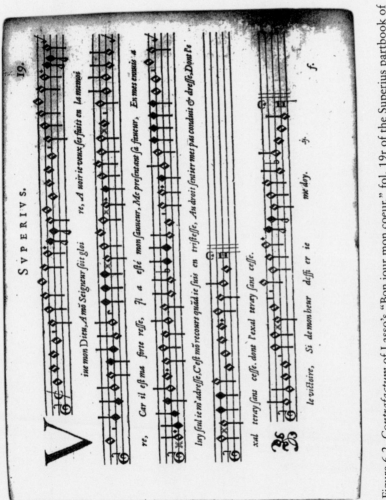
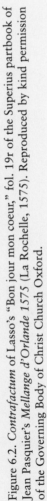

Figure 6.2. *Contrafactum* of Lasso's "Bon jour mon coeur," fol. 19r of the Superius partbook of Jean Pasquier's *Mellange d'Orlande 1575* (La Rochelle, 1575). Reproduced by kind permission of the Governing Body of Christ Church Oxford.

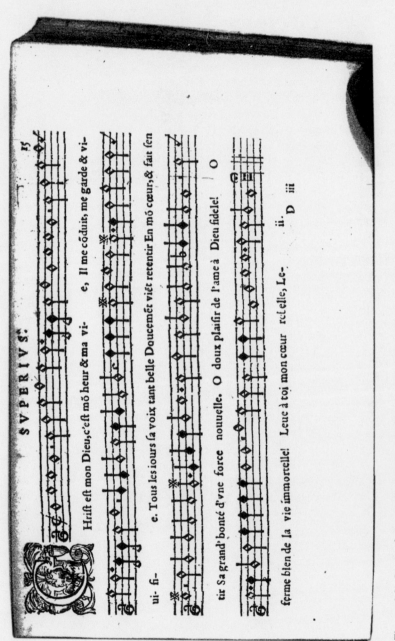

Figure 6.3. *Contrafactum* of Lasso's "Bon jour mon coeur," fol. 15r of the Superius partbook of Simon Goulart's *Thrésor de musique d'Orlande* (Geneva, 1576). Reproduced by kind permission of the Bayerische Staatsbibliothek, Munich.

for all voices) serves to emphasize the connection of that greeting with the ensuing line of verse (which includes the signal verbal motif of the entire poem). The gesture also works to undercut the rhyme scheme: we hardly notice the connection between "bon jour" and "mon amour".

Each of the spiritual versions redirects poetry to the contemplation of the divine: faith supplants the flora and fauna of Ronsard's lyrics. In so doing, both Pasquier and Goulart seem to have been careful to preserve the general form of Ronsard's poetry, with its elegant succession of differing combinations of line lengths and rhymes. The *contrafacta* offered by Pasquier and Goulart nevertheless tailor themselves to Lasso's music in surprisingly different ways. Pasquier has, of course, tailored his poem to fit the line lengths and pattern of rhymes that Lasso encountered in Ronsard's original text. To do less might have required significant change to the music itself. But beyond such correspondence at the metric or formal level, Pasquier's poem seems to avoid the imagery and iterative syntax of the original lyrics. Such restraint often comes at the expense of the close alliance between text and tone that was so evident in Lasso's setting of the poem. There is a vague echo, for instance, of the repetitive rhetoric of Ronsard's opening line in the first verse of Pasquier's poem ("Vive mon Dieu, à mon Seigneur") that aligns with Lasso's conventional division of the decasyllabic line into two complementary parts. The composer's treatment of lines 4 and 5 in Ronsard's text, it will be recalled, highlighted the subtle syntactic *enjambement* of those lines and the rhetorical echo of the opening of the poem. Pasquier's includes neither the *enjambement* nor the echo, an absence that makes Lasso's agogic accent (in measure 13) seem curiously misplaced.

Goulart's poem shares the devotional aim of Pasquier's lyric, but seems much more closely modeled upon the syntax, rhetoric, and even sound of Ronsard's poem. As result, many of the musical gestures that Lasso tailored to fit the character and language of the original verse suit the new words, too. Like Ronsard (and unlike Pasquier), Goulart joins lines 4 and 5 as a single syntactic unit ("Doucement vient retenir / en mon coeur") that Lasso's long musical gesture and agogic stress serve well to reflect. The second tercet of Goulart's poem likewise joins itself with surprising ease to the succession of contrasting harmonic gestures that Lasso crafted for the second tercet of Ronsard's lyric. "D'une force nouvelle," for instance, seems aptly embodied in the shift to the *durum* C sharp and G sharp, while the *mollum* B flats of the ensuing phrase suggest the comparatively "doux plaisir" of a faithful and pious heart (measures 17–21). Goulart's chosen end-rhymes, too, are at times the same as those of the original. The reuse, for example, of the subtle wordplay between line 3 and the concluding line of the poem ("belle" / "rebelle") seems at the very center of his *contrafactum*. Here the poetic persona addresses not the beloved, but the divine, which is called upon to save his own "coeur rebelle." That this final gesture should be set to music that itself recalls the very opening lines of the chanson ("Christ est mon Dieu") helps to enact in sound precisely the process of recollection proposed by the verbal text. Note, moreover, how this same music is used (in diminution) for the third line of the chanson, which is also the very line where Goulart establishes parallelism with the end of the poem.[6]

"Ren moy mon coeur"

Ronsard's sonnet "Ren moy mon coeur" also relies on the repetition of a short idea as a source of both emotional force and formal coherence. In this case, the motif is imperative rather than salutary, but the parallelisms and additive effects are in some ways related to those heard in the example just considered. In a formal sense, the repetitions of "Ren moy" serve to mark off several hierarchical levels in the first section of the poem, dividing the first and second hemistichs of lines 1 and 3, spelling out the parallelism of the first two couplets, and linking these two couplets with the second *quatrain*. At the same time, these verses also outline an existential progress, demanding the return first of heart, then of freedom, then of life itself, each of which is held captive by the beloved. The second half of the sonnet moves from the imperative mode to an epigraphic and narrative one, shifting suddenly to some posthumous future in which the speaker's own sufferings are described by a wandering visitor. In all, the poem can stand as a good example of Ronsard's ability to draw inspiration from long-standing poetic conventions, in this case the rather Petrarchan conceit of a lovesick poet whose very life is transformed into an epitaph in verse. Here the pangs of unrequited love are deferred into the idea of writing itself.

> *Ronsard's original poem as printed by Le Roy et Ballard:*[7]
>   Rendz moy mon coeur, rendz moy mon coeur, pillarde
>   Que tu retiens dans ton sein arresté
>   Rendz moy, rendz moy ma douce liberté
>   Qu'à tes beaux yeux, mal caut, je mis en garde:
>   Rendz moy ma vie, ou bien la mort retarde,
>   Qui me devance en aimant ta beauté
>   Par ne sçay quelle honneste cruauté
>   Et de plus prez mes angoisses regarde.
> [These lines were not set by Lasso]:
>   Si d'un trepas tu payes ma langueur
>   L'age a venir maugreant ta rigueur
>   Dira sur toy: "De ceste fier amie
>   Puissent les oz reposer durement
>   Qui de ses yeux occit cruellement
>   Un qui l'avoit plus chere que sa vie."

Translation:

> Give me back my heart, give me back my heart, thief, that you retain
> imprisoned in your breast. Give me back, give me back my sweet liberty
> that to your fair eyes, I imprudently gave into your keeping. Give me back
> my life, or else death delay which overtakes me in the love of your beauty
> by I know not what honest cruelty, and looks more closely upon my
> torment.

[These lines were not set by Lasso]:

> If you repay my pain with my death the ages to come, reviling your rigor,
> will say of you: "may the bones of this fierce beloved rest hard, who with
> her glances cruelly struck down on who held her more dear than his own
> life."

Lasso set only the first eight lines of Ronsard's sonnet. He also used a reading for the first line of text that differs somewhat from the version published in Ronsard's *Livre des amours* of 1552. It is possible that Lasso was here relying on some independent tradition of the great poet's work. Perhaps, too, the rhetorical shift from the language of the *quatrains* to the imagined speech of the *tercets* was simply too great to be effectively embraced in music. On the other hand, as Jean-Pierre Ouvrard has observed, many early settings of Ronsard's sonnets by French composers of the sixteenth century were of similarly incomplete poems.[8] No matter the precise reason for the truncation of the text, Lasso's setting beautifully balances the repetitive design of its text as a means to capitalize on the emotional force behind that pattern. The successive repetition of "Rendz moy mon coeur" and "Rendz moy" in lines 1 and 3, for instance, is emphasized through dramatic pauses in the individual voices (measures 1–4, 10–15), while the larger parallelism set up in the first and second couplets is similarly articulated via long overlapping contrapuntal ideas or prolonged sonorities that join line 1 with 2 and line 3 with 4 (measures 1–9, 10–21). Each of these syntactic units begins with similar verbal repetitions, and each corresponding musical idea comes to a close with an effective cadence only at the end of a pair of verses. The same syntactic *enjambement* is also used to treat lines 5 and 6, which contain some of Lasso's most characteristic representations of the moods and images at work in the poetry. The rapid ascent and then sudden contrast of a low choir of voices that come to rest on low E flat (see Ex. 6.2, measures 21–24) are an apt embodiment of the violently contrasting sentiments contained in that line of text, which calls at first for the return of life itself, or at least the delay of what seems an imminent death (measure 25). The blatant "cruauté" described at the end of line 7 similarly is joined to a melancholy tonal tension between F sharp and E flat in the deep cadence that marks the conclusion of that verse (measures 35–36). And the many repetitions of "et de plus" in his setting of the last of these eight lines acts both to recall the repetitions heard earlier

Example 6.2. Lasso, "Ren moy mon coeur," mm. 21–57.

Example 6.2, cont.

Example 6.2, cont.

Example 6.2, cont.

in the chanson and to direct the listener's attention to the remarkable expansion that follows for "mes angoisses regarde," which seethes with dissonant suspensions and evaded cadences that give voice to the emotional climax of the *quatrain* (measures 41–57).

The cadential structure of this composition, according to Bernhard Meier, illustrates Lasso's subtle use of tonal articulation within a given modal framework as a means of representing ideas, gestures, or emotional states at hand in its literary text. In Meier's view, the soft and languid qualities suggested in the phrase "Ren moy ma *douce* liberté" are enacted sonically in the similarly languid Phrygian cadences (E flat to D in measures 13–14 and B flat to A in measure 17) which introduce unexpected "softness" in the form of those inflections.[9] But there is more; Lasso brings back this same Phrygian motion (at measure 36—"cruauté") in a way that exaggerates its contrast with the "hard" F sharps and B naturals in the line "Rendz moy ma vie ou bien la mort." Through this setting, in sum, Lasso uses the power of musical space itself to inflect the affective conditions of the poetic speaker.

The *contrafacta* of this poem retain the affective language of the fifth and eighth lines of text, which, as we have just seen, also correspond to the most striking moments in the music. This pathos, however, is enlisted in an appeal for Divine clemency and for release from a current suffering brought on by transgression that began with Adam himself. It is thus with good effect that Vautrollier, Pasquier, and Goulart alike substitute "iniquité" for "cruauté" at the end of line 7. Supported by the poignant juxtaposition of E flat and F sharp noted above and by the low register of the voices, this moment serves well to articulate a theme central to Christian moralizing and penitence. The substitution, moreover, gives new meaning to the equally moving treatment Lasso afforded the "torment" of the final line of text.

Pasquier and Vautrollier:[10]
> Rendz moy, Seigneur, rendz moy, et plus ne tarde
> Le bien, qui est de moy tant escarté
> Rendz moy, rendz moy la douce liberté
> Qu'Adam mal caut m'a perdu par mesgarde.
> Rendz moy la vie, ou bien la mort retarde
> Qui me devance, O Dieu, par ta bonté
> Retire moy de mon iniquité
> Et de plus prés mes angoisses regarde.

Translation:
> Give me back, Lord, give me back and delay no more, the good that was set so far from me. Give me back, give me back the sweet liberty that Adam imprudently lost for me by negligence. Give me back the life, or delay death that approaches, O God, by your goodness. Relieve me of my iniquity and look more closely upon my torment.

Goulart:
> Ren moi mon coeur que d'une main pillarde
> Le peché tient en ses lacs arresté:
> Ren moi, Seigneur, ma douce liberté
> Qu'Adam seduit m'a perdu par mesgarde.
> Ren moi la vie, ou mon malheur retarde,
> Et me devance au cours de ta bonté
> Retire moi de toute iniquité
> Et de plus pres mes angoisses regarde.

Translation:
> Give me back my heart that by a thieving hand sin holds firm in his grasp.
> Give back to me, Lord, my sweet liberty that Adam, distracted, lost for me
> by carelessness. Give me back life, or slow down my misfortune, and move
> me towards your goodness. Relieve me of all iniquity, and look more
> closely upon my torment.

In the first four lines of poetry the makers of the *contrafacta* were careful to preserve both the rhyme scheme and something of the additive rhetoric and parallel syntactic design structuring the original poem and so effectively mirrored in Lasso's setting of these lines. Both of the *contrafacta* retain similar wording at the outset of lines 1 and 3, and both similarly use each of the first two couplets to embrace a single syntactic idea. Vautrollier and Pasquier, moreover, retain the parallel imperative language of the first verse, albeit with a direct plea to "Seigneur" in place of the original "mon coeur" in the first hemistich of that line. Goulart's poem seems to borrow from the *contrafacta* of his colleagues, lifting the allusion to Adam's original sin found in the texts by Pasquier and Vautrollier. Goulart's direct plea to the Deity, however, appears in the first hemistich of line 3 rather than line 1. The difference is subtle, but in some respects musically more effective than the approach taken by the other editors, for in this position Lasso's dramatic pause (measures 10–11), which originally supported the repeated imperative "rendz moy, rendz moy ma douce liberté" now serves to set off the cry to the Divine from the remainder of the text. As in the case of his reworking of Ronsard's "Bon jour mon coeur," in short, Goulart here takes care to craft a devotional poem that does more than suppress inappropriate meanings in the text it replaces. His is instead an attempt to recognize in the power of Lasso's music gestures which could move his fellow Protestant listeners even as it reformed Ronsard's lyrics.

"La terre les eaux va beuvant"

Lasso's setting of a single strophe from one of Ronsard's Anacreontic odes, "La terre les eaux va beuvant," challenged both composer and contrafacter in pronounced ways, since this verse in particular tended towards the sensual celebration of wine, women, and song (see Ex. 6.3a and 6.3b).[11] Ronsard and other writers of the Pléiade found in a repertory of Greek poetry ascribed to the ancient writer Anacreon (6th century, B.C.E.) a fresh source of inspiration and new means to elevate poetic language about laughter, drink, and erotic desire. This "Anacreontic" material first came to the attention of French writers in 1554, when the humanist editor Henri Estienne published a translation of some sixty short poems under this author's name. Imitations of this type of verse structure and especially its thematic emphasis on the apparently frivolous pleasures of drink, laughter, and love gave it a lasting place not only in sixteenth-century French poetry, but well into the nineteenth century in English, Italian, and German literature.[12]

Ronsard was drawn to this poetry in part because of its affinity with a literary program that extolled the power of poetic song to move listeners in the manner of classical verse. With their regular verse forms and strophic designs, odes such as "La terre les eaux va beuvant" (first issued in Ronsard's *Les meslanges* of 1555) neatly embody this ideal. Such poems, according to Kate van Orden, also gave Ronsard a means to elevate themes of erotic love, the pleasure of wine, and carnivalesque laughter itself by regarding them through a kind of philosophical lens.[13] The first strophe of "La terre les eaux va beuvant" touches on precisely this sentiment: it describes a kind of animistic landscape in which each of a succession of natural bodies consumes the next according to what the poem proposes as a "common law." It ends with an epigrammatic query: "Should we not also drink?" The rich natural tapestry of this text is in some respects reminiscent of the cosmos described in Du Bellay's "La nuict froide et sombre." Lasso's approach to Ronsard's text, too, recalls his famous setting of that sonnet, with its varied musical figures and reserved portrayal of the images assembled in the poetry. His treatment of line 3, for instance, with its low sonorities (measures 13–16), serves well to represent the depth and perhaps the stillness of the sea mentioned in that line. The expansive repetition of "tout boit" in line 6 (measures 26–28) similarly helps to recapitulate the several consumptions listed up to this point in the poem. The sudden shift to animated rhythm and melodic patter song for the final line of text in some ways supports an equally sudden shift in poetic voice (measures 40–47), which now turns to address the reader with an epigrammatic (and unanswerable) question.

The first strophe of Ronsard's poem as set by Lasso:[14]
    La terre les eaux va beuvant
    L'arbre la boit par sa racine
    La mer esparse boit le vent
    Et le soleil boit la marine.
    Le soleil es beu de la lune
    Tout boit soit en haut ou en bas
    Suivant ceste reigle commune
    Pourquoy donc ne burons nous pas?

Example 6.3a. Lasso, "La terre les eaux va beuvant," mm. 13–16.

Translation:

The earth drinks the water, the tree drinks it through its roots, the wide ranging sea drinks the wind, and the sun drinks the sea. The sun is consumed by the moon—everything drinks, either above or below. Following this common law, why, then, should we not also drink?

Pasquier:

Mon coeur s'en va tout languissant
Comblé d'ennuy doint il souspire.
O Seigneur mon Dieu tout puissant,
Tu vois les maux que n'ose dire.
Ces gens de toy ne font que rire
Pensans que tu n'es point au cieux.
Ton Nom sans cesse vont maudire.
Abysme donc ces furieux.

Translation:

My heart is all along in pain, filled with a weariness over which it sighs. O Lord my God all mighty, you see the evils of which I dare not speak. This crowd laughs you to scorn, thinking that you are not in heaven. Your Name they curse incessantly. Therefore dash down these raving beasts.

Goulart:

La terre son Dieu va louant
Et chante sa bonté notoire.
La mer bruit son nom bien souvent,
Et le soleil presche sa gloire:
Au Soleil s'accorde la lune.

Tout dit soit en haut ou en bas
Le los de Dieu de voix commune.
Quoy donques? le lou'rons nous pas?

Translation:
The earth goes in praise of its God, and sings of his acknowledged goodness. The sea sounds his name very often, and the sun preaches his glory.
With the sun the moon agrees. Everything speaks, whether high or low, the
praises of God in a single voice. What then? Shall we not praise him?

Pasquier's text entirely discards the substance (and rhyme) of Ronsard's
ode, proposing instead a prayer that at once articulates the speaker's languishing heart and the gross public impiety that prompts it. His is not an
elevation of some "common law" but instead a rebuke of ignorance and of
Ronsard's sublime drunkenness. Small wonder that this *contrafactum* clashes
awkwardly with Lasso's music, as in the case of line 6, where the repeated
motives designed to set "tout boit" repeat "pensans" with almost comic
effect (could the ridicule of disbelievers possibly have been Pasquier's point?).
Goulart's *contrafactum,* in contrast, is a model of careful thought, and
indeed, thanks to his efforts, the result reads (and with the music, sounds)
a good deal like "La nuict froide et sombre." He does not discard the original language so much as adjust it, replacing the "drinking" of the model
with singing the Lord's praises. For Goulart, the various elements in the
natural world each offers a form of oral praise for the divine: in his poem
the sun itself assumes the role of the Protestant preacher ("le Soleil presche
sa gloire"). In this context, the repeated musical motives that set "tout
boit" in line 6 of Ronsard's poem take on a new significance, for through
them the verbal eloquence of Goulart's universe quite literarlly speaks "en
haut ou en bas." And with a turn of phrase echoing both the poetic model
and the insistent interrogative of sermons, Goulart's parting challenge to his
readers finds similar support in Lasso's musical setting, with its frequent repetition (and thus intensification) of the final line (see Ex. 6.3b, measures 40–
47). In so doing Goulart does not so much rebuke Ronsard's imitation of
Anacreon's philosophy as focus its spiritual meanings more acutely.[15]

Our exploration of the *contrafacta* based on Ronsard's poetry has shown
how Lasso's subtle musical idiom was particularly suited to the concise
structures and expansive range of themes found there. In the hands of their
Protestant editors, these chansons yield some compelling moments. In these
revised chansons Lasso's musical gestures intersect with the spiritual messages of the *contrafacta* in particularly effective ways, as we have heard in
Goulart's approach to the iterative rhetoric of "Bon jour mon coeur" and
"Rendz moy mon coeur," as well as in the enacted "preaching" of "La
terre son Dieu va louant." These spiritual revisions, in short, embrace nearly
the entire range of musical techniques and literary voices encountered elsewhere in the *contrafacta* repertory based on Lasso's chansons.

Example 6.3b. Lasso, "La terre les eaux va beuvant," mm. 26–47.

Example 6.3b, cont.

Example 6.3b, cont.

Chapter 7

Lasso's Chansons in Printed Sets

In revising Lasso's individual chansons for spiritual purposes, the editors of the *contrafacta* volumes remind us how music can move between realms of experience—heavenly and mundane—normally thought of in opposition. But the albums prepared by Vautrollier, Pasquier, and Goulart are not simply republications of chansons with expurgated texts. The books that contain the individual *contrafacta* are also significant for the ways in which they appropriate, revise, and reinterpret the choices made by editors of still other books, in this case the important set of *chansonniers* prepared by the Parisian printer Adrian Le Roy during the 1570s, perhaps with the help of Lasso himself. Lasso, as we will discover in the final chapter of our study, was in the 1570s granted a remarkable level of authorial control over the distribution of his music in France. This condition is witnessed in the title page of the 1576 edition of *Les meslanges d'Orlande*, which announces itself as "corrected by the composer himself" (see Figure 7.1).[1] The relationship among these books is often rather complex, for it hinges upon patterns of organization (by genre, by number of voice parts, and by modal category) that fluctuate from one collection to the next. Despite these vagaries, careful attention to the connections and contrasts at hand among the Lasso–Le Roy *chansonniers* and the Huguenot *contrafacta* volumes revising them reveals how editorial priorities could shape the ways in which readers encountered musical texts. For Le Roy, the series of Lasso chansonniers emerged as an increasingly comprehensive and authoritative assimilation of Lasso to the broader story of the French musical Renaissance. In the hands of his Protestant editors, the chansonniers provide opportunities to correct not only the spiritual failings of the individual Lasso chansons, but also a way of imposing spiritual significance upon the entirety of his chanson production.

Each of the sets of *contrafacta* approaches the problem of how to revise the chansonnier as a whole with different perspectives (see Figure 7.2 for a summary of the relationships among the *contrafacta* sets and their models). Vautrollier's is a highly selective redaction of the Le Roy et Ballard *Mellange d'Orlande* of 1570, but manages to chart something of a narrative reordering of some of the works it assembles. Pasquier's two-volume *Mellange d'Orlande* books take a characteristically passive approach to

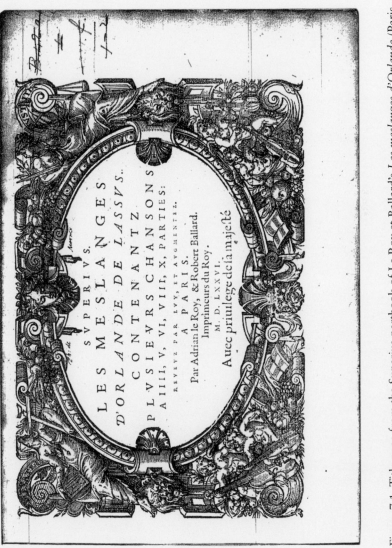

Figure 7.1. Title page from the Superius partbook of Le Roy et Ballard's *Les meslanges d'Orlande* (Paris, 1576). Reproduced by kind permission of the British Library (shelf mark Music K5a3).

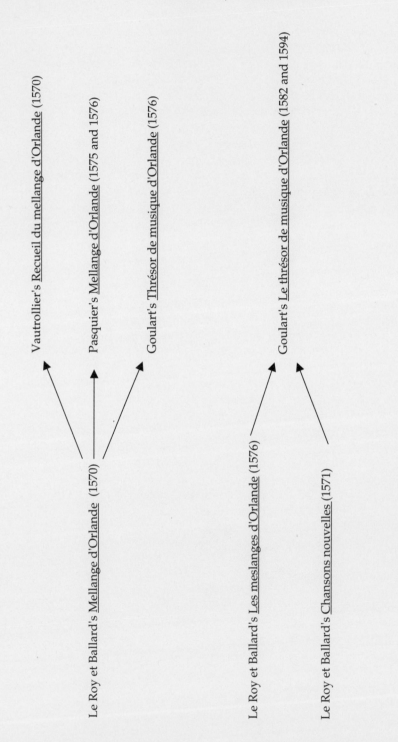

Figure 7.2. The Lasso *Contrafacta* books and their models.

rescripting the Le Roy et Ballard prints, and largely acquiesce to the original plan of that book. (Much as Pasquier often corrected the texts of the chansons with comparatively little regard for how they might relate to Lasso's music.) Simon Goulart's *Le thrésor de musique d'Orlande,* in contrast, thoroughly revises the musical organization of his Parisian models, but not with the aim of crafting any kind of *literary* sequence. Instead Goulart's approach was to reshape the contents of the Lasso chansonnier according to musical principles, in this case a scheme of organization by mode. *Le thrésor de musique d'Orlande* thus emerges as something more than a collection of edited songs. It is instead a carefully organized site where spiritual meanings are inscribed and framed for pious listeners. In order to understand the complexity of these transformations, however, we must first explore the musical organization of Le Roy et Ballard's *Les meslanges d'Orlande.*

The Musical Organization of Le Roy's *Les meslanges d'Orlande*

Each edition of *Les meslanges d'Orlande* (first issued in 1570, but printed in an expanded form in 1576) is organized according to the vocal forces required by the pieces it assembles: music for four parts comes before that for five, six, eight, or ten voices (see Table 7.1). This sort of arrangement, of course, was absolutely conventional in sixteenth-century music prints, which employed such schemes as both a typographical convenience and as an aid for performers. Renaissance music was typically issued in part books rather than score, and this arrangement by number of voice parts made the most effective use of space given for this printed format. Adrian Willaert's celebrated *Musica nova* of 1559, to cite one famous model for this scheme, likewise puts four-voice works before those for five, six, and seven parts, an arrangement neatly mirrored in two great generic divisions, one devoted to motets, the other to madrigals.[2] The bulk of the *Mellange d'Orlande* of 1570 thus consists of forty-four works for four voices (chansons and two motets), followed by forty-six pieces for five parts (chansons, plus a madrigal and thirteen motets), plus another nine works for six, eight, and ten voices (all but one of them motets). The 1576 version of *Les meslanges d'Orlande* of 1576 preserves this same basic scheme: fifty-nine works for four voices (chansons and now three motets) are followed by fifty-seven pieces for five parts (chansons, now with six madrigals and sixteen motets), and finally thirteen works for six, eight, and ten voices (three chansons, a madrigal, and some motets).

We should also note that while in the edition of 1570 Le Roy was content simply to interfile the relatively small number of motets and the lone madrigal among the chansons for similar forces, in the case of the expanded *Les meslanges d'Orlande* of 1576 the preference was instead to put all the motets and all the madrigals (now that there were enough of them to war-

Table 7.1 Le Roy et Ballard's *Les meslanges d'Orlande*: The 1570 and 1576 Editions Compared

1570	1576	Incipit	Voices	System	Clef	Final
1	1	Las! Voulez-vous qu'une personne chante	4	natural	C1	A
	2	L'heureux amour qui esleve et honore	4	natural	C1	A
2	3	Si le long tems à moy trop rigoreux	4	natural	C1	A
3	4	Un advocat dit à sa femme	4	natural	C1	A
	5	Sauter, danser, faire les tours	4	natural	C1	A
6	6	Si par souhait je vous tenoye	4	flat	G2	G
7	7	En un chateau madame par grand cure	4	flat	G2	G
16	8	Monsieur l'Abé et monsieur son varlet	4	flat	G2	G
17	9	Qui dort icy? Venus y dort	4	flat	G2	G
19	10	Soyons joyeux sur la plaisant verdure	4	flat	G2	G
18	11	Quand mon mari vient de dehors	4	flat	G2	G
20	12	Ardant amour souvent me fait instance	4	flat	G2	G
21	13	A ce matin ce seroit bonne estreine	4	flat	G2	G
	14	Si je suis brun et ma couleur trop noir	4	flat	G2	G
	15	La nuict froide et sombre	4	natural	C1	D
8	16	O vin en vigne gentil joy vin en vigne	4	natural	C1	D
13	17	Avecques vous mon amour finira	4	flat	C1	G
11	18	Un jour vis un foulon qui souloit	4	flat	C1	G
12	19	Je l'aime bien et l'ameray	4	flat	C1	G
14	20	Fleur de quinze ans si Dieu vous sauve et gard	4	flat	C1	G
9	21	Un doux nenny avec un doux sourire	4	natural	G2	D
4	22	Helas quel jour seray-je à mon vouloir	4	natural	G2	D
10	23	Le temps passé je soupire	4	natural	G2	D
	24	Si du malheur vous aviez cognoissance	4	natural	G2	D
23	25	En espoir vis et crainte me tourmente	4	natural	C1	E
5	26	Je suis quasi prest d'enrager	4	flat	G2	A
24	27	Du corps absent le coeur je te presente	4	natural	C1	E
25	28	J'ay cherché la sçience	4	natural	C1	E
26	29	La morre est jeu pire qu'aux quilles	4	natural	C1	E
27	30	Si vous n'estes en bon point bien a-point	4	natural	C1	E
28	31	Le vray amy ne s'estonne de rien	4	natural	C1	E
	32	Or sus filles que l'on me donne	4	natural	C1	E
	33	Qui bien se mire, bien se void	4	natural	C1	E
	34	Scais tu dire l'Avé? disoit il	4	natural	C1	E
22	35	O tems divers qui me deffend de veoir	4	natural	C1	E
	36	De vous servir ne me puis contenir	4	natural	C1	E
29	37	Trop endurer sans avoir allegeance	4	flat	G2	F
30	38	Vray Dieu disoit une fillette	4	flat	G2	F
32	39	Il estoit une religieuse	4	flat	G2	F
31	40	Le tems peut bien un beau teint effacer	4	flat	G2	F
33	41	Petite folle estes vous pas contente	4	flat	G2	F
34	42	Fuyons tous d'amour le jeu	4	flat	G2	F
35	43	Hatez vous de me faire grace	4	flat	G2	F
36	44	En un lieu ou l'on ne void goutte	4	natural	G2	C
	45	Si pour moy avez du souci	4	natural	G2	C
37	46	Mes pas seméz et loings alez	4	natural	G2	C
	47	Un jeune moine est sorti du convent	4	natural	G2	C
	48	Beau le cristal beau l'albastre et l'ivoyre	4	natural	G2	C
41	49	Si froid et chaut mis ensemble ne dure	4	natural	G2	G
38	50	Je ne veux rien qu'un baiser de sa bouche	4	natural	G2	G
40	51	Bon jour mon coeur	4	natural	G2	G
42	52	Margot labourez les vignes	4	natural	G2	G
43	53	Ce faux amour d'arc et de fléches s'arme	4	natural	C1	G
44	54	En m'oyant chanter quelque fois	4	natural	C1	G
	55	Quand un cordier cordant	4	natural	C1	G
	56	Ton feu s'esteint de ce que le mien ard	4	natural	C1	G

Table 7.1 Cont.

1570	1576	Incipit	Voices	System	Clef	Final
39	57	Fertur in conviviis	4	natural	G2	G
	58	Pronuba Juno tibi det longae tempora	4	natural	G2	G
15	59	Deus qui bonum vinum creasti	4	flat	C1	G
49	60	Noblesse gist au coeur du vertueux	5	natural	C1	D
50	61	La terre les eaux va beuvant	5	natural	C1	D
84	62	Vive sera et tousjours perdurable	5	flat	G2	G
45	63	Mon coeur se recommande à vous	5	flat	G2	G
46	64	Rendz moy mon coeur	5	flat	G2	G
47	65	Mon coeur ravi d'amour fort variable	5	flat	G2	G
48	66	Sur tous regretz le mien plus pitieux pleure	5	flat	G2	G
52	67	Susanne en jour d'amour solicitée	5	flat	G2	G
51	68	De tout mon coeur j'ayme la Marguerite	5	flat	C1	G
53	69	J'endure un tourment des tourmens le pire	5	flat	C1	D
80	69.2	Mais à quel propos	5	flat	C1	G
54	70	Vous qui aymez les dames	5	flat	C1	G
55	71	J'atendz le tems ayant ferme esperance	5	flat	C1	G
79	72	Chanter je veux la gente damoiselle	5	flat	C1	G
90	73	Un mesnagier viellard recreu d'ahan	5	flat	C1	F
	74	Dix ennemis tous desarmez et nudz	5	flat	C1	G
	75	S'il y a compagnon	5	flat	C1	G
57	76	Et d'ou venez vous madame Lucette	5	natural	G2	D
56	77	Veux tu ton mal et le mien secourir	5	natural	G2	D
59	78	Las! me faut il tant de mal supporter	5	natural	C1	E
60	79	Un triste coeur remply de fantasie	5	natural	C1	E
61	80	Ardant amour souvent de fait instance	5	natural	C1	E
62	81	Je ne veux plus que chanter de tristesse	5	flat	G2	A
63	82	Au feu au feu, venez moy secourir	5	flat	G2	F
64	83	Au tems jadis amour s'entretenoit	5	flat	C1	F
65	84	Elle s'en va de moy la mieux aymée	5	flat	C1	F
67	85	Le Rossignol plaissant et gratieux	5	natural	G2	C
66	86	Est il possible à moy pouvoir trouver	5	flat	C1	F
	87	Une puce j'ay dedans l'oreill' helas	5	natural	G2	C
68	88	Le departir est sans departement	5	natural	C1	G
70	89	Comme la Tourterelle	5	natural	C1	G
69	90	Puisque fortune a sur moy entrepris	5	natural	C1	G
77	91	Quand me souvient de ma triste fortune	5	natural	C2	E
58	92	Toutes les nuitz que sans vous je me couche	5	natural	G2	A
	93	Qui veult d'amour sçavoir tous les esbatz	5	natural	G2	A
91	94	I vo piangendo I miei passati tempi	5	flat	C1	G
	95	Soleasi nel mio cor star bell'e viva	5	natural	G2	G
	96	Madonna sall'amor fel ver dic'io	5	natural	C1	E
	97	Che piu d'un giorno è la vita mortale	5	natural	C1	G
	98	Ove le luci giro un tenebrose horrore	5	natural	G2	G
	99	Con lei fuss'io da che si part' il sole	5	natural	G2	A
82	100	Quid prodest stulto habere divitas	5	natural	C1	D
	101	Bestia curvasia Pulices proch posoniensis	5	natural	G2	A
85	102	Quis mihi, quis te rapnit	5	flat	G2	G
81	103	Alma venus vultu languentem	5	flat	G2	G
	103	Alma Venus vultu	5	flat	G2	G
86	104	Ave color vini clari	5	flat	G2	G
73	105	Ut radios, edit rutilo	5	flat	C1	F
74	106	Non tenuit Musae	5	flat	C1	F
75	107	Quis valet eloquio munus	5	flat	C1	C
78	108	Beatus ille qui procul negociis	5	natural	G2	D
76	109	Stet quincunque volet poteus	5	flat	C1	G
87	110	Cernere virtutes qui vult	5	natural	G2	D

Table 7.1 Cont.

1570	1576	Incipit	Voices	System	Clef	Final
88	111	Dulces exuviae	5	natural	C1	E
72	112	Delitiae Phaebi Musarum	5	flat	G2	A
89	113	Super flumina	5	flat	C1	F
71	114	Te spectant Reginalde poli	5	natural	C1	G
	115	Agimus tibi gratias	5	natural	C1	D
	116	Nunc guadere licet	6	flat	C1	F
93	117	Heroum soboles amor orbis celebrates Musica	6	flat	C1	F
94	118	Pacis amans cultorque deum	6	flat	C1	F
95	119	Tyture tu patulae recubans	6	natural	C1	G
96	120	Si qua tibi obtulerint	6	flat	C1	G
97	121	Un jour l'amant et l'amye	8	natural	C1	G
	122	Que dis tu, que fair-tu, pensive Tourterelle	8	natural	C1	G
	123	Di moy mon coeur quelle sera ma vie	8	natural	C1	D
99	124	Edite Ceasro Boiorum sanguine	8	flat	G2	F
100	125	Dic mihi quem portas	8	flat	C1	F
98	126	Vinum bonum et soave	8	natural	G2	G
	127	Su'na fede. Un languir voce	8	natural	G2	D
101	128	Quo properas facunde nepos Atlantis	10	natural	C1	G

rant a special section for each genre) together at the *end* of the chansons with the same number of voice parts. "Deus qui bonum," for instance, appeared in the *Mellange d'Orlande* of 1570 as No. 15, in the midst of chansons for four voices. In the edition of 1576 this piece instead appears as No. 59, along with other motets, at the very end of the segment of the print devoted to works for four voices. "Fertur in conviviis" was similarly displaced from amidst a group of chansons (No. 39 in the 1570 edition,) to a corpus of motets (No. 57 in the revised edition of the print). Thus, in the edition of 1576, arrangement according to vocal forces is further divided according to language of the literary texts Lasso chose to set.[3]

Modal Categories and Renaissance Polyphony

Within these broad divisions, the two editions of Le Roy's Lasso chansonnier also share a basic impulse to gather together compositions according to musical mode. For Lasso, as for Le Roy and many other musicians of the sixteenth century, the musical modes were a complex and often changing set of assumptions about the melodic and tonal resources of musical practice. At the heart of this system were the eight melodic modes—or scale types—of ecclesiastical plainsong, themselves the subject of theoretical and practical discussions for centuries in treatises written by Catholic musicians (see Table 7.2). How (and even whether) this system of complementary modalities relates to polyphonic practice of the sixteenth century was the subject of much debate in Lasso's time, and has remained a topic for debates about theory, practice, and method among modern scholars as well.

At the very least, the distinctive aspect of the so-called "authentic" and "plagal" melodic modes, with their important differences of range, are substantially undermined by the very nature of most vocal polyphony, with its overlapping registers of adjacent parts. If we identify a Tenor as "authentic Mode 1," for instance, the Bassus might well align more neatly with the characteristics of "plagal Mode 1." If this were not enough, the very identity of the broad families of modal pairs (*Protus*=Modes 1/2 centered on D; *Deuterus*=Modes 3/4 centered on E; *Tritus*=Modes 5/6 centered on F; *Tetrardus*=Modes 7/8 centered on G), familiar from the late medieval system was certainly made problematic by the increasingly adventuresome chromatic compass employed by composers of Lasso's generation. Among works considered in earlier chapters of this study, for instance, we should recall how in pieces such as "Ce faux amour" how readily Lasso used an expansive range of tones (including F sharp, C sharp, G sharp, and B flat all in the same work) never embraced by any single mode. We also saw how in a composition such as "Si du malheur" he managed to craft cadences in tonal contexts rarely heard in strictly modal compositions of the sixteenth century. All of this suggests that musical modality was at work in Lasso's music in subtle and often unconventional ways.

Even as modal practice became more problematic and complex, theoretical justifications for the continued validity of some sort of modal system became more rather than less earnest. Indeed, the continued profession of some sort of modal system has been seen as something of an act of faith, particularly in an age when accepted teachings of all kinds were subject to intense interrogation or outright disregard. During the middle years of the sixteenth century, writers like the Swiss humanist Heinrich Glarean and the Venetian choirmaster Gioseffo Zarlino proposed new categories of modal classification that could embrace changing compositional practice under a single system, in this case consisting of twelve rather than the traditional eight polyphonic modes (authentic and plagal pairs on each of six principal tones). Although these two twelve-mode systems have some important differences, they both served to accommodate a large (and growing) corpus of compositions centered on C and A, two tonal centers absent from the old eight-mode system. Ironically, although Lasso himself composed a good number of works "in" C and A, he never embraced the new theoretical constructions, either in his cyclic compositions or in music prints he supervised.[4]

In some respects these theoretical debates appear less as discussions of what polyphonic modality actually *was* than what one or another theorist *believed it to be*. Adrian Le Roy's instruction manual for the lute (originally issued by 1568 but surviving today only in an English translation printed in 1574) obliquely acknowledges the problem of these colliding systems of theoretical belief. "All our Musicke," he writes, "consisteth of eight tunes although *Glarian* and some other would devide them into a greater number, as farre as twelve."[5] As it happens, Le Roy took his ex-

Table 7.2
The Eight Basic Musical Modes

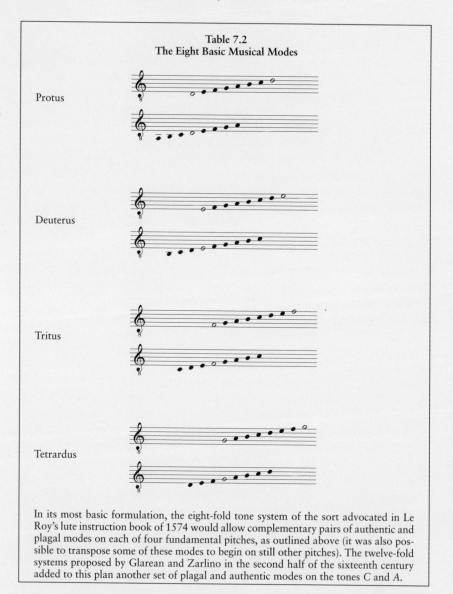

In its most basic formulation, the eight-fold tone system of the sort advocated in Le
Roy's lute instruction book of 1574 would allow complementary pairs of authentic and
plagal modes on each of four fundamental pitches, as outlined above (it was also possible to transpose some of these modes to begin on still other pitches). The twelve-fold
systems proposed by Glarean and Zarlino in the second half of the sixteenth century
added to this plan another set of plagal and authentic modes on the tones C and A.

amples of these eight modes almost exclusively from his own publication
of Lasso's great chansonnier of 1570 (see Table 7.3). This book will shortly
provide us with clues about how Lasso and his editor are likely to have
conceived of the modal organization of that book and its 1576 revision.
But before turning to the modal scheme of *Les meslanges d'Orlande*, we
should first pause to consider some of the complexities of modal representation in Renaissance polyphony.

One basic challenge of understanding the polyphonic presentation of modal categories is that in practice, the individual modes could appear in both an original register (*Protus* modes centered on D; *Deuterus* on E, etc.) or transposed downwards by a fifth (*Protus* on G, *Deuterus* on A, etc.). This transposition was normally indicated by a change from *cantus durus* (so called on account of the "hard"—for moderns, natural—B in this musical space) to *cantus mollis* (named for the "soft"—or flatted—B's that are found here), necessitated in order to preserve the precise sequence of diatonic intervals that characterize each scale type. And depending on the range of a particular piece, composers would score their compositions in either of two sets of clefs ("high" and "low"), normally abbreviated in modern discussions according to the position of the sign used in the uppermost part: G2 (G clef on the second line of the staff) for the high clefs; C1 (C clef on the first line of the staff) for the low ones. The high clefs kept higher music on the staves while the low clefs brought lower music up to sit on the staves where one could read it without the use of ledger lines. In all, Renaissance musicians theoretically had at their disposal some twenty-four combinations of these tonal resources: six final tones (C, D, E, F, G, and A), two background registers (the *cantus durus* and *cantus mollis* systems), and two sets of clefs (high/G2 and low/C1).

Harold Powers, among others, has encouraged modern scholars to recognize in these "tonal types" a means by which Renaissance composers (and editors) could "represent" a succession of modal categories, although not in a simple one-to-one correspondence. The point, according to this line of thought, is less to decide how Lasso understood the melodic or cadential properties of one or another of the eight musical modes as embodied in particular pieces, but instead to recognize how contrasting elements among the tonal types might here stand in for those modal categories. "A tonal type," as Powers succinctly put the distinction, "need not 'be' a mode, but should rather be thought of as having been chosen to 'represent' a mode, to stand as the embodiment of a traditional category."[6]

The chansons selected by Adrian Le Roy as illustrations of the eight basic modes can help to show how Lasso's editor interpreted the tonal features of a given piece in light of this theoretical backdrop (see Table 7.3). According to this practice, the same mode might be represented by two different combinations of tonal elements. Here, for instance, both Lasso's "Quand mon mari" and Arcadelt's "Si le bien" are understood as Mode 1. In the second of these works the mode appears in its original position in musical space, centered on the tone D, and using *cantus durus* (that is, with B naturals in the staves) throughout. The choice of musical clefs is such that the Superius part uses C on the first line of the staff. The tonal type natural/C1/D thus can signify Mode 1. Lasso's "Quand mon mari," in contrast, uses a different tonal type to represent the same mode in its transposed position: *cantus mollis* (B flat in all voice parts), a set of high clefs that accommodate a Superius part that moves well above middle C, and G as the lowest tone of the final sonority.

As Le Roy's examples suggest, in Lasso's publications (as in the publications of other sixteenth-century music printers), the individual modes are at times represented by more than one tonal type (the standard and transposed versions of Modes 1, 2, and 6, for instance). At times, too, the same tonal type is used to represent more than one mode, as in the case of Modes 3 and 4, notorious for their ambiguity, even in the sixteenth-century theoretical literature. For Lasso, some tonal types, although compositionally valid, simply remained beyond the scope of the octenary system as he envisaged it. Compositions using the tone A as the lowest note of a final sonority are a good case in point, and occupy unusual or marginal positions in collections of compositions organized according to musical mode. Adrian Le Roy admits as much in his lute instruction book, offering as an appendix to his main discussion of the eight modes an additional example ("Las voulez vous"—the very first piece in both the 1570 and 1576 editions of the Le Roy–Lasso chansonnier, the modal assignment of which is patently uncertain (see Table 7.3). On one hand Le Roy follows what he calls "the common opinion, whiche place it under the seconde Tune." But he also allows that "to many it semeth otherwise."[7] Renaissance publishers had a penchant to order their musical anthologies by mode, and Le Roy's little treatise here serves as a practical aid to performers who encountered just these sorts of editorial schemes of organization. Le Roy's lute manual thus provides us with a unique opportunity to hear Lasso's French editor

Table 7.3
Musical Examples, Modes, and Tonal Types
from Le Roy's Lute Instruction Book of 1574

Mode	Incipit	Location in *Mellange d'Orlande* of 1570	Tonal Type
1 transposed	*Quand mon mari*	18	flat/G2/G
1	Arcadelt's *Si le bien*		natural/C1/D
2 transposed	*Je l'ayme bien*	12	flat/C1/G
2	*Un doux Nennin*	9	natural/G2/D
3	*En espoir vy*	23	natural/C1/E
4	*Du corps absent*	24	natural/C1/E
5	*Trop endurer* and *Vray Dieu disoit*	29 and 30	flat/G2/F
6	*En un lieu*	36	natural/G2/C
7	*Je ne veux rien*	38	natural/G2/G
8	*Ce faux amour*	43	natural/C1/G
?	*Las voulez vous*	1	natural/C2 A

Le Roy's treatise follows the same organization by modal category used in the *Mellange d'Orlande* of 1570 (see Table 7.5). The anomalous works "in A" appear at the end rather than at the outset of the collection, but they are nevertheless "outside" the main sequence of eight modes.

voice his views on how individual pieces aligned with the background of basic modal categories. It is also remarkable that his chosen examples come from precisely the same Lasso monument that served as the central model for the Huguenot *contrafacta* prints.

Lasso and the Octenary Modal System

Throughout his creative career, Lasso used the eight-mode system both as a template for organizing cyclic compositions and as a convenient way of organizing groups of related pieces. In an often-cited letter from 1593, one of Lasso's pupils from his years in Munich, Leonhard Lechner, recalled his teacher's long-standing advocacy of the octenary system (presumably over the system of twelve modal categories proposed by theorists such as Glarean and Zarlino). In this letter Lechner recalls a Lasso motet book from 1562 (the *Sacrae cantiones quinque vocum,* issued by Lasso's friend and collaborator Adam Berg), which is organized in a way to effect an orderly representation of the basic eight modes.[8] Similar octenary schemes, as Harold Powers has demonstrated, are at work on a number of other printed books in which Lasso himself seems to have had an editorial hand. Berg's 1577 edition of twenty-four vocal duos by Lasso, for instance, follows a clear plan of contrasting tonal types intended to represent the eight modal categories in each of two sequences (one for texted pieces, another for textless compositions).[9]

Lasso seems also to have used the modal system itself as a means of articulating a basic unity or symbolizing a narrative progression presumed to inhere in some chosen "set" of texts. His seven *Penitential Psalms* (which unfold in their Biblical order) plus Psalm 150 ("Laudate Dominum"*),* printed together by Adam Berg in 1584, find tidy correspondence in the tonal forces that the composer chose for the individual settings, which here recapitulate in turn each of the eight modes of the octenary system.[10] Likewise in our composer's setting of the *Lagrime di San Pietro,* a set of twenty Italian madrigals to texts by Luigi Tansillo, plus a single Latin motet (in the voice of Jesus), the octenary modal system once again serves as backdrop, but (as Powers has nicely articulated) with an added twist:

> The sequence of Italian madrigals and modes in the *Lagrime di San Pietro* ends with nos. 19, "Queste opere e più," and 20, "Negando il mio Signor," representing mode 7. There is no representation of mode 8; the concluding item, number 21, is a Latin motet, "Vide homo, quae pro te patior," not part of Tansillo's cycle, and set with the anomalous tonal type A-natural-G2. [David] Crook accepts my suggestion that in this collection the A tonality stands outside the broken-off modal sequence, that it is a "religious symbol"—or rather, part of a religious symbol, for the Latin text too stands outside the madrigal cycle, and it

replaces not only the language but also the speaker, who has been Peter "Negando il mio Signore" (no. 20), but now becomes the crucified Lord himself, speaking perhaps to Peter, perhaps to the composer, perhaps to all mankind: "Vide homo, quae pro te patior" (no. 21).[11]

Here, in short, the eight-fold system of ecclesiastical musical modes is not just a convenient organizing scheme. It is instead a means of supporting the rhetorical and narrative structures of the text at hand. This sort of semiotic ploy on Lasso's part suggests that here we confront a composer especially aware of modal systems and the power of tonal types to signify them. Among prints brought out by Le Roy et Ballard as well we can detect Lasso's continuing interest in ways of articulating modal schemes, or at least of organizing groups of previously composed works in coherent (if abstract) musical patterns. According to Peter Bergquist, all of the Le Roy et Ballard volumes devoted to Lasso's music were organized according to the eight-mode system encountered elsewhere in Lasso's output.[12] The *Chansons nouvelles* of 1571, for instance, offers a middle ground between sets in which texts followed a prescribed precompositional order (one recapitulated by a succession of modes), and the patently postcompositional ordering found in the retrospective *Les meslanges d'Orlande*. The *Chansons nouvelles* (see Table 7.4) opens with texts especially chosen to honor royal patrons, suggesting that Lasso similarly "chose" a modal category (Mode 1) that would put these pieces at the beginning of a modally organized print.

We should also note the characteristically anomalous standing of the tonal type "natural/C1/A," used in two pieces found in this collection (see

Table 7.4 The *Chansons nouvelles* of 1571: Contents and Modal Organization

Chansons Nouvelles	Incipit	Voices	System	Clef	Final	Mode
1	Comme un que prend une couppe	5	flat	G2	G	1
2	Ton nom que mon vers dira	5	flat	G2	G	1
3	J'espere et crain, je ma tais et supplie	5	flat	G2	G	1
4	Un bien petit de pres me venez prendre	5	flat	G2	G	1
5	Ores que je suis dispos	5	flat	C1	G	2
6	Soufflons d'autant amis et faisons feste	5	flat	C1	G	2
7	O foible esprit, chargé de tant de peines	5	natural	G2	D	2
8	Parens sans amis	5	natural	C1	A	?
9	Helas mon Dieu, te me fais tant de biens	5	natural	C1	E	3/4
10	Paisible demaine	5	flat	G2	F	5
11	Bon jour, et puis, quelles nouvelles	5	flat	G2	F	5
12	D'amours me va tout au rebours	5	flat	C1	F	6
13	Pour courir la poste a la ville	5	flat	C1	F	6
14	Je vous donne en conscience	5	natural	G2	G	7
15	De plusieurs choses Dieu nous garde	5	natural	C1	G	8
16	Amour, amour, donne moy paix ou treve	5	natural	C1	A	?
17	Hola Caron, nautonnier infernal!	8	natural	C1	F	5
18	O doux parler, dont l'apast doucereux nourrit	8	natural	G2	A	?

Nos. 8 and 16). As Peter Bergquist and Harold Powers have noted, the tonal types using A as a final occupy an exceptional position in Lasso's musical production (and therefore in his "modal" prints—recall the example of the *Lagrime di San Pietro*). Unlike his contemporaries, they observe, Lasso (and significantly for our purposes, his editor, Le Roy) normally understood "natural/C1/A" as standing *outside* the customary eight modes of polyphonic practice, and as such normally placed such pieces at the margins of the ordered sets of works intended to recapitulate the basic modal system: before the pieces representing Mode 1 or following those representing Mode 8; or just between the pieces representing Mode 2 and those standing in for Modes 3 and 4.[13] Chanson No. 8 from the *Chansons nouvelles* illustrates the latter approach; Chanson No. 16 is an example of the former.

The exceptional standing of compositions "in A" seems again to have been among Le Roy's concerns in 1587, when he issued a collection of Lasso's motets, the *Sacrarum cantionum moduli quatuor vocibus contexti auctore Orlando Lassusio*. As Harold Powers has convincingly shown, in this print Le Roy restructured according to eight modal categories the contents of volumes previously issued by Lasso's Munich printer Adam Berg in 1582 and 1585, books that were originally planned according to tonal type (but not mode). Of signal importance, according to Powers, is the treatment of the tonal type "natural/G2/A," which in Le Roy's print stands as a representative of Mode 3. Throughout Lasso's other modally organized sets or publications (as we have seen) this type stands *outside* the usual scheme of octenary representation, and as such is normally placed only after the main corpus of compositions that follow the normative sequence of tonal types and corresponding modal categories. In the case of Le Roy's 1587 motet publication, Powers suggests, we should detect editorial initiative rather than compositional intent.[14] This print is thus an exception to the general pattern by which Lasso and Le Roy handled compositions "in A."

The exceptional standing (with respect to his version of the octenary modal system) of these pieces "in A" notwithstanding, Lasso hardly refrained from using such tonal types often in his compositions—among his chansons alone there are over a dozen examples of it. The trouble came, as we have noticed, when Lasso or one of his editors attempted to assimilate these pieces to the modal plan of some particular book. For instance, whereas the two editions of Le Roy's Lasso chansonnier (the *Mellange d'Orlande* of 1570 and *Les meslanges d'Orlande* of 1576) positioned such compositions outside the main body of modal categories, the second and third editions of Goulart's Lasso album assimilated the works "in A" to a neat, eight-mode plan. Such differences among rival editions of the same basic repertory can be revealing, for they show that the modal identity of an individual chanson can change depending on the context in which it appears. Anthologized, reprinted, and reorganized, works contained in the *Mellange d'Orlande* and *Les meslanges d'Orlande* and in the Protestant *contrafacta* books, in short, offer compelling evidence of the ways that different authorial and editorial conceptions could shape how musicians encountered Lasso's music.

The Modal Plan of *Les meslanges d'Orlande*

In the broadest sense, each of the editions of Le Roy's great Lasso chansonnier has been organized according to the vocal forces required by the pieces it assembles: music for four parts comes before that for five, six, eight, or ten voices. Within these broad divisions, the two editions of this set also share a basic impulse to gather together compositions according to tonal disposition (*cantus durus* or *mollis*; high or low cleffing; and final sonority), and to arrange these tonal types to illustrate a succession of modal categories. Of course nothing in either of the editions of Le Roy's book alludes directly to the presence of a modal plan. But Le Roy's previously mentioned lute instruction book (recall that it was originally issued in 1570, the same year as the first edition of the Lasso chansonnier) leaves little doubt that the Parisian editor (and presumably, his readers) was well aware of the modal design circumscribed here. In presenting his advice on how to intabulate vocal models for the lute, Le Roy draws almost exclusively upon works from Lasso's *Mellange d'Orlande* (adding a single chanson by Arcadelt), selecting four-voice pieces that represent each of the eight modes and their common transpositions. Moving from Le Roy's cited examples to the tonal forces that these pieces use, we can readily see that the four- and five-voice sections of *Mellange d'Orlande* articulate the same basic octenary scheme presupposed by Le Roy's treatise (compare Table 7.3 with Table 7.5), and that once again the compositions "in A" stand outside the normal sequence.

The plans of the two editions of Le Roy's Lasso chansonniers are not quite identical, of course, but the ways in which they differ, as well as the ways in which they treat anomalous tonal types, are especially revealing, for as Lasso and his editor Le Roy expanded the *Mellange d'Orlande* of 1570 as *Les meslanges d'Orlande* of 1576, they also rethought the sequence of some of the music offered here in ways that clarified the modal plan and resolved some of its ambiguities (see Tables 7.5 and 7.6). Perhaps the most striking of these "exceptional" pieces come at the very outset of each edition of the great Lasso chansonnier, for here we find a group of compositions that use a tonal type ("natural/C1/A") that finds no unequivocal corresponding category in Lasso's (and Le Roy's) conception of the octenary system articulated here. Indeed, the A tonalities at hand among the chansons present an interesting set of exceptions and problems for the modal scheme of the two editions of this album.

Table 7.5
Principal Tonal Types and Modal Categories
of the *Mellange d'Orlande* of 1570

Nos.	Tonal Type	Modal Category	Remarks
1–3	natural/C1/A	?	Le Roy *Brief instruction*: mode uncertain
4	natural/G2/D	2	1576 *Meslanges* groups as Mode 2
5	flat/G2/A	3/4 transposed	1576 *Meslanges* groups as Mode 3 or 4
6–7	flat/G2/G	1 transposed	Le Roy *Brief instruction*: Mode 1 Transposed
8	natural/C1/D	1	Le Roy *Brief instruction*: Mode 1
9–10	natural/G2/D	2	Le Roy *Brief instruction*: Mode 2
11–15	flat/C1/G	2 transposed	Le Roy *Brief instruction*: Mode 2 Transposed
16–21	flat/G2/G	1transposed	
22–28	natural/C1/E	3 or 4	Le Roy *Brief instruction*: Mode 3 or 4
29–35	flat/G2/F	5	Le Roy *Brief instruction*: Mode 5
36–37	natural/G2/C	6 transposed	Le Roy *Brief instruction*: Mode 6
38–42	natural/G2/G	7	Le Roy *Brief instruction*: Mode 7
43–44	natural/C1/G	8	Le Roy *Brief instruction*: Mode 8
45–48	flat/G2/G	1 transposed	
49–50	natural/C1/D	1	
51	flat/C1/G	2 transposed	
52	flat/G2/G	1 transposed	
53–55	flat/C1/G	2 transposed	
56–57	natural/G2/D	2	
58	natural/G2/A	?	
59–61	natural/C1/E	3 or 4	
62	flat/G2/A	3 or 4 transposed	
63	flat/G2/F	5	
64–66	flat/C1/F	6	
67	natural/G2/C	6 transposed	
68–71	natural/C1/G	8	
72–91	various	?	Chansons and motets not organized by mode
92–96	various	?	Motets not organized by mode
97–100	natural/C1/G	8	Motets
101	natural/C1/G	8	Motets

Le Roy's *Mellange d'Orlande* unfolds according to a scheme of eight musical modes. Some of the musical works found here are used as examples in his lute instruction book of 1574 (see Table 7.3). Among works that here in the *Mellange d'Orlande* stand outside the main sequence of eight modes, chansons nos. 4 and 5 were in the 1576 revision of this print assimilated to modes 2 and 3/4 respectively.

The first three pieces from the 1570 edition and the first five from the edition of 1576 share a tonal disposition ("natural/C1/A") used nowhere else among the four-voice chansons. What is more, in expanding this brief "prelude" of compositions in tonalities that stand outside the main modal sequence, Le Roy has in the 1576 edition of *Les meslanges d'Orlande* also reclassified two other pieces from early in the previous edition in ways that subordinate them to the modal design at hand: the fourth piece from the 1570 edition ("Helas quel jour"), with the tonal type "natural/G2/D" is now grouped with others of the same disposition (as Mode 2), while the fifth work ("Je suis quasi prest d'enrager"), which uses the unusual tonal

Table 7.6
Principal Tonal Types and Modal Categories
of *Les meslanges d'Orlande* of 1576

Nos.	Tonal Type	Modal Category	Remarks
1–5	natural/C1/A	?	In Goulart *Thrésor* of 1582: Mode 3/4
6–14	flat/G2/G	1 transposed	
15–16	natural/C1/D	1	
17–20	flat/C1/G	2 transposed	
21–24	natural/G2/D	2	
25	natural/C1/E	3 or 4	
26	flat/G2/A	3 or 4 transposed	
25–36	natural/C1/E	3 or 4	
37–43	flat/G2/F	5	
44–48	natural/G2/C	6 transposed	
49–52	natural/G2/G	7	
53–56	natural/C1/G	8	
57–59	various	?	Motets; not organized by mode
60–61	natural/C1/D	1	
62–67	flat/G2/G	1 transposed	
68–75	flat/C1/G	2 transposed	
76–77	natural/G2/D	2	
78–80	natural/C1/E	3 or 4	
81	flat/G2/A	3 or 4 transposed	
82	flat/G2/F	5	
83–84	flat/C1/F	6	
85	natural/G2/C	6 transposed	
86	flat/C1/F	6	
87	natural/G2/C	6 transposed	
88–90	natural/C1/G	8	
91	natural/C2/E	?	
92–93	natural/G2/A	?	
94–99	various		Madrigals; not organized by mode
100–115	various		Motets; not organized by mode
116–120	various		Motets; not organized by mode
121–27	various		Motets; not organized by mode

Les meslanges d'Orlande clarifies the basic scheme of modal representation proposed in the
Mellange d'Orlande of 1570 (see Table 7.5). Chansons nos. 1 through 5, which here stand
outside the main sequence of musical modes, were in Simon Goulart's *Thrésor de la musique
d'Orlande* of 1582 and 1594 positioned as representations of modes 3 and 4 (see Table 7.11).

type "flat/G2/A" was reinterpreted (as both Lasso and Le Roy often did) as
a transposed form of Mode 3.[15] It seems reasonable to assume that our
editor viewed Lasso's five-voice setting of "Je ne veux plus que chanter de
tristesse" in a similar way, for in both editions of the Lasso chansonnier he
staged it just after the pieces in E tonalities that normally represent that
mode, which appropriately enough for the theme of this particular poem,
suits the general emotional disposition Le Roy identified with a musical
ethos that he felt should serve (in the words of his English translator) "onely
for Melancholie and doolefull matters."[16]

Among the five-voice works, too, Le Roy included chansons by Lasso that used tonal types centered on A. In the *Mellange d'Orlande* of 1570, for instance, Le Roy placed "Toutes les nuitz," (with tonal type "natural/ G2/A") just between the compositions representing Modes 2 and 3 (as No. 58). By the 1576 edition this work and another sharing the same tonal forces, "Qui veult d'amour," were both moved to the margins of the main modal cycle that comprises the five-voice section of this print (see Nos. 92 and 93).[17] And these same dual tendencies, whereby the edition of 1576 both confirms and revises choices made for that of 1570, are also at work elsewhere among the pieces assembled for *Les meslanges d'Orlande*. In the 1570 edition, for instance, "De tout mon coeur" and "Susanne un jour" (Nos. 51 and 52) were apparently interchanged, confusing the otherwise neat arrangement of works representing transposed versions of Modes 1 ("flat/G2/G") and 2 ("flat/C1/G"). The editor of *Les meslanges d'Orlande* reverses the order of these two works (they are now No. 68 and 67 respectively), thereby clarifying the arrangement by mode.

The 1570 and 1576 editions of Le Roy's Lasso album, in short, speak to the enduring validity that the octenary modal system held for editor and composer alike, for in these books we can detect the workings of a plan in which various tonal types were assembled according to a clear and reasonably consistent plan. Some tonal types (especially those on A with *cantus durus*) seem for Le Roy and Lasso to stand outside the usual bounds of this sort of modal representation, and as such were placed in positions well suited to their marginal status in the system. With this plan firmly in mind, we now turn to the Protestant editors who prepared the volumes of spiritual *contrafacta* based directly upon the *Mellange d'Orlande* and *Les meslanges d'Orlande*.

The Modal Organization of Pasquier's *Mellange d'Orlande*

Pasquier's *Mellange d'Orlande* of 1575 and 1576 differs from the 1570 edition of Le Roy's own *Mellange d'Orlande* in two fundamental ways: it divides the album into two separate volumes (one for the four-voice compositions and another for the five-voice works), and it includes only the chansons, omitting the motets and the lone madrigal from the print upon which it was based (see Tables 7.7 and 7.8, which list the contents of these books and their relationship to *Mellange d'Orlande* of 1570).[18] In other respects, however, the book depends almost too closely upon the organization of its model, reproducing the same plan of modal categories, and even retaining some of the more glaring anomalies found there. The same set of four-voice works that stood outside the remainder of the modal plan at the outset of the Le Roy's *Mellange d'Orlande,* for instance, appears in Pasquier's book in the very same position. Likewise, in Pasquier's book of chansons

Table 7.7 Pasquier's *Mellange d'Orlande* of 1575 and Its Source

Mellange d'Orlande 1575	Contrafactum	System	Clef	Final	Mellange d'Orlande	Incipit
1	Las voulez vous que le fidele chant	natural	C1	A	1	Las! Voulez-vous qu'une personne chante
2	Si le long tems à moy trop rigoureux	natural	C1	A	2	Si le long tems à moy trop rigoureux
3	A toy seigneur sans cesser crie	natural	C1	A	3	Un advocat dit à sa femme
4	Helas quel jour pourray je voir, O Dieu	natural	G2	D	4	Helas quel jour seray-je à mon vouloir
5	Je suis quasi au plus profond	flat	G2	A	5	Je suis quasi prest d'enrager
6	Et vois estiez entrez en joye	flat	G2	G	6	Si par souhait je vous tenoye
7	L'homme mortel contemplant par grand cure	flat	G2	G	7	En un chateau madame par grand cure
8	Grace divine, Qui la mort nous extermine	natural	C1	D	8	O vin en vigne gentil joy vin en vigne
9	J'ayme mon Dieu et l'ameray	natural	C1	G	12	Je l'aime bien et l'ameray
10	Le temps passé je souspire	natural	G2	D	10	Le temps passé je soupire
11	Un jour vis un Neron qui souloit	flat	C1	G	11	Un jour vis un foulon qui souloit
12	Un jour l'esprit tachant la chair distraire	natural	G2	D	9	Un doux nenny avec un doux sourire
13	Avec mon Dieu mon amour finira	flat	C1	G	13	Avecques vous mon amour finira
14	Fleur de quinze ans Dieu vous conserve et gard	flat	C1	G	14	Fleur de quinze ans si Dieu vous sauve et gard
15	Qui dort icy? Un paresseux	flat	G2	G	17	Qui dort icy? Venus y dort
16	Quand mon mari s'en va dehors	flat	G2	G	18	Quand mon mari vient de dehors
17	Soyons joyeux sur la belle verdure	flat	G2	G	19	Soyons joyeux sur la plaisant verdure
18	Ardant amour fit Dieu du ciel descendre	flat	G2	G	20	Ardant amour souvent me fait instance
19	A ce matin ce seroit chose sainte	flat	G2	G	21	A ce matin ce seroit bonne estreine
20	O tems divers, o tems qui nous fait voir	natural	C1	E	22	O tems divers qui me deffend de voir
21	En espoir vis, et crainte me tourmente	natural	C1	E	23	En espoir vis et crainte me tourmente
22	Du cors captif je coeur je te presente	natural	C1	E	24	Du corps absent le coeur je te presente
23	Ceste haute puissance	natural	C1	E	25	J'ay cherché la sçience
24	L'esprit nous dit et nous avise	natural	C1	E	26	La morre est jeu pire qu'aux quilles
25	Dieu voit des tyrans l'orgueil de son oeil	natural	C1	E	27	Si vous n'estes en bon point bien a-point
26	L'homme chrestien ne s'estonne de rien	natural	C1	E	28	Le vray amy ne s'estonne de rien
27	Trop endurer force la patience	flat	G2	F	29	Trop endurer sans avoir allegeance
28	Vray dieu disoit une fillette	flat	G2	F	30	Vray Dieu disoit une fillette

No.	Title		Clef		No.	Title
29	Le tems peut bien les honneurs effacer	flat	G2	F	31	Le tems peut bien un beau teint effacer
30	Petite troupe estes vous pas contente	flat	G2	F	33	Petite folle estes vous pas contente
31	Fuyons le vice en tout lieu	flat	G2	F	34	Fuyons tous d'amour le jeu
32	Il estoit une religieuse	flat	G2	F	32	Il estoit une religieuse
33	Haste toy de me faire grace	flat	G2	F	35	Hatez vous de me faire grace
34	En un lieu ou l'on ne voit goutte	natural	G2	C	36	En un lieu ou l'on ne void goutte
35	Mes pas semez et loin et lez	natural	G2	C	37	Mes pas seméz et loings alez
36	Je ne veux rien que de Christ le merite	natural	G2	G	38	Je ne veux rien qu'un baiser de sa bouche
37	Vive mon Dieu a mon Siegneur soit gloire	natural	G2	G	40	Bon jour mon coeur, bon jour ma douce vie
38	Le froit et chaut estre ensemble ne peuvent	natural	G2	G	41	Si froid et chaut mis ensemble ne dure
39	Ce faux Sathan quand il s'equipe et arme	natural	C1	G	43	Ce faux amour d'arc et de fléches s'arme
40	Faites labourer la vigne vigne vigne vignolet	natural	G2	G	42	Margot labourez les vignes vigne vigne vignolet
41	En m'oyant chanter quelque fois	natural	C1	G	44	En m'oyant chanter quelque fois
42	Monsieur l'Abbé et monsieur son varlet	flat	G2	G	16	Monsieur l'Abbé et monsieur son varlet

Table 7.8 Pasquier's *Mellange d'Orlande* 1576 and Its Source

Mellange d'Orlande 1576	Contrafactum	System	Clef	Final	Mellange d'Orlande	Incipit
1	Mon coeur se rend a toys seigneur	flat	G2	G	45	Mon coeur se recommande à vous
2	Mon Dieu, y a il rien plus desirable	flat	G2	G	47	Mon coeur ravi d'amour fort variable
3	Sur tous regrets une chose je pleure	flat	G2	G	48	Sur tous regretz le mien plus pitieux pleure
4	Renz moy, Seigneur, rendz moy, et plus ne tarde	flat	G2	D	46	Rendz moy mon coeur, rend moy mon coeur pillarde
5	Mon coeur s'en va tout languissant	natural	C1	D	50	La terre les eaux va beuvant
6	Noblesse gist au coeur du vertueux	natural	C1	D	49	Noblesse gist au coeur du vertueux
7	De tout mon coeur j'aime la marguerite	flat	C1	G	51	De tout mon coeur j'ayme la Marguerite
8	Susanne un jour	flat	G2	G	52	Susanne en jour d'amour solicitée
9	J'endure en tourment sujet au martire	flat	C1	D	53	J'endure un tourment des tourmens le pire
10	Vous qui viviez en crainte	flat	C1	D	54	Vous qui aymez les dames
11	J'attens le tems avec ferme asseurance	flat	C1	G	55	J'atendz le tems ayant ferme esperance
12	Vien tost, Seigneur, ton peuple secourir	natural	G2	D	56	Veux tu ton mal et le mien secourir
13	Toutes les nuits que le Chrestien se couche	natural	G2	A	58	Toutes les nuitz que sans vous je me couche
14	Las! me faut il tant de mal supporter	natural	C1	E	59	Las! me faut il tant de mal supporter
15	Un triste coeur trouble de fantasie	natural	C1	E	60	Un triste coeur remply de fantasie
16	Ardant amour fit Dieu du ciel descendre	natural	C1	E	61	Ardant amour souvent de fait instance
17	Je ne veux plus que chanter de tristesse	flat	G2	A	62	Je ne veux plus que chanter de tristesse
18	Au feu au feu, las! vien moy secourir	flat	G2	F	63	Au feu au feu, venez moy secourir
19	Au tems jadis amour s'entretenoit	flat	C1	F	64	Au tems jadis amour s'entretenoit
20	Elle viendra des bons la paix aymée	flat	C1	F	65	Elle s'en va de moy la mieux aymée
21	Est il possble à l'homme de trouver	flat	C1	F	66	Est il possible a moy pouvoir trouver
22	Le rossignol oyselet gracieux	natural	G2	C	67	Le Rossignol plaissant et gratieux
23	Le departir est sans departement	natural	C1	G	68	Le departir est sans departement
24	Si les meschans ont sur nous entrepris	natural	C1	G	69	Puisque fortune a sur moy entrepris
25	Comme la Tourterelle	natural	C1	G	70	Comme la Tourterelle
26	La foy en Christ est tousjours perdurable	flat	G2	G	84	Vive sera et tousjours perdurable
27	Le souvenir de ma vie passée	natural	C2	E	77	Quand me souvient de ma triste fortune
28	Chanter je veux de l'Eglise fidelle	flat	C1	G	79	Chanter je veux la gente damoiselle
29	Mais à quel propos	flat	C1	G	80	Mais à quel propos
30	Que gaignez vous Chrestiens	flat	G2	G	83	Que gaignez vous
31	Dedans l'enfer un riche homme brusloit	flat	C1	F	90	Un mesnagier viellard recreu d'ahan

for five voices he similarly retains an obvious error from the original *Mellange d'Orlande,* namely the way in which "J'endure un tourment" (No. 53) and its response "Mais à quel propos" (No. 80) were separated from one another in that print.[19] And in skipping over the motets and the madrigal from the five-voice section of the *Mellange d'Orlande* of 1570, Pasquier and his printer Haultin made no effort to integrate the other chansons from that portion of the print back into the main corpus of modally organized chansons (see Nos. 26–31 in Pasquier's 1576 print).

There are, as it happens, a few instances in which the sequence of compositions in Pasquier's *Mellange d'Orlande 1575* differs marginally from that of Le Roy's album: in Pasquier's book, Nos. 9–12 and 30–33 slightly shuffle the sequence of pieces relative to the 1570 edition of Le Roy's *Mellange d'Orlande.* The same sort of local rearrangement recurs in Nos. 1–4 and 5–6 of Pasquier's book of 1576. But these differences are of little or no significance for the coherence of the modal plan as set out in the Paris print, since each of these groups of pieces shares a common tonal type (or pair of types) intended to represent a single modal category. The only significant change in this respect appears in Pasquier's book of chansons for four voices, which closes (No. 42) with Lasso's "Monsieur l'Abbé," a chanson that in Le Roy's print appeared with other compositions representing Mode 1 (as No. 16). Clearly the placement of this piece at the end of the book of *contrafacta* makes no sense from the standpoint of a scheme of modal organization. We can only guess that Pasquier gave this piece—one of a few in which the poetic text remains exactly as it was in Lasso's original—pride of *last* place on account of its overtly anticlerical theme. Conversely (and inexplicably) Pasquier *omits* another chanson from Le Roy's *Mellange d'Orlande* that would have seemed an obvious favorite among Huguenot listeners: Lasso's famous setting of "Susanne un jour," the famous *chanson spirituelle* by the Protestant poet and editor Guillaume Guéroult. Pasquier and his printer Haultin, in short, seem to have been largely unconcerned with—and perhaps even unaware of—the modal organization of Le Roy's *Mellange d'Orlande,* and instead rather slavishly copied the succession of chansons there. Their principal concern, evident in Pasquier's dedicatory preface, was instead with the character and purpose of the music and its poetic texts, not with the theoretical background according to which they were organized.

Goulart's *Le Thrésor de musique d'Orlande* and Its Modal Organization

The three editions of Simon Goulart's *Le thrésor de musique d'Orlande* contrast starkly with the relatively passive approach taken by Pasquier when it came to the modal organization of the chansons. Goulart's first edition

Table 7.9 Goulart's *Le thrésor de musique d'Orlande* and Its Sources [sorted according to the 1582 edition]

Thrésor 1576	1582	1594	Contrafactum	Voices	System	Clef	Final	Les meslanges 1576	Chansons nouvelles 1571	Incipit
10	1	4	Soyons joyeux sur la plaisant verdure	4	flat	G2	G	10		Soyons joyeux sur la plaisant verdure
44	2	2	Si par souhait je te tenoie	4	flat	G2	G	6		Si par souhait je vous tenoye
49	3	3	L'homme mortel contemplant par grand cure	4	flat	G2	G	7		En un chateau madame par grand cure
25	4	1	Qui dort en nous? La vanité	4	flat	G2	G	9		Qui dort icy? Venus y dort
27	5	5	Monsieur l'Abbé et monsieur son varlet	4	flat	G2	G	8		Monsieur l'Abbé et monsieur son varlet
26	6	6	Quand l'homme honneste va dehors	4	flat	G2	G	11		Quand mon mari vient de dehors
28	7	7	L'avare veut avoir sa bourse pleine	4	flat	G2	G	13		A ce matin ce seroit bonne estreine
7	8	8	La ferme foi souvent me fait instance	4	flat	G2	G	12		Ardant amour souvent me fait instance
23	9	9	Du fonds de ma pensee	4	flat	G2	G			See Note A
31	10	10	Si je suis brun et ma couleur trop noire	4	flat	G2	G	14		Si je suis brun et ma couleur trop noir
55	11	11	Bonté divine, vien et monstre ta puissance	4	natural	C1	D	16		O vin en vigne gentil joy vin en vigne
58	12	12	La nuict froide et sombre	4	natural	C1	D	15		La nuict froide et sombre
59	13	13	Deus qui bonum vinum creavit	4	flat	C1	G	59		Deus qui bonum vinum creasti
30	14	14	Ta voix, O Dieu avec ton doux sourire	4	natural	G2	D	21		Un doux nenny avec un doux sourire
29	15	15	O comme heureux, j'estimerois mon coeur	4	natural	G2	D			See Note B
33	16	16	Helas quel jour aurai-je un bon vouloir	4	natural	G2	D	22		Helas quel jour seray-je à mon vouloir
34	17	17	Le temps perdu je souspire	4	natural	G2	D	23		Le temps passé je souspire
32	18	18	De ce malheur tu as la connaissance	4	natural	G2	D	24		Si du malheur vous aviez cognoissance
19	19	19	En espoir vis, et crainte me tourmente	4	natural	C1	E	25		En espoir vis et crainte me tourmente
17	20	20	Las voulez vous que le fidele chant	4	natural	C1	A	1		Las! Voulez-vous qu'une personne chante
56	21	21	L'heureux amour qui esleve et honore	4	natural	C1	A	2		L'heureux amour qui esleve et honore
11	22	22	Puisque peché à mon trop rigoureux	4	natural	C1	A	3		Si le long tems à moy trop rigoreux
40	23	23	L'homme de bien dit à son ame	4	natural	C1	A	4		Un advocat dit à sa femme
57	24	24	Sauter, danser, faire les tours	4	natural	C1	A	5		Sauter, danser, faire les tours
43	25	25	Je suis quasi prest de mourir	4	flat	G2	A	26		Je suis quasi prest d'enrager
14	26	26	Du corps absent le coeur je te presente	4	natural	C1	E	27		Du corps absent le coeur je te presente
15	27	27	J'ai du ciel la science	4	natural	C1	E	28		J'ay cherché la science
37	28	28	Les dez, c'est jeu pire qu'aux quilles	4	natural	C1	E	29		La morre est jeu pire qu'aux quilles
38	29	29	Si vous n'estes en boin point bien à point	4	natural	C1	E	30		Si vous n'estes en bon point bien a-point
16	30	30	Le vertueux ne s'estonne de rien	4	natural	C1	E	31		Le vray amy ne s'estonne de rien
51	31	31	Sus, je vous pri' que l'on me donne	4	natural	C1	E	32		Or sus filles que l'on me donne
39	32	32	Qui bien se mire, bien se void	4	natural	C1	E	33		Qui bien se mire, bien se void
52	33	33	Sais-tu dire bien: disoit il	4	natural	C1	E	34		Scais tu dire l'Avé? disoit il

13	34	34	Maudit peché qui me deffens de voir	4	natural	C1	E	35	O tems divers qui me deffend de voir	
53	35	35	De te servir ne me veux contenir	4	natural	C1	E	36	De vous servir ne me puis contenir	
9	36	36	Trop endurer de peché la puissance	4	flat	G2	F	37	Trop endurer sans avoir allegeance	
24	37	37	Vray Dieu disoit un ame sainte	4	flat	G2	F	38	Vray Dieu disoit une fillette	
45	38	38	Si j'estoi ou mon ame desire	4	flat	C1	F	39	Il estoit une religieuse	
1	39	39	Avec mon Dieu mon amour finira	4	flat	C1	G	17	Avecques vous mon amour finira	
2	40	40	Fleur de quinze ans si Dieu vous sauve et gard	4	flat	C1	G	20	Fleur de quinze ans si Dieu vous sauve et gard	
3	41	41	On ne peut le so amour saouler	4	flat	C1	G	18	Un jour vis un foulon qui souloit	
4	42	42	J'ayme mon Dieu et l'aimera	4	flat	C1	G	19	Je l'aime bien et l'ameray	
8	43	43	Le tems peut bien un beau taint effacer	4	flat	G2	F	40	Le tems peut bien un beau teint effacer	
6	44	44	Troupe fidele es-tu pas bien contente	4	flat	G2	F	41	Petite folle estes vous pascontente	
	45	45	Fuyons des vices le jeu	4	flat	G2	F	42	Fuyons tous d'amour le jeu	
5	46	46	Haste toi de me faire grace	4	flat	G2	F	43	Hatez vous de me faire grace	
21	47	47	En ce monde où l'on ne voit goute	4	natural	G2	C	44	En un lieu ou l'on ne void goutte	
46	48	48	Quand mon coeur a quelque souci	4	natural	G2	C	45	Si pour moy avez du souci	
22	49	49	Mes pas Seigneur, tant esgarez	4	natural	G2	C	46	Mes pas seméz et loings alez	
	50	50	Quitte le monde	4	natural	G2	C	47	Un jeune moine est sorti du convent	
48	51	51	Beau le cristal beau l'albastre et l'ivoyre	4	natural	G2	G	48	Beau le cristal beau l'albastre et l'ivoyre	
60	52	52	Si froid et chaut mis ensemble ne dure	4	natural	G2	G	49	Si froid et chaut mis ensemble ne dure	
18	53	53	Je ne veux rien que deux mots de ta bouche	4	natural	G2	G	50	Je ne veux rien qu'un baiser de sa bouche	
20	54	54	Christ est mon Dieu, c'est mon heur et ma vie	4	natural	G2	G	51	Bon jour mon coeur, bonjour ma douce vie	
42	55	55	Qui laboure champ out vigne est heureux si humblement	4	natural	G2	G	52	Margot labourez les vignes vigne vignolet	
12	56	56	Ce faux Satan de ma vanité s'arme	4	natural	C1	G	53	Ce faux amour d'arc et de fléches s'arme	
35	57	57	En m'oyant chanter quelque fois	4	natural	C1	G	54	En m'oyant chanter quelque fois	
54	58	58	Quand un cordier cordant	4	natural	C1	G	55	Quand un cordier cordant	
36	59	59	Mon feu s'estient quand celui de Dieu	4	natural	C1	G	56	Ton feu s'esteint de ce que le mien ard	
50	60	60	Gratia summi Dei	4	natural	G2	G	58	Pronuba Juno tibi det longae tempora	
41	61	61	Tristis ut Euridicen Orphaeus ab orco	4	natural	G2	F	57	Fertur in conviviis	
47	62	62	Celebrons sans cesse	4	flat	C1	D		*See Note C*	
75	63	63	Noblesse gist au coeur du vertueux	5	natural	C1	D	60	Noblesse gist au coeur du vertueux	
76	64	64	La terre son Dieu va louant	5	natural	C1	G	61	La terre les eaux va beuvant	
69	65	65	Mon coeur se rend à toi seigneur	5	flat	G2	G	63	Mon coeur se recommande à vous	
68	66	66	Vive sera et tousjours perdurable	5	flat	G2	G	62	Vive sera et tousjours perdurable	
70	67	67	Ren moi mon coeur que d'une main pillarde	5	flat	G2	G	64	Rendz moy mon coeur, rend moy mon coeur pillarde	
71	68	68	Sur tous regretz le mien plus pitieux pleure	5	flat	G2	G	66	Sur tous regretz le mien plus pitieux pleure	
	72	69	O dieu, mon vers te dira	5	flat	G2	G		Ton nom que mon vers dira	2
	73	70	J'espere et crain, je me tais et supplie	5	flat	G2	G		J'espere et crain, je ma tais et supplie	3

Table 7.9 Cont.

Thrésor			Contrafactum	Voices	System	Clef	Final	Les meslanges 1576	Chansons nouvelles 1571	Incipit
1576	1582	1594								
88	71	71	Que malheureuse est la troupe	5	flat	G2	G		1	Comme un que prend une couppe
64	72	69	Mon coeur ravi d'amour non variable	5	flat	G2	G	65		Mon coeur ravi d'amour fort variable
	73	70	Susanne en jour d'amour solicitée	5	flat	G2	G	67		Susanne en jour d'amour solicitée
	74	74	Un bien de pres me venez prendre	5	flat	G2	G		4	Un bien petit de pres me venez prendre
	75	75	D'ou vient cela, Seigneur	5	flat	G2	G			Que gaignez vous See Note D
63	76	76	De tout mon coeur j'aime ceste Parole	5	flat	C1	G	68		De tout mon coeur j'ayme la Marguerite
86	77	77	J'endure en tourment des tourmens le pire	5	flat	C1	D	69		J'endure un tourment des tourmens le pire
87	78	78	Vous qui aimez le monde	5	flat	C1	G	70		Vous qui aymez les dames
67	79	79	J'atten le tems, aiant ferme esperance	5	flat	C1	G	71		J'attendz le tems ayant ferme esperance
62	80	80	Chanter je veux l'heur de l'ame fidele	5	flat	C1	G	72		Chanter je veux la gente damoiselle
	81	81	Mes vains desirs, tous desarmés et nuds	5	flat	C1	G	74		Dix ennemis tous desarmez et nudz
	82	82	Il n'y a que douleur	5	flat	C1	G	75		S'il y a compagnon
	83	83	Ores que tu sois dispos	5	flat	C1	G		5	Ores que je suis dispos
	84	84	Cerchons ailleurs soulas, ne faisons festes	5	flat	C1	G		6	Soufflons d'autant amis et faisons feste
	85	85	Las, je n'iray plus jouer au boys	5	flat	C1	G			Las, je n'iray plus See Note E
77	86	86	Las! me faut il tant de mal supporter	5	natural	C1	E	78		Las! me faut il tant de mal supporter
92	87	87	Sentant l'effort, et la triste misere	5	natural	C2	E	91		Quand me souvient de ma triste fortune
	88	88	Parens sans amis	5	natural	C1	A		8	Parens sans amis
80	89	89	Divine armour qui eschauffe mon ame	5	natural	C1	E	80		Ardant amour souvent de fait instance
	90	90	Helas mon Dieu, te me fais tant de biens	5	natural	C1	E		9	Helas mon Dieu, te me fais tant de biens
74	91	91	Je ne veux plus que chanter de tristesse	5	flat	G2	A	81		Je ne veux plus que chanter de tristesse
89	92	92	Au feu au feu, las! vien moy secourir	5	flat	G2	F	82		Au feu au feu, venez moy secourir
61	93	93	Au tems jadis amour s'entretenoit	5	flat	C1	F	83		Au tems jadis amour s'entretenoit
85	94	94	Elle perit ma chair qu'ai tant aimée	5	flat	C1	F	84		Elle s'en va de moy la mieux aymée
	95	95	Que est-ce que Dieu donne	5	flat	G2	F		10	Paisible demaine
	96	96	Bon coeur, amis, ouvrez l'oreille	5	flat	G2	F		11	Bon jour, et puis, quelles nouvelles
	97	97	Le monde va tout à rebours	5	flat	C1	F		12	D'amours me va tout au rebours
	98	98	Pour courir la poste a la ville	5	flat	C1	F		13	Pour courir la poste a la ville
84	99	99	Est-il possible en ce monde trouver	5	flat	C1	F	86		Est il possible à moy pouvoir trouver
	100	100	Du monde vain, qui me tien en ses laz	5	flat	C1	F	73		Un mesnagier viellard recreu d'ahan
	101	101	Que devenez vous, ô troupe fidele	5	natural	G2	D	76		Et d'ou venez vous madame Lucette
	102	102	Puis qu'en mon mal tue me peux secourir	5	natural	G2	D	77		Veux tu ton mal et le mien secourir
82	103	103	Toutes les nuits que le Chrestien se couche	5	natural	G2	A	92		Toutes les nuitz que sans vous je me couche

	104	104	Que de peché veut savoir les apasts	93	A	natural	5	Qui veult d'amour sçavoir tous les esbatz	14
	105	105	Dieu nous doint en conscience		G	natural	5	Je vous donne en conscience	15
	106	106	De plusieurs vices Dieu nous garde		G	natural	5	De plusieurs choses Dieu nous garde	16
91	107	107	Seigneur, seigneur, donne moy paix ou treve		A	natural	5	Amour, amour, donne moy paix ou treve	7
90	108	108	O foible esprit, chargé de tant de peines		D	natural	5	O foible esprit, chargé de tant de peines	
79	109	109	Peché infame a sur moi entrepris	90	G	natural	5	Puisque fortune a sur moy entrepris	
81	110	110	Partir d'ici, c'est un departement	88	G	natural	5	Le departir est sans departement	
	111	111	Comme la Tourterelle	89	G	natural	5	Comme la Tourterelle	
	112	112	Le Rossignol plaissant et gratieux	85	C	natural	5	Le Rossignol plaissant et gratieux	
	113	113	I vo piangendo I miei passati tempi	94	G	flat	5	I vo piangendo I mie passati tempi	
	114	114	Che piu d'un giorno è la vita mortale	97	G	natural	5	Che piu d'un giorno è la vita mortale	
	115	115	Ove le luci giro un tenebrose horrore	98	G	natural	5	Ove le luci giro un tenebrose horrore	
	116	116	Con lei fuss'io da che si parr' il sole	99	A	natural	5	Con lei fuss'io da che si parr' il sole	
	117	117	Christe, Patris verbum, lapsi spes unica mundi	103	G	flat	5	Alma Venus vultu	
	118	118	Ave Christi, fili Dei	104	G	flat	5	Ave color vini clari	
	119	119	Quid prodest stulto habere divitas	100	D	natural	5	Quid prodest stulto habere divitas	
	120	120	Agimus tibi gratias	115	D	natural	5	Agimus tibi gratias	
	121	121	Stet quincunque volet poteus	109	G	flat	5	Stet quincunque volet poteus	
	122	122	Dulces exuviae	111	E	natural	5	Dulces exuviae	
	123	123	Delitiae Phaebi Musarum	112	A	flat	5	Delitiae Phaebi Musarum	
	124	124	Ut radios, edit rutilo	105	F	flat	5	Ut radios, edit rutilo	
	125	125	Non tenuit musae	106	F	flat	5	Non tenuit Musae	
	126	126	Quis valet eloquio munus	107	C	flat	5	Quis valet eloquio munus	
	127	127	Beatus ille qui procul negociis	108	D	natural	5	Beatus ille qui procul negociis	
	128	128	Or sus, esgaion nous, chassons soin et douleur	116	F	flat	6	Nunc guadere licet	
	129	129	Heroum soboles amor orbis celebrates Musica	117	F	flat	6	Heroum soboles amor orbis	
	130	130	Pacis amans cultorque deum	118	F	flat	6	Pacis amans cultorque deum	
	131	131	Tyture tu patulae recubans	119	G	natural	6	Tyture tu patulae recubans	
	132	132	Da pacem, Domine		G	flat	6	See Note F	
	133	133	Domine, Dominus noster		G	flat	6	See Note G	
	134	134	Surge, propera		D	natural	6	See Note H	
	135	135	Concuspiscendo concupiscit anima mea		D	natural	6	See Note I	

Explanatory Notes for Table 7.9

A few of the works in the 1582 and 1594 editions of Goulart's *Le Thrésor de musique d'Orlande* derive from books other than the Le Roy *Les meslanges d'Orlande* of 1576 and the *Chansons nouvelles* of 1571. They are (the letters refer to notations under **Incipit** in the right-hand column above).

Note A. Du fonds de ma pensée, Lasso's setting of Marot's translation of Psalm 130, did not figure in either edition of Le Roy's *Les meslanges d'Orlande.* But this

Explanatory Notes to Table 7.9, Cont.

composition had been in print since 1564, when it appeared in Susato's *Premier livre* of Lasso compositions. The work also appeared in Vautrollier's and Pasquier's books of *contrafacta*. Perhaps Goulart borrowed the piece from one of these imprints. In all instances the work remains unchanged from its original form.

Note B. O comme heureux did not appear in the Le Roy *Les meslanges d'Orlande* books. Goulart may have found this work, which also figured (likewise without changes relative to the original chanson) in Bavent's *Fleur des chansons* of 1574. Goulart had also featured this piece in the 1576 edition of his *Thrésor de musique d'Orlande*. The piece does not appear in either Pasquier's or Vautrollier's books of *contrafacta*.

Note C. Celebrons sans cesse is a four-voice canon found uniquely in Goulart's *Thrésor de musique d'Orlande*.

Note D. Goulart's *D'ou vient cela* is a *contrafactum* of *Que gaignez vous*, which appeared in the 1570 edition of Le Roy's *Mellange d'Orlande* but was dropped from *Les meslanges d'Orlande* of 1576. Goulart seems to have borrowed the *contrafactum* text from Vautrollier's *Recueil du mellange d'Orlande*.

Note E. Las, je n'iray first appeared in Adam Berg's *Der dritte theil* of 1576 (reprinted in 1581). It was the only chanson included in that work, and did not otherwise figure in the Le Roy *Les meslanges d'Orlande* books of 1570 and 1576. It did not appear in the 1576 edition of Goulart's *Thrésor de musique d'Orlande*.

Note F. Not in Goulart's principal source, Le Roy's *Les meslanges d'Orlande* of 1576. The work first appeared in print in 1556, and was reprinted several times, including in Le Roy's *Moduli quatuor* of 1577, a source that Goulart may well have seen (see Note G, below). The work appears in the *Le thrésor de musique d'Orlande* without textual change.

Note G. Not in Goulart's principal source, Le Roy's *Les meslanges d'Orlande* of 1576. The work first appeared in Le Roy's *Moduli quatuor* of 1577, a source that Goulart may well have seen (see Note F, above). The work appears in the *Le thrésor de musique d'Orlande* without textual change.

Note H. Not in Goulart's principal source, Le Roy's *Les meslanges d'Orlande* of 1576. The work first appeared in print in 1564, and was included in Le Roy's *Moduli sex, septem et duodecim vocum* of 1573 and in Goulart's own *Theatrum musicum orlandi de Lassus* of 1580. The work appears in the *Le thrésor de musique d'Orlande* without textual change.

Note I. Not in Goulart's principal source, Le Roy's *Les meslanges d'Orlande* of 1576. The work first appeared in print in 1565. Goulart's immediate source is unclear, but the motet appears in the *Le thrésor de musique d'Orlande* without textual change.

of the *Thrésor de musique d'Orlande* (1576), for instance, largely ignores the organization by modal category set out in the 1576 edition of Le Roy's *Les meslanges d'Orlande,* preferring instead a completely new sequence of compositions presented according to background system and cleffing, but *not* final sonority. There was apparently no attempt to represent a succession of modal categories, nor is the basic scheme of system and cleffing played out consistently: the last section of the pieces for four voices, for example, are a jumble of tonal types (see Table 7.10, Nos. 46–60). Goulart's basic strategy, however, is both clear and distinct from the one used in the Le Roy chansonnier and slavishly reproduced by Pasquier and Haultin. Indeed, a note from Goulart's printer blames the apparent lack of comprehensiveness in the selection and organization of the volume on the sheer scope of Lasso's chanson production and on "a great difficulty that arose." (For the complete text and a translation of this preface, see Appendix A.)

Exactly what sort of "great difficulty" neither the printer nor Goulart was able to say, but apparently the second and third editions were produced under easier conditions. These books offer a fuller range of works from Le Roy's *Les meslanges d'Orlande* of 1576 (motets and madrigals ignored by the Goulart's *Thrésor de musique d'Orlande* of 1576) and undertake what seems to have been a systematic effort to gather chansons from still other prints, such as works from the *Chansons nouvelles* of 1571, which were assimilated to *Le thrésor de musique d'Orlande* (1582) in their entirety. The title page of this edition of *Le thrésor de musique d'Orlande* explicitly celebrates the enhancement of a book now "bigger by half." (For the complete text and a translation of this preface, see Appendix A.)[20]

What is more, Goulart and his printer here impose a systematic scheme of modal organization that attempts to frame all of these chansons in a single musical design that we may understand as forming a kind of site where spiritual transformation takes place. The 1582 and 1594 editions of *Le thrésor de musique d'Orlande* are thus more than republications of chansons with expurgated texts. They instead represent a thorough rethinking of Lasso's collected chanson production, here redacted according to Goulart's literary sensibilities and organized according to a musical scheme that refines in important ways those of the models from which its contents were drawn. As in the case of the Le Roy *Mellange d'Orlande* and its own republication in 1576, the differences between the Goulart books and *Les meslanges d'Orlande* and the differences among the various editions of *Le thrésor de musique d'Orlande* itself are as significant as the similarities (see Tables 7.10 and 7.11).

Le Roy (and in close imitation of him, Pasquier) began both editions of his Lasso chansonnier with a small set of works for four voices with tonal types that stand outside the main sequence of modes represented in the body of the print. The second and third editions of Goulart's *Le thrésor de musique d'Orlande* (1582 and 1594), in contrast, gather these four-voice

Table 7.10
The 1576 Edition of Goulart's *Thrésor de musique d'Orlande:*
Tonal Types and Their Sequence

Nos.	System and Cleffing	Remarks
1–4	flat/C1	
5–10	flat/G2	
11–17, 19	natural/C1	Nos. 18 and 19 apparently reversed?
18, 20–22	natural/G2	Nos. 18 and 19 apparently reversed?
23–28, 31	flat/G2	No. 31 out of sequence?
29–30, 32–34	natural/G2	
35–40	natural/C1	
41–42	natural/G2	
43–45	flat/G2	
46	natural/G2	
47	flat/C1	
48	natural/g2	
49	flat/G2	
50	natural/G2	
51–58	natural/C1	
59	flat/C1	
60	natural/G2	
61–63	flat/C1	
64–74	flat/G2	
75–80	natural/C1	
81–83	natural/G2	
84–87	flat/C1	
88–89	flat/G2	
90–92	natural/C1	

The basic sequence used by Goulart in this first edition of the *Thrésor de musique d'Orlande* groups together works that share background system (*cantus durus* or *cantus mollis*) and cleffing (high clefs = G2 for Superius; low clefs = C1 for Superius). The print is not organized according to a scheme of modal representation.

pieces "in A" together with the other four-voice works representing Modes 3 and 4 in the main sequence of modal categories (see Nos. 20–24 in the 1582 edition of the Goulart print), just before "Je suis quasi prest" (à 4; No. 25), with its curious tonal type "flat/G2/A," which Le Roy had considered as a transposed version of one of the Deuterus modes.[21] Except for "En espoir vis" (No. 19 in *Le thrésor de musique d'Orlande* of 1582), the pieces representing Modes 3 and 4 are here offered in exactly the same succession as in the Le Roy issue of 1576, but now all as a contiguous group within the four-voice section of *Le thrésor de musique d'Orlande*. In sum, whereas Lasso and Le Roy were content to regard some works for four voices as simply beyond the system of eight modal categories, Goulart preferred to see all works as embodiments of one or another of these basic types.

Among the pieces for five voices from Le Roy's *Les meslanges d'Orlande* of 1576, too, was a small group of chansons, madrigals, and motets that apparently stood outside the modal sequence represented elsewhere in that

Table 7.11
1582 and 1594 Editions of Goulart's *Le thrésor de musique d'Orlande*:
Tonal Types and Modal Categories

Nos.	Tonal Type	Mode	Remarks
1–10	flat/G2/G	1 transposed	
11–12	natural/C1/D	1	
13	flat/C1/G	2 transposed	nos. 39–42 belong here, too?
14–18	natural/G2/D	2	
19	natural/C1/E	3 or 4	
20–24	natural/C1/A	3 or 4	In Le Roy *Les meslanges d'Orlande* of 1576: outside modal scheme
25	flat/G2/A	3 or 4 transposed	
26–35	natural/C1/E	3 or 4	
36–38	flat/G2/F	5	
39–42	flat/C1/G	2 transposed	These belong with no. 13?
43–46	flat/G2/F	5	
47–51	natural/G2/C	6 transposed	
52–55	natural/G2/G	7	
56–59	natural/C1/G	8	
60–62	various	?	Motets; too few for attempt at modal representation.
63–64	natural/C1/D	1	
65–75	flat/G2/G	1 transposed	Includes *Chansons nouvelles*, nos. 1–4
76–85	flat/C1/G	2 transposed	Includes *Chansons nouvelles*, nos. 5–6
86–90	natural/C1/E	3 or 4	Includes *Chansons nouvelles*, nos. 8–9
91	flat/G2/A	3 or 4 transposed	
92–100	flat/G2 and C1/F	5 or 6	Includes *Chansons nouvelles*, nos. 10–13
101–112	various		Not organized by mode, but includes *Chansons nouvelles*, nos. 7 and 14–16
113–116	various		Madrigals à 5; not organized by mode.
117–127	various		Motets à 5; not organized by mode.
128–135	various	Motets	à 6; not organized by mode.

In the second and third editions of Goulart's *Le thrésor de musique d'Orlande* the chansons have been grouped according to tonal type, each of which represents one of the eight musical modes. Nos. 20–24 represent modes 3 or 4; in Le Roy's *Les meslanges d'Orlande* these same pieces stand outside the usual set of eight basic modal categories (see Table 7. 6).

chansonnier. Goulart's *Thrésor de musique d'Orlande* made no serious attempt to assimilate the madrigals and motets to the main succession of modal categories outlined by the chansons. One of the chansons from this tonal miscellany, "Quand me souvient" (No. 87; tonal type "natural/C2/ A"), now appears among the works representing Modes 3 and 4, apparently in an effort to make the modal or tonal organization of *Le thrésor de musique d'Orlande* a little neater than its model.[22]

The 1576 edition of Goulart's *Thrésor de musique d'Orlande* included a single work, "O foible esprit," drawn from the *Chansons nouvelles* that Le Roy issued in 1571. Dedicated by Lasso to King Charles IX at a time of close connections between the composer and his prospective French patron, the latter album was never assimilated by Le Roy to the expanded edition of *Les meslanges d'Orlande*, but was instead reissued by the French printer (and by Pierre Phalèse in Louvain) as a separate book. Goulart, in contrast, did not respect the autonomy of this "royal" print, for the 1582 and 1594 editions of his *Le thrésor de musique d'Orlande* included all sixteen of the five-voice works from Lasso's 1571 book. The *Chansons nouvelles* is itself an exemplary model of how tonal forces might be understood as representations of modal categories (see Table 7.4), and Goulart seems to have been well aware of the scheme at work here. Works from the *Chansons nouvelles* do not appear in *Le thrésor de musique d'Orlande* of 1582 as a contiguous group, but instead individually assume their appropriate places in the sequence of tonal types and corresponding modal categories circumscribed by the other five-voice chansons in *Le thrésor de musique d'Orlande* (see Table 7.12).[23]

The 1594 edition of Goulart's book in general affirms the scheme by which the *Chansons nouvelles,* a print itself organized according to mode, was assimilated to the 1582 edition of *Le thrésor de musique d'Orlande,* a publication remarkable for the ways in which it sought to impose a clear modal plan upon all of the chansons it revised. The 1594 edition continues this process, not by adding newly published material to the 1582 edition, but instead by diligently correcting the offerings from 1582 ("Revue et corrigé diligement en ceste troisieme Edition" is the phrase on the title page). One small trace of this renewed diligence can be seen in Goulart's treatment of the first four chansons drawn from the *Chansons nouvelles,* the sequence of which had been slightly jumbled in the 1582 version of *Le thrésor de musique d'Orlande.* The confusion really had no effect on the clarity of the modal plan for Goulart's book, since all four chansons share the same tonal type with each other and with the works that surround them. The 1594 edition of *Le thrésor de musique d'Orlande* nevertheless offers the four chansons as a contiguous set in their original order—with good reason: the first two works of the *Chansons nouvelles* were each settings of lyrics by Ronsard in praise of Henri II and Catherine de' Medici, with careful homorhythmic presentation by Lasso of allusions in the poetry to Florence and France. Goulart was himself keen to convert these songs to serve rather different ends, offering his decidedly political trope of Ronsard's panegyrics and thus of Lasso's supporting musical gestures.[24]

The *Thrésor* as a Spiritual Site

Goulart's publications of *Le thrésor de musique d'Orlande* were, of course, first and foremost enterprises intended to address the character of literary texts and their relation to music. The Genevan preacher appears to have been a keen student of Lasso's music, a listener and reader particularly adept at crafting pious lyrics to the sense and expressive sensibilities of the music that carried them. But differences among the three editions of his

Table 7.12 The Five-Voice Compositions in the *Chansons nouvelles* of 1571 as Assimilated to Goulart's *Le thrésor de musique d'Orlande* [Sorted according to the 1582 edition of the *Le Thrésor de musique d'Orlande*]

Chansons Nouvelles	Incipit	Le thrésor 1582	1594	Contrafactum	Voices	System	Clef	Final
2	Ton nom que mon vers dira	69	72	O dieu, mon vers te dira	5	flat	G2	G
3	J'espere et crain, je ma tais et supplie	70	73	J'espere et crain, je me tais et supplie	5	flat	G2	G
1	Comme un que prend une couppe	71	71	Que malheureuse est la troupe	5	flat	G2	G
4	Un bien petit de pres me venez prendre	74	74	Un bien de pres me venez prendre	5	flat	G2	G
5	Ores que je suis dispos	83	83	Ores que tu sois dispos	5	flat	C1	G
6	Soufflons d'autant amis et faisons feste	84	84	Cerchons ailleurs soulas, ne faisons festes	5	flat	C1	G
8	Parens sans amis	88	88	Parens sans amis	5	natural	C1	A
9	Helas mon Dieu, te me fais tant de biens	90	90	Helas mon Dieu, te me fais tant de biens	5	natural	C1	E
10	Paisible demaine	95	95	Que est-ce que Dieu donne	5	flat	G2	F
11	Bon jour, et puis, quelles nouvelles	96	96	Bon coeur, amis, ouvrez l'oreille	5	flat	G2	F
12	D'amours me va tout au rebours	97	97	Le monde va tout à rebours	5	flat	C1	F
13	Pour courir la poste a la ville	98	98	Pour courir la poste a la ville	5	flat	C1	F
14	Je vous donne en conscience	105	105	Dieu nous doint en conscience	5	natural	G2	G
15	De plusieurs choses Dieu nous garde	106	106	De plusieurs vices Dieu nous garde	5	natural	C1	G
16	Amour, amour, donne moy paix ou treve	107	107	Seigneur, seigneur, donne moy paix ou trevce	5	natural	C1	A
7	O foible esprit, chargé de tant de peines	108	108	O foible esprit, chargé de tant de peines	5	natural	G2	D

Lasso chansonnier also reveal that Goulart was especially concerned to have all of the music unfold according to a systematic design. The organizational system itself may have manifested a spiritual plan, or at least a prepared a "place" where spiritual meanings were inscribed in familiar sounds.

The system in question, of course, is in some important respects both highly conventional and impenetrably abstract. But the special care with which *Le thrésor de musique d'Orlande* of 1582 and 1594 attend to modal organization—an organization that comes to exceed its models even as it acknowledges them—should at least suggest that the modal "set" had, for Goulart, assumed a significance nearly as important as the chansons it framed. Indeed, some of the other books of *contrafacta* prepared by Goulart during the years between the publication of the first edition of the *Thrésor de musique d'Orlande* and its expanded revision in 1582 were based on books that themselves self-consciously used a modal plan to represent—and perhaps to express—a parallel "set" of poetic stances in sonnets by Ronsard.

In 1578, for instance, Goulart brought out spiritual versions of two collections of poems by Ronsard that had been set to music by Guillaume Boni, choirmaster of the Cathedral of Saint Étienne in Toulouse. According to Kate van Orden, in Boni's *Sonetz de P. de Ronsard mis en musique a. IIII. parties* (issued by Le Roy et Ballard in 1576) the composer has set texts that appear close together in Ronsard's publications. These pieces unfold according to a sequence of eight musical modes.[25] The plan in question is not radical by the conventions of Renaissance octenary system, but it does provide a direct model for the identification of the tonal type "natural/ C1/A" with Modes 3 and 4 (this tonal type is the only one used for these modes in the *Sonetz de P. de Ronsard*). This, of course, was how Goulart chose to interpret the pieces "in A" from *Les meslanges d'Orlande* when he brought out his own second edition of *Le thrésor de musique d'Orlande* in 1582.

Goulart may also have found models for rethinking the modal organization and significance of his versions of the Lasso chansons among the publications of another composer based in Toulouse, Anthoine de Bertrand. Bertrand's two books of *Les amours de P. de Ronsard mises en musique à quatre parties* (Le Roy et Ballard, 1576 and 1578), as Jeanice Brooks has amply demonstrated, is remarkable for the extent to which it uses an unusual succession of modal categories—with the Phrygian/Deuterus group taking pride of place at the outset of the volume—in order to trope a love story narrated by a series of sonnets drawn from Ronsard's famous *Amours* cycle of 1552.[26] This book opens idiosyncratically with nine pieces that use the tonal type "natural/C1/E (or even A)," a set of dispositions encountered nowhere else in this volume, which otherwise proceeds in a way that represents Modes 1, 2, 3, 6, 7, and 8 in a very conventional sequence. The overwhelmingly melancholic themes of the opening nine sonnets, Brooks argues, find fitting conjunction in Bertrand's theories of modal ethos, which identify in particular melodic types the power to engender particular emotional responses.

Goulart acquiesces quite readily to the idiosyncratic arrangement presented in Bertrand's *Premier livre* of Ronsard settings, offering his spiritualized versions of Ronsard's sonnets in the same sequence just described. It is tempting to detect in the language of Goulart's edited sonnets an attempt to mirror the melancholic sentiments so carefully collected here at the outset of Bertrand's book: many of his texts, for instance, dwell on sin and suffering as preconditions of redemption and joy in ways that find apt correspondence in the modalities assembled at the outset of the book. If so, however, it is curious that the liminary materials to Goulart's version of this book suppress Bertrand's humanist philosophizing on the effects of music, and preserve only his concluding remarks on the need for careful observation of the various chromatic inflections found in the notation.[27]

Bertrand's *Second livre* of Ronsard settings is conspicuous for its avoidance of somber lyrics of the sort that opened the *Premier livre,* and its corresponding avoidance altogether of pieces representing *Deuterus* modes. Yet when Goulart approached this volume in order to make spiritual *contrafacta,* he did not simply reproduce this plan, but instead reintroduced the "missing" modalities (and poetic *topoi*) by drawing together in a single volume works not only from Bertrand's *Second livre* but also his *Tiers livre de chansons* (Paris, 1578), a book of previously issued chansons that embraced a full set of modal categories in the conventional sequence (see Table 7.13 for the plan and sources of Goulart's combined version of the *Second* and *Tiers livres*).

Vautrollier's *Recueil du mellange d'Orlande* was the first systematic attempt by a Protestant printer to assimilate Le Roy's great Lasso chansonnier of 1570 to the ideals of Huguenot musical devotion. In acknowledging the title of Le Roy's *Mellange d'Orlande* in the title of his own imprint Vautrollier's project reveals a certain self-consciousness about his publication as a "set" that owes its selection at least in part to those already made by another editor. He emulated, for instance, the broad and entirely routine division of Le Roy's book into sets of pieces grouped by language and musical forces, while ignoring the further organization by Le Roy of these groups of pieces according to musical mode (see Table 7.14). In this respect Vautrollier's print contrasts strongly with those of Pasquier and Goulart, who variously reproduce Le Roy's modal plan and even improve upon it. But in other respects it was also the most modest of these books in terms of scope and thoroughness of editorial intervention. The *Recueil du mellange d'Orlande*—the word "recueil" alone suggests a kind of derivative "gleaning from a miscellany"—offers only thirty-eight French and six Latin works from the much larger *Mellange d'Orlande* upon which it was based. What

Table 7.13

Goulart's *Second livre de Sonets chrestiens* (Geneva, 1580) and Its Sources

No. in Goulart	Tonal Type	Mode	No. in Bertrand's Second livre	No. in Bertrand's Tiers livre
1–2	G natural/C1	1	1–2	
3	D/natural/C1	2	3	
4	G/flat/G2	1 transposed	5	
5–7	D/flat/G2	3/4 (transposed?)		9, 11, 7
8–11	F/flat/G2	5		15, 12, 13, 14
12	G/flat/C1	2 transposed	8	
13	F/flat/C1	6		18
14–16	D/natural/G2	1	9–11	
17	G/natural/G2	7	13	
18–19	C/natural/G2	6 transposed		22–23
20–23	G/natural/G2	7	17, 18, 19, 16	
24–25	C/natural/G2	6 transposed	20–21	
26–29	G/natural/C1	8	22–25	

Goulart's *Second livre de Sonnets chrestiens* borrows chansons from two independent volumes by Guillaume Bertrand. Bertrand's own *Second livre* was remarkable for its avoidance of compositions in the *deuterus* group of modes (modes 3 and 4). In selecting compositions from both the *Second livre* and Bertrand's *Tiers livre*, Goulart creates a single volume in which all eight modes are represented in turn. Note Bertrand's idiosyncratic use of the tonal type D/flat/g2 to represent modes 3 and 4. This same type recurs in other of his publications from the 1570s and 1580s. It is not found among Lasso's chansons.

is more, despite the claims maintained in Vautrollier's preface that the chansons presented here were "joined with a serious text, and far from all impurity,"[28] fully half of these pieces appear in the *Recueil du mellange d'Orlande* unchanged. We have already surmised that Protestant readers would have found nothing wrong (and perhaps a little vindication) in Marot's anticlerical poem "Monsieur l'Abbé" (it appears in each of the books of *contrafacta* without alteration), although we can only guess whether Vautrollier's Catholic dedicatee, Lord Arundel, would have thought well of this poem. Somewhat more surprisingly, however, intensely erotic lyrics such as "Quand me souvient" and "Toutes les nuitz" also appear in Vautrollier's Lasso book uncensored.

Joseph Kerman has suggested that the presence of a lone work for four voices, Lasso's setting of the Calvinist hymn tune, "Du fonds de ma pensée," in the midst of the portion of Vautrollier's print given over to works for five voices might be understood as a gesture of concealment: by "hiding" this Protestant hymn among the chansons and motets, Vautrollier could have been attempting to avoid offending the sensibilities of his Catholic patron.[29] Kerman also allowed that the placement of the piece here could simply have been a mistake (apparently one of the early owners of the lone surviving copy of the Superius and Quintus partbooks noticed the error, for the notation "Du fonds de ma pensée is but for 4. voc." appears in each of those books in a sixteenth- or seventeenth-century hand). It also should be noted that of the pieces printed in the *Recueil du mellange d'Orlande* only this one was drawn from a source other than Le Roy's *Mellange d'Orlande*. Perhaps, then, the odd placement relative to the prevailing plan of the *Recueil du mellange d'Orlande* recalls the "additional" status of "Du fonds de ma pensée," and marginal generic status, too, since it is more properly a French motet than a chanson.

We might also infer a latent devotional narrative in Vautrollier's plan, particularly among the *contrafacta* that round out the book. Whereas in the 1570 edition of Le Roy's *Mellange d'Orlande* the relatively small number of motets were simply interlaced among the chansons for a similar number of vocal parts, here in the *Recueil du mellange d'Orlande* we find one group of chansons for five voices, then a group of motets, and at last a final group of chansons (all for five voices). This last group concludes with a set that stresses the literary theme of attentive fidelity. Such sentiments are by no means unique to just these *contrafacta,* of course, but given the nearly equal representation in this print of works with "purified" and "original" texts, it does not seem coincidental that the print would conclude with several works whose texts articulate so consistent a theme. The poetic persona of "D'où vient cela" (a reworking of "Que gaignez vous"), for instance, worries aloud about a Deity that has seemingly withdrawn from the world. In "Comme la tourterelle" (this chanson appears without change from the original) the speaker compares his heart to the turtledove, a Biblical symbol of chastity and faithful love, which waits even unto death for an absent mate. And finally "J'attens le tems" (it shares an incipit with the chanson it revises) professes constant devotion to God: "I await the time with solid hope that in living faith my days will end." It seems an especially fitting subject with which to close a newly "spiritual" collection of chansons.

The selection and sequence of pieces "gleaned" in Vautrollier's *Recueil du mellange d'Orlande,* in short, now seems somewhat less arbitrary than we might have supposed. Understood in this way, it is not just a gathering together of a portion of Le Roy's *Mellange d'Orlande*. It is instead a place where Vautrollier can inscribe new meanings to the Lasso chansons as a group and even "hide" a Protestant hymn among the chansons and motets. As we have noted, his central aim hinged on the power of music, when joined to appropriate texts, to sustain social harmony. And in closing with an almost narrative sequence that prepares the reader to wait with "solid hope" and "living faith," the book emerges as a site where spiritual meanings are discovered in familiar musical objects. As such, the book resembles what Catharine Randall has recently identified as the "salvific narratives" created in the tradition of the Protestant "cabinet," a kind of personal collection of emblematic objects arranged to prepare a spiritual journey or insight (see chapter 1).

The idea of a cycle or ordered "set" seems also to have been an explicit element of the literatures of devotion that circulated in sixteenth-century

Table 7.14
Thomas Vautrollier's *Recueil du mellange d'Orlande* and
Le Roy et Ballard's *Mellange d'Orlande*

Recueil du Mellange d'Orlande No.	Incipit	Mellange d'Orlande No.	Incipit	Tonal Type
[à 4]				
1	Las voulez vous	1	Las voulez vous	natural/C1/A
2	Un jour vis un foulon	11	Un jour vis un foulon	flat/C1/G
3	Je l'aime bien	12	Je l'aime bien	flat/C1/G
4	Monsieur l'abbé	16	Monsieur l'abbé	flat/G2/G
5	Soyons joyeux	19	Soyons joyeux	flat/G2/G
6	A ce matin	21	A ce matin	flat/G2/G
7	Avecques vous	13	Avecques vous	flat/G1/G
8	En espoir vis	23	En espoir vis	natural/C1/A
9	Le vray amy	28	Vray Dieu disoit	natural/C1/A
10	Un jour l'esprit	9	Un doux nenny	natural/G2/D
11	Si le long tems	2	Si le long tems	natural/C1/A
12	O tems divers	22	O tems divers	natural/C1/A
13	Petite troupe	33	Petite folle estes vous	flat/G2/F
14	Je ne veux rien	38	Je ne veux rien qu'un baiser	natural/G2/G
15	Helas! Quel jour	4	Helas quel jour	natural/G2/D
16	Ce faux Sathan	43	Ce faux amour	natural/C1/G
17	Hastez vous	35	Hatez vous de me faire	flat/G2/F
18	En m'oyont chanter	44	En m'oyont chanter	natural/C1/G
19	O vin en vigne	8	O vin en vigne	natural/C1/D
[à 5]				
20	Au tems jadis	64	Au tems jadis amour	flat/C1/F
21	Mon coeur se rend	45	Mon coeur se recommande	flat/G2/G
22	Mon coeur ravi	47	Mon coeur ravi d'amour	flat/G2/G
23	Sur tous regretz	48	Sur tous regretz	flat/G2/G
24	De tout mon coeur	51	De tout mon coeur	flat/C1/G
25	Susanne un jour	52	Susanne un jour	flat/C1/D
26	J'endure un tourment	53	J'endure un tourment	flat/C1/D
	Mais à quel propos [response]	80	Mais à quel propos [response]	natural/C2/E
27	Quand me souvient	77	Quand me souvient	natural/C2/E
28	Toutes les nuitz	58	Toutes les nuitz	natural/G2/A
29	Noblesse gist	49	Noblesse gist	natural/C2/D
30	Du fond de ma pensée [à 4]			flat/G2/G
31	Alma venus	81	Alma venus	flat/G2/G
32	Dulces exuviae	88	Dulces exuviae	natural/C1/E
33	Beatus ille	78	Beatus ille	natural/G2/D
34	Le rossignol	67	Le rossignol	natural/G2/C
35	Vive sera	84	Vive sera	flat/G2/G
36	Rendz moy Seigneur	46	Rendz moy mon coeur,	flat/G2/G
37	Chanter je veux	79	Chanter je veux	flat/G2/G
38	Pourquoy font bruit	59	Las, me faut il tant	natural/C1/E
39	D'où vient cela	83	Que gaignez vous	flat/G2/G
40	Comme la tourtourelle	70	Comme la tourterelle	natural/C1/G
41	J'attens le tems	55	J'attendz le tems ayant	flat/C1/G

France. Among Catholic readers, as Terence Cave has noted, penitential treatises modeled on the writings of men like the Spanish Dominican preacher Luis de Granada propose an orderly sequence of introspection and prayer, a kind of private, lisable liturgy that moves from the somber "Evening" meditations (with their contemplation of physical decay and moral transgression) to the joyous "Morning" ones (which turn instead to the cleansing power of Jesus and of Divine grace).[30] Cyclic elements also figure prominently in Protestant devotional literatures, in Protestant adaptations of humanistic writings, and in musical settings of them. Anthoine de la Roche de Chandieu's *Octonaires sur le vanité du monde,* for instance, proceeds as an orderly "set" of poems on related themes, a sequence that finds close correspondence in Claude Le Jeune's settings of three dozen eight-line strophes from this cycle, which uses groups of three pieces to represent each of the twelve ecclesiastical modes.[31] Le Jeune's *Dodecacorde* (first issued in 1598 by Pasquier's publisher, Haultin) similarly proposes a significant set hinging on an abstract (and ecclesiastical) musical design— in this case settings of Psalm texts chosen to engender a kind of social restoration. In dedicating his book to the Protestant sympathizer Henri de Bouillon, Le Jeune explicitly addresses the ethic effects of the ancient modalities as an aggregate with unique powers to bring religious and political harmony to a French nation wracked by division and warfare. By these, he hopes "to quench by the Dorian mode the rages which the Phrygian was able to arouse." He refrains, however, "from cloaking all the modes with their names," preferring instead to avoid the manifest confusion that reigns among rival ancient accounts of those categories.[32]

As we have seen, books by Boni and Bertrand that served as models for Goulart's books of *contrafacta* based on Lasso's chansons also use sequential plans as templates for a series of aesthetic categories or narrative designs. His own poetry, and some of the literary texts he edited, work in similar ways. Goulart's spiritual sonnets, issued together in one of the central documents of the Protestant devotional movement, Bernard de Montméja's *Poèmes chrestiennes* (Geneva, 1574), are grouped according to the literary *topoi* they share.[33] His expurgated version of the creation story, *La Sepmaine,* by the humanist Guillaume de Saluste du Bartas, assimilates that great cyclic poem to the rhetoric of Calvinist piety.[34] His *Quarante tableaux de la mort* of 1607 offers an ordered "set" of prose contemplations of biblical quotations on the themes of sin and its physical manifestation in illness and death.[35] All of this material offers striking parallels with Goulart's self-conscious reorganization of Lasso's chansons in the 1582 edition of his own *Le thrésor de musique d'Orlande,* which like the *Quarante tableaux* becomes a site of spiritual reflection that retreats from outward representation and instead highlights "inner" voices.

Whether any of the individual modes "represented" in *Le thrésor de musique d'Orlande* were understood by Goulart to embody a particular spiritual ethos is far from clear. But inasmuch as *Le thrésor de musique d'Orlande* attempts a systematic spiritual renovation of those chansons, it seems at least possible that casting these songs against a backdrop of a musical "set" with deep symbolic meaning was yet another way of hearing preparing the listener to attend to their "divins accords." The notion was hardly foreign to Lasso and his contemporaries, as Harold Powers has observed of some of the great modally ordered works of Lasso (the *Penitential Psalms*; the *Lagrime di San Pietro*) and Palestrina (the Petrarch *vergine* cycle; a set of spiritual madrigals), which may have embodied a similar sensibility for Catholic musicians and readers: "One cannot help but wonder if to order the musical setting of a cycle of pious texts according to the prescribed musical system of the church was not an affirmation of faith every bit as compelling as the choice of a pious cycle of texts to set in the first place."[36] Of course, the signal difference between the sets by Le Jeune, Lasso, or Palestrina and the one offered in Goulart's *Le thrésor de musique d'Orlande* is that the latter was an editorial, not authorial artifact, mediated through the printing press and its special affinities for the Protestant public.

In naming his book a "thrésor," Goulart may have signalled to his readers that this was not merely a miscellany of Lasso's music, but instead a set with a rather more ambitious meaning. The word "thrésor," of course, was used by writers of the years around 1600 as a title for a dictionary or encyclopedic project, as in Jean Nicot's edition of *Le thrésor de la langue française* of 1606.[37] But the word also can mean "treasury," either literally, in the sense of the physical space (a room or cabinet) where precious objects are kept, or in the figurative sense of an accumulation of useful or valued items. As Catharine Randall has shown us, Protestant writers of the late sixteenth century often used the figure of an interior space—a grotto, an enclosed garden or square, and often a cabinet—to prepare spiritual meanings and to invest existing objects with spiritual meanings (see chapter 1, above). By analogy with this tradition, Goulart's book can be understood not simply as an edition of expurgated chansons, but a "place" where spiritual meanings are inscribed in familiar musical objects through the judicious adjustment of literary texts. *Le thrésor de musique d'Orlande,* perhaps more than any of the other books of *contrafacta* based on the Lasso chansons, emerges as a space where Lasso's music can work to effect a program of spiritual solace and even social restoration. In so doing, this book reminds us of the dynamic way in which the medium of print could serve to create new meanings through the republication of old material.

In sum, we have seen how the Protestant editors of the Lasso *contrafacta* approached the challenge of organizing these spiritual songs as a cohesive "set" in different ways. Pasquier's prints adhere very closely to the scheme set out in the Paris prints that served as his immediate model. In light of how slavishly Pasquier imitates the books issued by Le Roy et Ballard, we may well wonder whether he was even aware of the musical plan that rests behind those volumes. The books issued by Vaultrollier and Goulart tell a rather different story, albeit in contrasting ways. They can be understood, moreover, as books that through their organization serve as "sites" of spiritual reflection through sound. Viewed in this context, the increasing comprehensiveness of the Le Roy–Lasso compilations bears witness to Lasso's own recognition of the importance of the press as a means of creative control. But that same medium became in the hands of Huguenot editors like Vautrollier and Goulart a means to impose their own spiritual meanings upon Lasso's "divins accords."

Chapter 8

Authorizing the Book

Privileges and Printing

We turn at last from discussion of the *contrafacta* of the individual Lasso chansons and exploration of the *contrafacta* publications as significant sets to broader concerns of authorship, piracy, and the culture of printed books. One remarkable feature of the books that offer *contrafacta* of the Lasso chansons, for instance, is the degree to which these prints acknowledge and play upon the peculiar power of Lasso's compositional voice, his poetic choices, and even the particular printed books from which his music has been appropriated. The prefaces to Pasquier's revisions of the Lasso chansons, as we have seen, explicitly acknowledge the superiority of Lasso's powers as a composer while simultaneously deploring his poetic choices: "Among all the musicians of our century Orlande de Lassus appears (and has good right) to deserve good standing, for the excellence and admirable sweetness of his music."[1] Goulart goes so far as to call upon the composer himself to reconsider his poetic choices: "it would be good to wish that Orlande use his graces, which the Holy Spirit has adorned in him above all, to recall and magnify the one from whom they derive, as he has done in several Motets and Latin Psalms. I deeply wish that these chansons might provoke the urge in him."[2]

Goulart also frequently acknowledges his debt to other prints of Lasso's music, including the "the books which have been printed in England" (Vautrollier's *contrafacta* album, no doubt) and those "printed in Paris and in Louvain" (that is, the Le Roy and the Phalèse publications).[3] Goulart's Geneva printer likewise overtly acknowledges the "Parisian" books that served as his models and the selective way in which the editor has handled their contents, explaining that "if in many the words remain just as they were in the Parisian books, that is precisely the intent of the corrector."[4] For comments such as these to make any sense we must, of course, assume that Goulart's readers would have been familiar with the Parisian books in question. The books by Pasquier and Goulart establish their credibility with readers not by representing themselves as identical to the "authentic" prints, but by persuading them that the *contrafacta* books are superior to those models, the contents of which have been made "authentic" by virtue of the devotional purposes now recovered for Lasso's music.

This editorial "troping" of other printed books was neither new nor unique to the Huguenot appropriation of Lasso. Indeed, from its very outset the Calvinist enterprise of making *chansons spirituelles* and *contrafacta* of secular chansons was self-consciously dependent upon printed books. This holds as firmly for Simon Du Bosc's and Guillaume Guéroult's *Tiers livre où sont contenues plusiers chansons . . . desquelles avons changé la verbe lubrique en lettre spirituelle et chrestienne* (Geneva, 1555) as for Jean Pasquier's *Premier* [and *Second*] *livre des Cantiques et Chansons spirituelles à quatre parties en quatre volumes, recueillies de plusieurs excellens musiciens* (La Rochelle, 1578).[5] Goulart's spiritual versions of Boni's and Bertrand's settings of sonnets by Ronsard, as we have already seen, even build upon compositional and editorial schemes that were essential to the integrity of those printed volumes.

It is worth noting, however, that Goulart's claims for the superiority of his Lasso *contrafacta* books were made at a time when Lasso himself commanded considerable prestige in France, for by 1571 he was uniquely (and suddenly) blessed with official sanction to control the distribution of his music. Lasso's stature as a composer grew steadily during the 1560s, thanks in large measure to the efforts of his printer and friend, Adrian Le Roy. The preface to Lasso's *Primus liber concentuum sacrorum* of 1564 already exemplifies Le Roy's special enthusiasm for our composer. Addressed to the royal counselor, Antoine Poart, this preface passes over the attributes of its nominal dedicatee in near silence, stressing instead the expressive power of Lasso's compositional voice and its effects upon listeners. "The differences between this preface and usual dedications," observes Peter Bergquist in his recent modern edition of this print, "are striking. The customary fawning over an exalted patron is almost completely lacking; in its place is a remarkably flattering evaluation of the composer, supported by unusually specific descriptions of his style."[6]

Throughout the 1560s Le Roy continued to issue more motets by Lasso, new compositions as well as ones previously published by printers in the Netherlands and in Italy. By the middle years of that decade, Lasso's name came to be prominently featured on the title pages of chanson anthologies issued by Le Roy and his partner Robert Ballard, eclipsing that of Jacques Arcadelt, who had previously held pride of place in those titles. Le Roy's lute instruction book (issued by 1568 but surviving only in an English translation of 1574) articulates this changing taste quite nicely, drawing upon a dozen of Lasso's chansons for its musical examples (Arcadelt is represented by but a single work).[7] Le Roy's official royal privilege of commercial protection, granted by the French King Charles IX in 1567, similarly puts

Lasso at the head of a long list of composers whose music was deemed particularly worthy of publication:[8]

Extrait du privilege.
Par lettres patentes du Roy données à Saint Maur le premier jour de May mil cinq cens soixante sept, signées par le Roy. Maistre Regnault de Beaune maistre des requestes ordinaires de l'hostel present, signées de Laubespine et scelées sur double queüe confirmatives d'autres precedentes Est permis et octroyé à Adrian le Roy et Robert Ballard Imprimeurs en musique de sa majesté, d'imprimer ou faire imprimer toute sorte de musique tant vocale que instrumentale de quelque sorte et composition d'auteurs que ce soit, specialement d'**Orlande de lassus**, Iosquin des prez, Mouton, Richaffort, Gascogne, Iaquet, Maillard, Gombert, Arcadet, et C. Goudimel: sans qu'il soit loysible à autre quelconque d'en imprimer, vendre ne distribuer en general ou particulier n'y en distraire aucune partie d'icelle durant le tems de dix ans. Ainsi qu'il est plus amplement contenu et declairé esdittes lettres, à peine de confiscation desditz livres, dommages, interests et amende arbitraire envers lesdits le Roy et Ballard. Lesquelles lettres sadite majesté veut sans autre formalité quelconque et l'extrait d'icelles mis et inferé au commencement ou fin de chacun desdits livres seulement estre tenues pour bien et duëment signifiées à tous imprimeurs à ce qu'ilz n'en puissent pretendre cause d'ignorance sans qu'il soit besoin d'aucune autre signification.

Translation:
Extract from the privilege.
By letters of patent of the King given at Saint Maur on the first day of May, 1567, signed by the King. Maistre Regnault de Beaune, master of requests general of the present household, signed by Laubespine and sealed with a double ribbon confirming previous letters. It is permitted and ordained for Adrian Le Roy and Robert Ballard, royal music printers, to print or have printed all sorts of music, vocal as well as instrumental, of whichever sort and type of any author, but especially that of **Orlande de Lassus**, Josquin des Prez, Mouton, Richaffort, Gascogne, Jaquet, Maillard, Gombert, Arcadet, et C. Goudimel. Without which privilege it will not be legal for any other to have these printed, sold, or distributed in general or in particular, or even to extract some part of these for a term of ten years. As it is amply contained and declared in these said letters, on pain of confiscation of the said books, damages, interests and arbitrary amends on behalf of the said Le Roy et Ballard. His Majesty desires that these provisions be understood without other formality—an extract from them can be put at the beginning or the end of each of the said books, and this alone will serve notice to all printers and on account of which they will not be able to feign ignorance.

By the 1570s, Le Roy et Ballard undertook an entire series of books devoted exclusively to the master's settings of French lyrics, most notably the *Mellange d'Orlande* of 1570 (and its expanded reprintings starting in 1576), and the *Chansons nouvelles* of 1571 (dedicated to members of the French royal family).[9] At about the time Le Roy brought out the *Chansons nouvelles* (and only a few weeks after Lasso himself had visited Paris and the royal household),[10] Charles IX granted the composer a special authorial privilege that gave him exclusive control over who might print, distribute, and sell his compositions (new as well as old) in France. Excerpts from this privilege, which was itself periodically renewed by Charles's successors, appeared in a few of the books of Lasso's music brought out by Le Roy et Ballard during the 1570s and 1580s:[11]

Par lettres patentes du Roy données à Fontainebleau le vingtcinquiesme jour de Julliet, M.D.LXXI. Signées par le Roy, de Neufville: et scellées du grand seau en cire jaune sur simple queuë. Et par autres lettres patentes de confirmation du Roy Henry, données à Paris le vingtcinquiesme jour d'Aoust M.D.LXXV. aussi signées, de Neufville: Il est permis au **sieur Orlande**: de faire imprimer par tel Imprimeur ou Libraire que bon luy semblera, toutes et chacunes les Oeuvres qu'il a faictes et composées, et pourra cy aprez faire et composer, jusques au temps et terme de dix ans, à compter du jour qu'elles seront achevées d'imprimer. Avec defenses tresexpresses à toutes personnes de quelque qualité qu'elles soyent, de les imprimer, faire imprimer, ou mettre en vente, sans le congé et consentement dudict **Orlande**, ou de celuy auquel il aura baillé ledict congé: Sur peine d'amende arbitraire contre les contrevenans, confiscation des livres, despens, dommages et interests. En outre veut ledict Seigneur que mettant au commencement ou à la fin desdictes livres un extraict sommaire desdictes presentes, elles soyent tenues pour suffisamment notifées et venues à la cognoissance particuliere de tous Libraires, Imprimeurs, ou autres, sans qu'ils en puissent pretendre cause d'ignorance.

Translation:
By *lettres patentes* of the King given at Fontainebleau the 25th day of July 1571, signed by the King by de Neufville on behalf of the King, and sealed with the great seal on yellow wax on a simple ribbon. And by other *lettres patentes* of confirmation of King Henry given at Paris the 25th day of August 1575 likewise signed by de Neufville. Granted to **Mr. Orlande** to have printed by whichever printer or bookseller he deems suitable, each and every work which he has made and composed, and may be able to create or compose in the future, for a term of ten years, counting from the day that they appear in print. With express prohibitions to all persons of any sort to print, to have printed, or to put on sale these works only with the approval and agreement of the said **Orlande**, or someone to whom he will have designated the said approval. Upon punishment of amends to be determined against the violators, confiscation of books, expense, damages, and interest. Furthermore the said *Seigneur,* in putting at the outset or conclusion of the said books a summary extract of what is said in this document, all booksellers, printers and others will thereby be sufficiently notified and informed of it, and cannot pretend ignorance.

It seems likely, as James Haar has recently observed, that Charles IX granted this privilege thinking that it offered Lasso an enticement to leave his permanent post at the Bavarian court and come to France to accept a

lucrative position with the French royal establishment.[12] But the chief effect of his proclamation was to reinforce the independence of composer
and printer from the royal household. Now free to choose whichever printer
he saw fit (no matter that the obvious choice was also the royal favorite Le
Roy), Lasso could assume a new level of control over the distribution of his
music without ever leaving the comforts of Munich. Indeed, the several
books issued by Le Roy et Ballard in the months immediately before and
after the granting of the new authorial privilege of 1571 are instructive in
this respect, showing the subtlety with which Lasso regarded his relationship to patrons in both Munich and Paris. In the dedication of a book of
motets issued shortly after his arrival in the French capital in May of 1571,
Lasso affirmed his enduring connection with the Bavarian court but simultaneously offered a book of *Chansons nouvelles* and another book of motets
to the French King Charles.[13] Subsequent volumes of music by Lasso issued
by Le Roy et Ballard continue this same pattern of dual allegiance.

In Imperial lands also, Lasso later astutely sought (and in 1581 was
granted) a special privilege of authority over publication of his music there,
thanks in part to the intercession of his Bavarian patron with Emperor
Rudolph II.[14] Soon thereafter Lasso's old Munich publisher, Adam Berg,
sought to prevent the composer's new partner in Nuremberg, Catherina
Gerlach, from issuing music on the grounds that Berg had exclusive right
to print those pieces that Lasso had sold him under a previous commerical
privilege held by the publisher. Berg, however, did not prevail in this instance, as Imperial magistrates ruled that the new authorial privilege allowed Lasso to reassign printing rights, regardless of the previous sale.

The French authorial royal privilege, and the remarkable authority it
invested in Lasso the composer, was wholly without precedent in the history of French music printing. We should recall, of course, that in the past
French privileges were in principle a form of commercial protection for
printers rather than a means of authorial control: the designation of royal
printer enjoyed by Le Roy and by Attaingnant before him was little more
than an institutionalized form of commercial protection. This privilege
brought with it special access (and perhaps obligation) to the royal musical
establishments from which so much of their repertories were drawn, as
well as a bulwark against unfair competition by rival firms who had not
incurred similar expense of time and capital in acquiring music and bring-
ing it to the public. No composer before Lasso had even been offered an
official voice in the control of his creative work in France. Even in the
literary world the notion of authorial privilege was exceedingly rare during
the late sixteenth century. The prolific essayist and humanist Michel de
Montaigne, for instance, was bound by a conception of property rights in
which printers, not authors, were understood to "own" published works.[15]
Given Lasso's extraordinary right to control the dissemination of his creative output in France, we must infer his approval behind the various prints

that Le Roy et Ballard offered the French musical public (the revised edition of *Les meslanges d'Orlande* promotes itself as having been inspected and approved by the composer himself (see Figure 7.1), who looks out from the pages of the print in a now celebrated engraving (see Figure 8.1). We must, in short, view the Protestant *contrafacta* of Lasso's chansons against the backdrop of this remarkable "authorial" presence.

The lasting effects of the new royal privilege were in some important respects both indirect and symbolic. The new alliance of interests among composer, merchant-printer, and royal authority, after all, served chiefly to confirm a state of affairs rather than to squelch any real competition for Lasso's musical works in France itself. Henri Vanhulst, for instance, has argued that, although the firm of Pierre Phalèse was a frequent (and often the first) publisher of many of Lasso's chansons during the 1560s, starting in the 1570s their publication of music by the great master became increasingly dependent on the Le Roy et Ballard prints, as we have seen.[16] Free from the legal restrictions imposed upon a would-be rival French printer by the new authorial privilege of 1571, Phalèse was nevertheless in no position to compete with Le Roy et Ballard's superior access to the composer's stock of compositions.

The books of *contrafacta* based on Lasso's chansons are similarly unlikely to have posed a real commercial threat to the composer's authorial rights to direct the dissemination of his music. Goulart in Geneva and Vautrollier in London were naturally not bound by commercial protections that applied only in France, while the Haultin firm (Pasquier's printer in the besieged Protestant stronghold of La Rochelle) could hardly have cared at all whether they violated royal copyright or not. We should thus view the authorial presence explicitly celebrated by Le Roy and pointedly troped by the Protestant editor as carrying a somewhat more symbolic meaning, one that Kate van Orden has recently characterized as the emblem of a musical culture newly preoccupied with lineages of prestige and patterns of ownership. In her view, the Le Roy–Lasso prints and the famous retrospective anthology, *Mellange de chansons tant des vieux autheurs que des modernes* (1572, a revision of the *Livre de meslanges* of 1560, with new prefatory material by Ronsard) betray an at times self-conscious attempt by the printer and the humanist poets of his circle to identify Lasso—and in particular his chansons—as the culmination of a long tradition of chanson composition stretching back through the generations of Willaert and Josquin.[17] The king, in "authorizing" Lasso to authorize Le Roy, lends his own official *imprimatur* to this enterprise, and with it a particular ideology that confers enduring worth upon a single representative of a prestigious past. Ignoring Lasso's pan-European career, his polyglot output, and even his nonresidence in France, the special privilege and the books that promoted the music of its bearer represent not just an attempt to gather his chanson production in a single set of partbooks. They represent for van

Figure 8.1. Portrait of Lasso, from fol. 1v of the Superius partbook of Le Roy et Ballard's *Les meslanges d'Orlande* (Paris, 1576). Reproduced by kind permission of the British Library (shelf mark Music K5a3).

Orden a focused attempt to assimilate Lasso himself to some notion of French musical tradition. Viewed in this light the Le Roy–Lasso books seem more than just the musical models for the Protestant *contrafacta* volumes. They are instead the ideological counterparts to those books, and as such use the medium of print to shape new and perhaps specifically French ways of hearing Lasso's secular songs.

Music and Cultures of the Printed Book

All of this activity can serve as a particular instance of what seems to have been a growing concern in Paris and in the Low Countries, too, during the 1570s, when established composers joined with influential printers in collecting together old and new material in a single issue, often with some clear generic focus, narrative or cyclic scheme, or even systematic musical plan. Of course, heavy editing was an established practice where musical anthologies were concerned. When the Parisian printer Nicholas Du Chemin, to take an example from the middle years of the century, obtained a royal privilege to print music books in the manner started in that city by Pierre Attaingnant during the late 1520s, he had to hire a house music editor (first Nicholas Regnes and later Claude Goudimel), whose duties included the selection of suitable music, the organization of these works into part books, and the supervision of the overall accuracy of the typesetting. But such obligations are only obliquely acknowledged by the books themselves, and certainly not in any direct address from editor to prospective readers.[18] Pierre de Ronsard's well-known preface to Le Roy et Ballard's *Mellange de chansons* (an anthology of music from many decades, not to be confused with the Lasso retrospectives), constitutes a clear departure from this general rule of editorial silence, for here we encounter a wealth of insight into the literary and musical ideas that governed the selection of works included in these books, which range widely among genres and styles from Josquin up to then current practice.[19] Jean de Castro's *Livre de meslanges*, issued by Phalèse and Bellère in Louvain and Antwerp in 1575, similarly uses the stabilizing function of print to impose an editorial framework (in this case a succession of works intended to recapitulate the ecclesiastical modes) upon chansons by various composers.[20]

It is, however, in books devoted to the works of individual composers that we may sense a budding notion of how the image of an author might be asserted through a process of redaction and textual repetition aimed to give new meanings (or at least new scope) to previously published compositions. Pierre Certon's *Meslanges*, issued by Du Chemin in 1570, casts a retrospective gaze over his own chanson production, assembling in systematic fashion works that themselves revised or borrowed from polyphonic works by some of his French and Franco-Flemish predecessors.[21] The royal composer Guillaume Costeley, to cite another example, collaborated with Le Roy in the publication of his collected secular works,[22] while in his *Livre de melanges* of 1585 Claude Le Jeune offers previously composed but heretofore privately consumed music to the public for the first time.[23] In all these books, as in the case of the Lasso–Le Roy collaborations of the 1570s and 1580s, retrospection and revision play important parts of the trade in musical ideas, revealing the extent to which even printed music could have a surprisingly fluid history and reception. These processes and practices, moreover, offer an important context for understanding the special publication history of the Lasso chansons and their self-conscious reception by Protestant editors and listeners.

A printer's workshop, according to Elizabeth Eisenstein's classic study of print in Renaissance Europe, was often the locus of a new kind of collaborative enterprise among authors, merchants, and guild craftsmen, an undertaking that in her view was to serve as a means and measure of cultural change.[24] At the very least the new medium and its means of production worked to transform relationships among authors, editors, and audiences. The power of the printing press to stabilize texts, she argues, afforded writers a new means to control language in ways that the vagaries of the scriptorium system could not have attempted, offering readers identical (or very nearly so) copies of a wide variety of texts. The example of the Lasso–Le Roy chansonniers and their appropriation by Huguenot audiences, however, shows that the "fixity" of printed books and the works they contained was largely relative, temporary, and a transitive property that depended as much on readers as it did on editors or authors. We have seen, for instance, how different editions of the assembled Lasso chansons intepret the modal significance of individual pieces according to a changing set of theoretical or editorial schemes. And of course the entire enterprise of the Huguenot *contrafacta* shows how different printed texts (and communities of readers) could coax radically different meanings from ostensibly the same musical notation.

Such concerns are not unique to the example of the books of *contrafacta* based on Lasso's chansons. The famous *Essais* of Michel de Montaigne, for instance, survive in a particularly rich tradition of printed sources, some of which were prepared under the direct supervision of the author. For generations, scholars have assumed that successive changes in these printed texts and annotated copies reflect the author's changing thoughts on individual topics. But recently George Hoffmann has shown that Montaigne's continuing process of revision and redaction of his writings may have been prompted as much by the legal technicalities of the French book privilege system and budding notion of intellectual property as by what previous writers had taken to be a largely internal process of authorial retrospection or elaboration.[25] What is more, Montaigne's *Essais* were also reprinted— often with significant editorial changes—by Goulart and other publishers active in Lyons and Geneva less keen to respect the author's best intentions for his writings than to redact them for Protestant readers.[26] Tessa Watt's recent exploration of the successive revision, adaptation, and reprinting of broadside ballads in the popular English press of the years around 1600 likewise demonstrates how the efforts of printers could both reflect and help to engender new religious beliefs or popular opinion.[27] In these and other ways, publication produced interpretation and dialogue, not merely the reproduction of a "fixed" text.

Roger Chartier views these kinds of transformations as entirely characteristic of the ways in which the advent of print requires us to study not so much the stability of texts that appear in identical copies of printed books, but instead the suprising fluidity with which such books are made and used. On one hand, he suggests, we must detail what he terms "historical modes of reading practice" and the ways in which they were differentiated according to time, place, social status, gender, and belief. Chartier also admonishes us to consider "printed matter as objects"—articles that served, through their format, design, or imagery, to impose certain editorial limits upon the free appropriation of the texts or ideas they offered.[28] At the heart of his work, then, is a concern to recognize how prints of the same text differ from one another and what those differences reveal about the sensibilities of their editors and readers. The example of Huguenot appropriation of the Lasso chansons offers a compelling instance of this process. It shows us how the meanings of these songs changed according to the sorts of possibilities deemed "correct" by a particular community of readers. The printed page, in short, is here invested with the power to stabilize texts, but only as such texts are framed by particular attitudes and assumptions about the ways in which music might "mean" in the first place. In this respect, the *contrafacta* found in Vautrollier's *Recueil du mellange d'Orlande,* in Pasquier's *Mellange d'Orlande,* and in Goulart's *Thrésor de musique d'Orlande* are not simply texts, they are instead reflections of the interior spaces and devotional sensibilities of those who read and heard these chansons.

Postscript

Given the close alliance between text and tone heard in many of Lasso's chansons, it would at first seem to a modern reader that any attempt to make a spiritual *contrafactum* of these chansons would inevitably fall short of the mark. Of course there is good reason to question the presumption that aesthetic criteria were paramount to the sixteenth-century editors who undertook to create such *contrafacta*. But the redacted versions of these chansons reveal that the problem of purification is rather more complex than we might initially suppose, for in the emended poems we may discover both the promise and the peril of the practice, which sought to correct "la lettre" while preserving the power of Lasso's "divins accords" for a morally suitable purpose.

This study has explored how Huguenot musicians felt in Lasso's chansons a spiritual essence patently at odds (for them) with the tenor of the lyric and narrative poetry the composer chose to set to music. In place of these verses Protestant editors crafted new poems—themselves often closely modeled on the language, syntax, and rhyme of the original ones—which embodied ideas and feelings more suited to their own devotional sensibilities than those of the original lyrics. For these editors, and for their largely Protestant audiences as well, Lasso's privileged idiom could be a suitable musical pursuit only if enlisted in the expression of an equally suitable spiritual text. The *contrafacta* thus reveal much about Huguenot assumptions concerning the relationship between words and tones, and about how this community sought to construct a spiritual self that did not so much suppress human emotion as direct it toward personal piety. In the hands of their Protestant editors, the Lasso chansons effect a series of remarkable transitions among categories of experience often viewed in isolation. As we have seen, the problems posed by crafting poetry to music that was itself already carefully molded to the needs of another text reminds us of the profound logocentrism that Lasso the composer shared with some of his ardent listeners. Slipping between secular and spiritual registers, the music of these chansons reminds us that sound *per se* could move between kinds of experience in ways that verbal texts or visual representations could not.

At another level, the books that contain the *contrafacta* are also interesting for the ways in which they appropriate, revise, and reinterpret the choices made in still other books, in this case important volumes that Lasso himself produced in collaboration with the Paris firm of Le Roy et Ballard. The increasing comprehensiveness of the Le Roy et Ballard–Lasso compilations, as we have seen, bears witness to a time of musical history increasingly concerned with lines of authority and cultural prestige. But that same medium became in the hands of Protestant editors a means to correct what they understood to be the spiritual failings of the Lasso chansons and the books that assembled them. In revising the modal plan of Le Roy et Ballard's *Les meslanges d'Orlande,* Goulart's books replace one editorial rendering of these chansons with another, using the unique fixity afforded by the printed book to prepare them as a site for spiritual contemplation. The *contrafacta* books are thus more than collections of edited chansons; they are instead artifacts of the processes by which those chansons were appropriated, reinterpreted, and disseminated in print according to the sensibilities of their Huguenot editors.

These books (and the *contrafacta* they contain) tell us much about the process of listening as it was constructed by this group of spiritual hearers. They also serve as an example of an obvious but often unsettling condition faced by any attempt to understand the music of a different time or place, namely that the meanings or emotional connotations that we attach to sounds "themselves" are rarely fixed, but instead vary according to the assumptions and attitudes of the listeners who encounter them. The *contrafacta* show us, moreover, that musical "texts" cannot be effectively understood apart from the books that preserve them, and that to focus on individual masterworks is to miss the ways in which such pieces were distributed (and redistributed) in sets compiled by editors according to particular criteria. As we have seen, the Lasso–Le Roy chansonniers were themselves prepared in remarkable circumstances, and show clear and self-conscious efforts to arrange their contents according to generic and modal schemes. The books of *contrafacta* prepared by Huguenot editors at times acknowledge and at times radically revise those "authorized" editions, replacing them with their own principles of selection and arrangement. Vautrollier's, Pasquier's, and Goulart's editions of Lasso, in brief, remind us that the process of "rehearing" music and reshaping its textual forms— even music by no less than the "divine Orlande"—was underway already during the composer's lifetime. What now remains is for us to turn the aural mirror upon our own musical and editorial selves in an effort to understand the assumptions that shape our understanding of the music that moves us still, even four centuries after it was first heard.

Appendix A

The Contrafacta Books and Their Prefaces

A. Thomas Vautrollier's dedication in and preface to *Recueil du mellange d'Orlande de Lassus contenant plusieurs chansons tant en vers latins qu'en ryme francoyse, à quatre, et cinq parties.* London, 1570.
B. Jean Pasquier's dedication in the *Mellange d'Orlande de Lassus contenant plusieurs chansons, à quatre parties desquelles la lettre profane a este changée en spirituelle.* La Rochelle, 1575.
C. Jean Pasquier's dedication in the *Mellange d'Orlande de Lassus contenant plusieurs chansons, à cinq parties desquelles la lettre profane a este changée en spirituelle.* La Rochelle, 1576.
D. Jean Pasquier's preface to *Premier livre des Cantiques et Chansons spirituelles a quatre parties en quatre volumes, recueillies de plusieurs excellens musiciens.* La Rochelle, 1578.
E. Simon Goulart's preface to *Le thrésor de musique d'Orlande contenant ses chansons à quatre, cinq et six parties.* [Geneva], 1576.
F. Printer's remarks from Simon Goulart's *Thrésor de musique d'Orlande de Lassus contenant ses chansons à quatre, cinq et six parties.* [Geneva, 1576].
G. Simon Goulart's preface from his *Le thrésor de musique d'Orlande de Lassus contenant ses chansons à quatre, cinq et six parties.* [Geneva, 1594].

A. Thomas Vautrollier's dedication in and preface to *Recueil du mellange d'Orlande de Lassus contenant plusieurs chansons tant en vers latins qu'en ryme francoyse, à quatre, et cinq parties.* London, 1570.

A Tresillustre et tresmag. Seigneur, Le Comte de Arondel,

Monseigneur, je confesse franchement, que je n'oy jamais la musique, qu'incontinent je n'en sente un merveilleux effect en moy: soit qu'un fredon delicatement recouppé, m'attache à la bouche d'un chantre, soit qu'une douce harmonye d'accords, me ravissent, là out le suject (selon qu'il est gay ou triste) guide ses tons allechants. Mais je puis dire aussi, que telle delectation, n'a presque aucune force sur mon ame, si elle est comparée au plaisir que je recoy, quand sous la consideration de ceste melodie, je me figure la beauté admirable de l'harmonye, dont les republiques sagement administrées, temperent l'accordante diversité de leurs estats: choses certes, qui ainsi qu'elle ne se peut veoir à l'oeil, si bien qu'elle se fait sentir par ses fruicts, aussi se represente-elle au vif dans un motet musical, au quel sous la conduite d'une partie, toutes les autres tiennent tellement mesure, qu'estant toutes diverses entres-elles, elles ne discordent en rien: Ainsi qu'en ce chrestien et fleurissant Reaulme (sous l'empire d'une sage et vertueuse Royne) la diversité des estats conspirée en union admirée, de tous les Royaumes voisins. Or Monseigneur, si en ce siècle, où Dieu fait revivre avec sa verité, toutes les sciences et disciplines liberales, il y a musique plus excellent, que celle d'Orlande de Lassus, j'en laisse le jugement aux maistres de l'art. Seulement je di cecy, que Platon qui s'est tant pleu à illustrer de ces proportions de musique, son harmonye politique, eust pris ses exemples des oeuvres d'un seul Orlande, s'ils eussent esté tout d'un temps. Voila pourquoy je les ay voulu imprimer, et communiquer principalement à ceux qui aiment la perfection de cest art, conjoincte avec une lettre grave, et eslongée de toute impurité. Et pource que d'un accueil fort humain, il vous a pleu recevoir les premices de mon Imprimerie, j'ay pensé que ce sien second fruict vous appartenoit aussi. A tant je baise les mains de vostre excellence, et prie Dieu, Monseigneur, qu'il vous enrichisse tousjours de ses graces les plus favorables.

De Londres ce 20. de Septembre 1570

De vostre excel. le plus humbl. et plus obeis. serviteur, T.V.

Translation:

To the most illustrious and most magnificent Lord, the Count of Arundel,

I freely admit that I never hear music without suddenly feeling a marvelous effect, whether on account of a light blended humming that draws me to the voice of a singer or from a sweet harmony of sounds that ravish me, especially when the topic of the text (according to whether it is happy or sad) guides its enticing tones. But I can also note that such delight has almost no influence over my soul if it is compared with the pleasure that I receive when, in regarding this melody, I imagine the admirable beauty of the harmony with which wisely administered republics temper the unified diversity of their various parts. Things of this certainty can not as readily be seen with the eyes as can their effects be felt. This is exemplified vividly in a musical motet, in which thanks to the leading of one part, all the others hold to a similar measure, for despite the differences among them they make no discord at all. In this same manner this Christian and flourishing realm (under the dominion of a wise and virtuous queen) the variety of estates joined in a union admired by all neighboring realms. Now, *Monseigneur,* if in this century when God revives with his Truth all liberal sciences and disciplines there is more excellent music than that of Orlande de Lassus I will leave it to the judgment of the masters of this art. I say only this: that Plato, who was delighted to illustrate with musical proportions his political harmony, would have taken his examples from the works of one such as Orlande, had they been contemporaries. This is why I wanted to print them and convey them mainly to those who love the perfection of this art conjoined with a serious text and far from all impurity. And because of a most human welcome it pleased you to receive the first fruits of my printing press, I have thought that the second fruit would belong to you, too. Indeed, I kiss the hands of your excellency, and beg God, *Monseigneur,* to enrich you always with his most favorable graces.

From London this 20th of September 1570

From your excellency's most humble and most obedient servant, T. V.

B. Jean Pasquier's dedication in the *Mellange d'Orlande de Lassus contenant plusieurs chansons, à quatre parties desquelles la lettre profane a este changée en spirituelle.* La Rochelle, 1575.

À TRES HAUTE, Trespuissante et vertueuse dame Catherine de Partenay dame de Rohan.

Madame, Apres m'estre retiré en ce lieu, pour me sauver des miseres et calamitez de ce tems tres difficile et dangereux, de peur que ne fusse trouvé oysif et inutile en L'eglise de Dieu, Je me deliberay y faire profession de la Musique: offrant à mes freres l'usage du petit talent que le Seigneur m'auroit commis, pour le faire proffiter à mon possible. Et pource qu'entre tous les Musiciens de notre siecle, Orlande de lassus semble (et a bon droit) devoir tenir quelque bon lieu, pour l'exellence et admirable douceur de sa Musique: Voyant icelle neantmoins employée à des chansons si profanes, si sales, et impudiques, que les oreilles chastes et chrestiennes en ont horreur: J'ay pensé que je ferois devoir de Chrestien, si repurgeant ces tresgracieux et plaisans accords de tant de villenies et ordures, dont ilz estoyent tous souillez, Je les remettois sur leur vray et naturel suject, qui est de chanter la puissance, sagesse et bonté de L'eternel. Ayant donc solicité aucuns de mes amis et emprunté d'eux quelques Cantiques de tel argument, au lieu de ces lascivetez et vaines resveries, Je les ay accommodez à la musique: voire tellement que l'harmonie de la voix respond à l'affection de la parolle, autant que faire se peut. Or Madame pource que entre plusieurs excellens dons, desquelz la divine bonté vous a liberalment enrichie, vous estes ornée de ceste douce, et plaisante discipline et y prenez (comme je scay) grande et singuliere delectation: J'ay bien voulu et ay deu vous presenter ceste petite reformation, afin qu'estant recommandée de vostre excellence, elle induyse la Jeunesse de nostre Eglise à s'y excercer plus volontier, et puisse aussy en general donner quelque rafraichissement aux pauvres ames chrestiennes comme alterées de tant d'afflictions dont nous sommes exercez de tous costez.

Madame Je prie Dieu augmenter de ses Graces vostre Excellence et grandeur, et vous maintenir en toute prosperité et santé. À la Rochelle Ce 20. Octobre, 1575.

De vostre excellence le treshumble et obeissant serviteur,

Pasquier

Translation:

To the most esteemed, most powerful and virtuous lady, Catherine de Partenay, de Rohan.

Madame, After retiring to this place, in order to save myself from the miseries and calamities of this most difficult and dangerous age, for fear that I not be found wasted or useless in the church of God, I decided to make music my calling, offering to my brothers the benefit of the little talent that the Lord imbued in me, in order to put it to good use. Among all the musicians of our century Orlande de Lassus appears (and has good right) to deserve good standing, for the excellence and admirable sweetness of his music. Seeing this nevertheless employed in chansons so profane, so salacious and impudent that chaste and Christian ears must recoil in horror, I thought that I might do my Christian duty by purging these very graceful and pleasant chords of such evils and filth with which they have been soiled. I returned them to their true and natural subject, namely to sing of the power, sagacity, and goodness of the Eternal. Having therefore solicited several of my friends and borrowed from them some *cantiques* of similar subject, in place of these lewd and vain reveries, I accommodated these verses to the music. Notice the extent to which the harmony of the voice corresponds to the affection of the word, as much as it is able. Now, Madame, among your many fine gifts, liberally endowed by Divine bounty, you are blessed with this sweet and pleasant discipline and undertake it (as I well know) with great and singular delight. I have therefore wished and am obliged to present you this small reformation, so that having been suggested by your excellency, it will lead the youth of our church to conduct itself more gladly, and might also in general give some refreshment to poor Christian souls that seem transformed by so many afflictions that press upon us from all sides.

Madame, I ask that God, by his Graces, increase your excellence and greatness, and keep you prosperous and healthy. At La Rochelle, this 20th of October, 1575.

Your excellency's most humble and obedient servant,

Pasquier

C. Jean Pasquier's dedication in the *Mellange d'Orlande de Lassus contenant plusieurs chansons, à cinq parties desquelles la lettre profane a este changée en spirituelle*. La Rochelle, 1576.

À Tres Illustre, et vertueux seigneur, Monseigneur de la Noüe.

Monseigneur, Comme j'estois a deliberer à qui je devois addresser ceste partie des mellanges d'Orlande de Lassus, avec la lettre changée et reformée en autre plus tolerable, et recevable entre personnes vertueuses que celle qu'au paravant on y souloit chanter, me representant l'integrité et pureté, de vos meurs, la constance et verité de voz propos, le plaisir aussy que j'ay cogneu que preniez en toutes sciences liberales. Et entre autres en la musique, mesmement d'Orlande, à cinq parties. Lors que sortant du travail de la guerre ou ennuys des conseils (pour prendre quelque respiration) me faisiez cest honneur, me commander d'aller faire la musicque en vostre maison, pour (par ce moyen) vous aider à tromper aucunement l'ennuy, et la tristesse, que ces guerres civiles vous apportoient. Je concluds que je ne pouvois mieux que d'appeller vostre Nom au commencement de ce livre, afin qu'a vostre exemple plusieurs de la noblesse fussent incitez a tels exercices, qui sont certes propres, et bien seants aux personnes illustres, et genereuses, pour leur adoucir l'amertume, et difficulté des labeurs, auquels la piéte, l'amour de leur patrie, la justice et honnesté les appelle, en ce tems miserable et calamiteux. Donques s'il vois plaist, Monseigneur, vous souffrirez, et prendrez en bonne part, que je vous addresse ce petit labeur, indigne veritablement de vostre grandeur, mais presenté de tres-bonne affection. Et de laquelle je prie Dieu vous conserver et accroistre les richesses de ses benedictions, dont il vous a honoré. De la Rochelle, ce premier Jour de Janvier, 1576.

Vostre treshumble serviteur, J. Pasquier.

Translation:

To the most illustrious and virtuous lord, Monseigneur de la Noüe.

Monseigneur, as I was deciding to whom I ought to address this part of the *Mellanges d'Orlande de Lassus* with the words changed and reformed to be more tolerable and acceptable among virtuous persons who were previously defiled through singing these words, it reminded me of the integrity and purity of your taste, of the constancy and truth of your purpose, and of the pleasure that I knew you to take in all the liberal sciences. And among other things in music, that of Orlande, too, in five voices. Now when taking leave of the work of war or the cares of councils (in order to revive yourself) you did me this honor of asking me to come make music in your house, in order (by this means) to help you to chase away care and sadness that these civil wars have brought you. I decided that I could do no better than to call your name at the outset of this book. On your example many of the nobility were induced to such activity, which is good and proper, and well suited to illustrious and generous folk in order to soften their bitterness and the difficulty of their labors, to which piety, love of country, justice and honesty call them in this miserable and calamitous period. Thus if it pleases you, *Monseigneur,* you will endure and accept in good spirit that I address this small labor to you, though truly unworthy of your greatness but granted your very good affection. And in this I ask that God will preserve you and accord you the richness of his benedictions which he has already honored you. From La Rochelle, this first day of January, 1576.

Your most humble servant, J. Pasquier

D. Jean Pasquier's preface to *Premier livre des Cantiques et chansons spirituelles à quatre parties en quatre volumes, recueillies de plusieurs excellens musiciens.* La Rochelle, 1578.

Ian Pasquier sezanien au lecteur fidele.

Je m'estudie tant que je puis (Ami lecteur) à ramener la Musique à son vray but, qui est de glorifier ce grand Dieu, qui l'a créée, et nous l'a donnée avec les autres arts et sciences liberales pour le soulagement de ceste vie. Ainsi t'ay donné premierement, un recueil des divins accords d'Orlande, les retirant de la poësie profane, comme pierres precieuses d'un vilain bourbier: et puis m'accommodant aux plus rudes ay dressé une briefve et facile instruction, pour les acheminer à ceste science: et maintenant pour la pratique d'icelle ay fait imprimer cest autre recueil, contenant plusieurs livres: au premier desquels seront cantiques et chansons les meilleures et plus faciles que i'ay peu choisir, dont le mot se trouvera tout au long en la partie de la taille, laquelle contient le chant ordinaire: aux autres livres seront certaines chansons tant vielles que modernes, fort bonnes et propres aux instruments, un peu plus difficiles que les premieres. Tu useras doncques de ce labeur, en attendant choses plus grandes. Bien te soit.

Translation:

Jean Pasquier, Sezanaien, to his faithful reader.

I have considered as well as I am able, Dear Reader, to return music to its true end, which is to glorify this great God, who created it, and who gave it to us along with the other liberal arts and sciences as comfort in this life. Thus I have initially given you a collection of the divine sounds of Orlande, retrieving them from profane poetry, like precious stones from a vile mud-pit, and applying myself to the most uncouth of these prepared a brief and simple introduction in order to direct them back to this science. And now in order to do this I have had printed this other collection comprising several books, the first of which will be the best and easiest *cantiques* and chansons that I have been able to select, in which the words will be found throughout in the tenor part, which contains the *chant ordinaire*. In the other books will be certain chansons, old as well as recent, quite nice and suitable for instruments, a little more difficult than the first. You will make use of this endeavor, therefore, awaiting still greater things. You should be well.

E. Simon Goulart's preface to the *Thrésor de musique d'Orlande contenant ses chansons à quatre, cinq et six parties* ([Geneva], 1576).

A Philippe de Pas, Gentilhomme françois,
S.[imon] G.[oulart] S.[enlis]

Monsieur, il y a long temps que je vous ay ouy desirer ce que je vous presente maintenant: asavoir, Les chansons d'Orlande de Lassus, tellement changées, qu'on les peust chanter de la voix et sur les Instruments, sans souiller les langues ni offenser les oreilles Chrestiennes. Et pource que vous m'exhortastes d'y mettre la main, je prins vostre desir comme pour commandement. Et selon que la fantasie me prenoit, je changeay en quelques unes ce qui me sembloit devoir este osté. Depuis, ceste entreprise demeura comme ensevelie, à cause des terribles changemens que nous avons veus. Et comme je pensois laisser là tout, un de mes Amis m'envoia ceste Musique d'Orlande accommodée à une lettre spirituelle: ce qu'aiant veu, je reprins courage pour agencer ce que j'en avois commencé: en telle sorte neantmoins que ce qui m'en a esté envoié par cest Ami, avec les livres qui on esté imprimez en Angleterre, m'a reclué de peine en divers endroits. L'ordre que j'ai tenu, a esté tel. La Lettre accommodée à la Musique d'Orlande imprimée à Paris et à Louvain, estoit sotte, lascive et profane, presque en toutes les chansons. En ostant quelques mots ou plusieurs, et les accommodant (au moins mal qu'il m'a esté possible) à la Musique, j'ai rendu ces chansons honnestes, et Chrestiennes pour la pluspart. Quelques unes sont restées plus gayes (peut estre) qu'aucuns ne desireroient: mais je pense qu'il n'y aura rien qui puisse offenser les gens de bien. Je ne doute point que plusieurs ne se plaignent que la Musique aura perdu sa grace, d'autant que Orlande l'avoit appropriée à la lettre, en quoi il est excellent (comme en tout ce qui est de ceste science liberale) pardessus tous les Musiciens de nostre temps. Mais je m'asseure que ceste plainte ne partira jamais que de la bouche de ceux dont le coeur est souillé de ces puantises et lascivetez, que beaucoup de poetes François ont semées pou infecter le monde. Or je pren plaisir à desplaire à telles gens: et si ces livres les faschent (comme j'en suis bien content) qu'ils achevent de se corrompre du tout par leur vilaine musique. Il seroit bien à desirer qu'Orlande emploiast ces graces dont le S. Esprit l'a orné par dessus tous, à reconoistre et magnifier celui de qui il les tient, comme il l'a fait en quelques Motets et Pseaumes Latins: et je desire grandement que ces chansons lui en puissent donner la volonte: à fin que nous aions une chaste Musique Françoise. Ce pendant, jouissez de ceste cì, qui pourra estre mieux changée par quelques autres ci apres: car il s'en faut beaucoup que j'aie rendu l'oeuvre accompli, comme j'eusse bien voulu. Au reste, si lon estime ce temps plein de troubles, n'estre encor du tout propres pour mettre ceci en lumiere: et qu'il faudroit plustost pleurer que chanter: je respondrai qu'il n'est point defendu aux gens de bien, de s'esiouir en Dieu avec honneste moderation, pour adoucir aucunement leurs ennuis. Comme de ma part j'ai trouvé en la Musique, d'Orlande specialement, des remedes souverains contre diverses blesseures de l'ame. D'entrer ici es louanges de la Musique, et d'Orlande aussi, ce seroit mal à propos et me pourroit on bien mettres au devant ce qu'Antalcidas respondit à quelqu'un qui vouloit louanger Hercules, Et qui est-ce (dit-il) qui le blasme? Qui est celui aussi, tant rude et barbare soit-il, qui n'ait l'ame picquée et comme tirée doucement du corps par les accords melodieux d'une si belle Musique que celle d'Orlande? A l'espreuve on orra si je di vrai ou non. Pourtant, Monsieur, vous recevrez de bon oeil ce present: et s'il vous contente, il me chaut bien peu du jugement qu'en seront les envieux. Et si les gens modestes et vertueux m'en savent gré, j'en serai bien aise: car je n'aurai du tout perdu mon temps en desirant leur complaire.

Translation:

To Philippe de Pas, French gentleman, S.G.S

Monsiegneur, for some time now I have heard that you wanted me to present to you this volume of the chansons of Orlande de Lassus, so altered that one may sing them or play them upon instruments without soiling the tongues or offending Christian ears. Since you exhorted me to put my hand to it, I took your wish as my command. As I allowed my imagination to take hold, I changed in several of these chansons that which appeared to me detestable. This undertaking remained shrouded on account of the terrible events we have seen of late. I thought to leave the work entirely aside, but one of my friends sent me this *Musique d'Orlande* accommodated to a spiritual text. Having seen it, I regained the courage to complete what I had started. In this manner nevertheless, that which was sent to me by my friend in the books that were printed in England revealed to me the similar efforts undertaken in various places. The order that I have held was just this: the text accommodated to the music of Orlande printed in Paris and in Louvain was silly, lascivious, and profane in nearly all of the chansons. In removing several or many of these words and accommodating them (as well as it has been possible for me) to the music, I rendered these chansons for the most part honest and Christian. Certain ones remain too merry (perhaps) for some. But I think that there remains nothing here that might offend honest folk. I have no doubt that many will grumble that the music will have lost all its grace, inasmuch that Orlande designed it according to the words, in which respect he is excellent (as he is in all aspects of this liberal science) beyond all musicians of our era. But I assure myself that this complaint will spring only from the lips of those in whom the heart is soiled by this filth and lewdness that many French poets have brought forth to infect the world. Now I take pleasure to displease such folk. And if these books anger them (which would be fine with me) they can manage to corrupt themselves totally by their villainous music. It would be good to wish that Orlande use his graces, which the Holy Spirit has adorned in him above all, to recall and magnify the one from whom they derive, as he has done in several Motets and Latin Psalms. I deeply wish that these chansons might provoke the urge in him, so that we have a chaste French Music. Pending this, rejoice in what is here, which could also be better changed by others hereafter, for there is much to do before I complete the work as I would have wished. For the rest, if one considers that in this time so full of troubles it is not proper to bring all of this material to light and that one ought sooner to cry than to sing, I would reply that it is in no way forbidden for good folk to rejoice in God with honest moderation, in order to assuage their sorrow in some way. For my part I have found in music, and especially in [that] of Orlande, powerful remedies for various wounds to the soul. To enter here with praises of music, and that of Orlande, too, would be inappropriate, and I would instead present that which Antalcides said to one who wished to praise Hercules, "And who (he said) would criticize him?" Who, however rude and barbarous he may be, has not had his soul touched and sweetly drawn forth from the body by the melodious accords of such beautiful music as that of Orlande? In the end one will see whether I am right or not. For this, sir, you will look kindly upon this offering, and if you agree it will show me of poor judgment when others become envious. If modest and virtuous folk are grateful, I would be well at ease, for I will in no way have wasted my time in wishing to please them.

F.   Printer's remarks from Simon Goulart's *Thrésor de musique d'Orlande de Lassus contenant ses chansons à quatre, cinq et six parties.* [Geneva, 1576], (Bassus, fol. 88v).

L'imprimeur aux musiciens S.

Je pensoi' bien (Messieurs) vous fournir toutes les chansons d'Orlande à cinq et six parties, commes celles a quatre: mais voyant les livres assez gros, et pour un notable empeschement survenu, je me suis contenté de vous donner ceste Centaine, esperant à la seconde edition (si Dieu le permet) vous presenter un thresor accompli et tout ce qui pourroit sembler non assez propre, si bien agencé qu'aurez contentement. Vous m'excuserez, si je n'ai esté si cler-voyant à bien ordonner toutes choses, comme il y a trois ou quatre chansons transposées, à quoi toutesfois l'indice remedie. Item parmi celles à cinq il y en a deux de Philippes de Monté, lesquelles se sont glissées sans que celui qui a corrigé la lettre, s'en soit apperceu qu'incontinent apres qu'elles ont este imprimées. Ces deux sont, *L'homme inconstant ne peut vaincre le monde,* et *Las! je n'ai point victoire sur le monde.* Au demeurant, je n'ai point mis l'indice des chansons profanes, encor que je ne doute qu'aucuns ne veuillent voir comment ceste ci ou ceste là sont changées. Car la Musique demeure en son entier, et est expedient qu'on ne se souvienne jamais plus de cette lettre lascive. Les deux chansons Latines à six faisans la conclusion, ne vous desagrèront. Et si en plusieurs la lettre est demeuree telle qu'elle est es livres de Paris, cela est procédé de la volonté du correcteur, qui ne s'est voulu ingerer de ragencer ce qui est passable.

Translation:

From the printer to the musicians S.

I thought well (Sirs) to provide you with all of the chansons of Orlande for five and six voices, as well as those for four voices. But seeing books so big, and for a great difficulty that arose, I am content to give you only these one hundred, hoping in the second edition (if God grants it) to offer you a complete *Thrésor.* If things do not all seem just so, please understand. You will pardon me, too, if I have not been so clairvoyant as to organize everything, as there are three or four displaced chansons, which will in any case be remedied by the index. Similarly among the chansons for five voices there are two by Philippe de Monté which have slipped past he who was to have corrected the text, which was noticed only after they had been printed. These two are, "L'homme inconstant ne peut vaincre le monde" and "Las! je n'ai point victoire sur le monde." I have not, moreover, indexed the secular chansons, as I have no doubt that no one will want to see how one or another of them has been changed. For the music remains in its entirety, and it is better that one never recall again the lascivious words. The two Latin chansons for six voices at the end should not displease you. And if in many the words remain just as they were in the Parisian books, that is precisely the intent of the corrector, who has not been inclined to censor that which is acceptable.

G. Simon Goulart's preface from his *Le thrésor de musique d'Orlande de Lassus contenant ses chansons à quatre, cinq et six parties.* [Geneva, 1594].

Note: The same preface was evidently issued in the second edition of 1582, as the text in this 1594 imprint alludes to six years passing since the first edition of 1576.

A. Philippe de Pas, Gentilhomme françois, S.G.S

Monsieur, il y a six ans passes, que, satisfaisant à vostre desir, je changeay la lettre de quelques chansons d'Orlande de Lassus, pour pouvoir estre chantées de la voix et sur les instruments, sans souiller les langues ny offenser les oreilles Chrestiennes. Il est advenu, que le recueil qui en fut mis en lumiere puis apres a esté mieux receu que je n'osois esperer. Tellement que l'imprimeur estant sur le poinct se mettre la main à ceste second [sic] edition je me suis enhardi de l'enricher d'une cinquantaine de chansons du mesme Auteur, esquelles, depuis quelques mois, j'ay changé ce qui me sembloit n'estre supportable. L'ordre que je tins au commencement, et que j'ay suyvi ceste seconde fois, a esté tel: la lettre accommodée à la musique d'Orlande imprimée à Paris et à Louvain, estoit soite lascive et profane, presque en toutes les chansons. En ostant quelques mots ou plusieurs, et les accommodant (au moins mal qu'il m'a esté possible) à la Musique, j'ai rendu ces chansons honnestes, et Chrestiennes pour la pluspart. Quelques unes sont restées plus gayes (peut estre) qu'aucuns ne desireroient: mais je pense qu'il n'y aura rien qui puisse offenser les gents de bien. Je ne doute point que plusieurs ne se plaignent que la Musique aura perdu sa grace, d'autant qu'Orlande l'avoit appropriée à la lettre, enquoi il est excellent (comme en tout ce qui est de ceste science liberale) par dessus tous les Musiciens de nostre temps. Mais je m'asseure que ceste plainte ne partira jamais sinon de la bouche de ceux dont le coeur est souillé de ces puantises que beaucoup de Poëtes François ont semées pour infecter le monde. Or je pren plaisir à desplaire à telles gents. Et si ces livres les faschent (comme j'en suis bien content) qu'ils achevent de se corrompre du tout par leur vilaine Musique. Il seroit bien à desirer qu'Orlande emploiast ces graces dont le S. Esprit l'a orné par dessus tous, à recongnoistre et magnifier celui de qui il les tient, comme il l'a fait en quelques Motets et Pseaumes Latins: et je desire grandement que ces chansons lui en puissent donner la volonte: à fin que nous aions de luy une chaste Musique Françoise. Cependant, jouisse de ceste-cì, qui pourra estre mieux changée par quelques autres ci apres: car il s'en faut beaucoup que j'aie rendu l'oeuvre accompli, comme j'eusse bien voulu. Au reste, si l'on estime ce temps plein de troubles, n'estre propres pour mettre ceci en lumiere: et qu'il faudroit plustost pleurer que chanter: je respondrai qu'il n'est point defendu aux gens de bien, de s'esiouir en Dieu avec honneste moderation, pour adoucir aucunement leurs ennuis. Comme de ma part j'ai trouvé en la Musique, d'Orlande specialement, des remedes souverains contre diverses blesseures de l'ame. D'entrer ici es louanges de la Musique d'Orlande, ce seroit mal à propos et me pourroit on bien mettres au devant ce qu'Antalcidas respondit à quelqu'un qui vouloit louanger Hercules, Et qui est-ce (dit-il) qui le blasme? Qui est celui aussi, tant rude et barbare soit-il, qui n'ait l'ame picquée et comme tirée doucement du corps par les accords melodieux d'une si belle Musique que celle d'Orlande? A l'espreuve on orra si je di vrai ou non. Pourtant, Monsieur, vous recevrez encor une fois de bon oeil ce present: et s'il vous contente, il me chaut bien peu du jugement qu'en seront les envieux. Et si les gents modestes et vertueux m'en scavent gré, j'en serai bien aise: car je n'aurai du tout perdu mon temps en desirant leur complaire.

Translation:

To Philippe de Pas, French gentleman, S.G.S

Monseigneur, it was six years ago [*sic*: this wording repeated even in the 1594 edition] that, in satisfying your wish, I adapted the text of several chansons of Orlande de Lassus, in order that they be performable by voice and upon instruments, without soiling the tongues or offending Christian ears. It has happened that the collection that was brought out has been better received than I could have hoped. So much so that the printer being ready to put his hand to this second [*sic*] edition, I emboldened myself to enrich it by another fifty chansons by the same composer, of which several months ago I altered that which to me appeared insupportable. The order that I have continued to hold was just this: the text accommodated to the music of Orlande printed in Paris and in Louvain were silly, lascivious, and profane in nearly all of the chansons. In removing several or many of these words and accommodating them (as well as it has been possible for me) to the music, I rendered these chansons for the most part honest and Christian. Certain ones remain too merry (perhaps) for some. But I think that there remains nothing here that might offend honest folk. I have no doubt that many will grumble that the music will have lost all its grace, inasmuch that Orlande designed it according to the words, in which respect he is excellent (as he is in all aspects of this liberal science) beyond all musicians of our era. But I assure myself that this complaint will spring only from the lips of those in whom the heart is soiled by this filth that many French poets have brought forth to infect the world. Now I take pleasure to displease such folk. And if these books anger them (which would be fine with me) they can manage to corrupt themselves totally by their villainous music. It would be good to wish that Orlande use his graces, which the Holy Spirit has adorned in him above all, to recall and magnify the one from whom they derive, as he has done in several Motets and Latin Psalms. I deeply wish that these chansons might provoke the urge in him, so that we have a chaste French Music. Pending this, rejoice in what is here, which could also be better changed by others hereafter, for there is much to do before I complete the work as I would have wished. For the rest, if one considers that in this time so full of troubles it is not proper to bring all of this material to light and that one ought sooner to cry than to sing, I would reply that it is in no way forbidden for good folk to rejoice in God with honest moderation, in order to assuage their sorrow in some way. For my part I have found in music, and especially in [that] of Orlande, powerful remedies for various wounds to the soul. To enter here with praises of the music of Orlande would be inappropriate, and I would instead present that which Antalcides said to one who wished to praise Hercules, "And who (he said) would criticize him?" Who, however rude and barbarous he may be, has not a soul touched and sweetly drawn forth from the body by the melodious accords of such beautiful music as that of Orlande? In the end one will see whether I am right or not. For this, sir, you will look kindly upon this offering, and if you agree it will show me of poor judgment when others become envious. If modest and virtuous folk are grateful, I would be well at ease, for I will in no way have wasted my time in wishing to please them.

Appendix B

Printing Privileges Mentioned in Publications of Lasso's Music Issued by Le Roy et Ballard

A. Books that mention some privilege on the title page, but surviving books offer no other details of the arrangements

RISM-A Number	Title of Print	Indication of Privilege	Location in Print
L1564b	*Primus liber concentuum sacrorum, quos motetos vulgo nominant, quinque et sex vocibus compositorum, Orlando de Lassus auctore.*	Cum privilegio Regis	Title page: CT, B, T
L1565a	*Modulorum Orlandi de Lassus. Quaternis, quinis, sénis, septenis, octonis et denis vocibus modulatorum Secundum volumen*	Cum privilegio Regis ad decennium	Title page: CT
L1565d	*Novem quiritationes divi Iob. Quaternis vocibus ab Orlando de Lassus. Modulatae.*	Cum privilegio Regis ad decennium.	Title page: CT
L1571a	*Moduli quinis vocibus nunquam hactenus editi monachii Boioarae compositi, Orlando Lassuo Auctore*	Cum privilegio Regis ad decennium.	Title page: T, B, CT, S, Q

L1573b	*Moduli sex, septem et duodecim vocum, Orlando Lassussio Auctore.*	Cum privilegio Regis ad decennium	Title page: S, CT, B, Q
L1576	*Les meslanges d'Orlande de Lassus*	Avec privilege de sa majesté	Title page: S, CT, T, B
L1577e	*Moduli. quatuor 5.6.7.8. et novem vocum. Orlando Lassusio auctore.*	Cum privilegio Regis ad decennium.	Title page: S, CT, B, Q
L1578g	*Moduli duarum vocum nunquam hactenus editi monachii boioariae compositi Orlando Lasso auctore.*	Cum privilegio Regis ad decennium.	Title page: S, T
L1581g	*Libro de villanelle, moresche, et altre canzoni, A. 4.5.6. et 8 voci. Di Orlando di Lasso*	Con privileggio de sua Magestà per dieci anni.	Title page: C, A, T, B
L1582a	*Missa ad imitationem moduli (Quand'io penso al martire.) Auctore Orlando de Lassus. Cum quatuor vocibus.*	Cum privilegio Regis, ad decennium.	Title page
L1582b	*Missa ad imitationem moduli (Quinti Toni.) Auctore Orlando de Lassus. cum quatuor vocibus.*	Cum privilegio Regis, ad decennium.	Title page
L1587a	*Missa ad imitationem moduli Beatus qui intelligit*	Cum privilegio Regis, ad decennium.	Title page
L1587b	*Missa ad imitationem moduli Locutus sum*	Cum privilegio Regis, ad decennium.	Title page
L1587d	*Sacrum cantionum moduli quatuor vocibus contexti, Auctore. Orlando Lassussio*	Cum privilegio Regis ad decennium	Title page: C, S, B, T

RISM-A Number	Title of Print	Indication of Privilege	Location in Print
L1587i	*Octo cantica divae Mariae virginis. quorum initium est Magnificat, secundum octo modos, seu tonos in templis decantari solitos singula quaternis vocibus constantia: Auctore ORLANDO LASSUSIO*		Foot of title page trimmed too closely.
L1588d	*Moduli quinque vocum. Auctore. Orlando Lasso*	Cum privilegio Regis ad decennium.	Title page
L1588e	*Moduli sex vocum. Auctore. Orlando Lasso.*	Cum privilegio Regis ad decennium.	Title page: S
L1597f	*Beatissimae Virginis Mariae. Octo cantica modis tonorum octo quaternisque vocibus distincta. Adiectus adhaec duplici Salve Regina. Missa Quinti toni. Veni Creator. Te Deum laudamus. Adoramus te Christe, 3, et 4 voc. et Tibi laus. Auctore Orlando Lasso.*	Cum privilegio Regis ad decennium.	Title page: CT, S, T

B. Books that contain an excerpt from a General Printer's Privilege

RISM-A Number	Title of Print	Indication of Privilege	Location in Print
L1570a	*Mellange d'Orlande de Lassus*	Avec privilege de sa majesté	Title page: S, T, CT, B, and Q.
		General privilege of 1567 (see below for full text).	Last page of Q.

L1571c	*Primus liber modulorum quinis vocibus constantium, Orlando Lassusio Auctore*	Cum privilegio Regis ad decennium / General privilege of 1567 (see below for full text).	Title page: T, B, CT, S, Q / Last page of B
L1571e	*Secundus liber modulorum Quinis vocibus constantium Orlando Lassusio Auctore*	Cum privilegio Regis ad decennium / Extract from general privilege of 1567 (see below for full text).	Title page: T, B, C, S, Q / Last page of C
L1572f	*Novem quiritationes divi Iob. Quaternis vocibus ab Orlando de Lassus. Modulata.*	Cum privilegio Regis ad decennium. / Extract from general privilege of 1567 (see below for full text).	Title page: S, T, CT, B. / Last page of S, T, CT, B
L1576d	*Moduli nondum prius editi monachii Boioarie ternis vocibus, ab Orlando Lasso Compositi.*	Cum privilegio Regis ad decennium. / Extract from general privilege of 1567 (see below for full text).	Title page: S, T, B. / Last page of S.
L1581c	*Octo cantica divae Mariae virginis. quorum initium est Magnificat, secundum octo modos, seu tonos in templis decantari solitos singula quaternis vocibus constantia: Auctore ORLANDO LASSUSIO*	Cum privilegio Regis, ad decennium (see below for full text).	Title page.

RISM-A Number	Title of Print	Indication of Privilege	Location in Print
L1607a	*Missa ad imitationem*	Cum privilegio Regis. General privilege (see below for full text).	Title page. Last page of choirbook.
L1607b	*Missa ad imitationem*	Cum privilegio Regis. General privilege (see below for full text).	Title page. Last page of choirbook.
L1608a	*Missa ad imitationem moduli Credidi Auctore Orlando de Lassus, cum quinque vocibus*	Cum privilegio Regis. General privilege (see below for full text).	Title page. Last page of choirbook.
L1613	*Missa ad imitationem In te Domine speravi*	Cum privilegio Regis. General privilege (see below for full text).	Title page. Last page of choirbook.

Text of the General Privilege found in L1570a, L1571c, L1571e, L1572d, L1572f, L157d, L1581c:

Extrait du privilege

Par lettres patentes du Roy donnés à Saint Maur le premier jour de May mil cinq cens soixante sept, signées par le Roy. Maistre Regnault de Beaune maistre des requestes ordinaires de l'hostel present, signées de Laubespine et scelées sur double queüe confirmatives d'autres precedentes Est permis et octroyé à Adrian le Roy et Robert Ballard Imprimeurs en musique de sa majesté, d'imprimer ou faire imprimer toute sorte de musique tant vocale que instrumentale de quelque sorte et composition d'auteurs que ce soit, specialement d'**Orlande de lassus**, Iosquin des prez, Mouton, Richaffort, Gascogne, Iaquet, Maillard, Gombert, Arcadet, et C. Goudimel: sans qu'il soit loysible à autre quelconque d'en imprimer, vendre ne distribuer en general ou particulier n'y en distraire aucune partie d'icelle durant le tems de dix ans. Ainsi qu'il est plus amplement contenu et declairé esdittes lettres, à peine de confiscation desditz livres, dommages, interests et amende arbitraire envers lesdits le Roy et Ballard. Lesquelles lettres sadirte majesté veut sans autre formalité quelconque et l'extrait d'icelles mis et inféré au commencement ou fin de chacun desdits livres seulement estre tenues pour bien et devëment signifiées à tous imprimeurs à ce qu'ilz n'en puissent pretendre cause d'ignorance sans qu'il soit besoin d'aucune autre signification.

L1607a:

Extraict du privilege

Par lettres patentes du Roy, données à Paris le vingt-cinquiesme iour de Mars, l'an de grace mil six cens sept, et de nostre regne le dix-huictiesme: Signées HENRY, et plus bas par le Roy, de Lomenie. Scellées du grand scel en cire jaune sur simple queuë: Il est permis à Pierre Ballard Imprimeur de Musique de sa Majesté, d'imprimer, vendre et distribuer toute sorte de Musique tant vocalle qu'instrumentalle, de quelque autheur que ce soit: faisant deffences à toutes autres d'imprimer vendre ny distribuer, extraire aucune partie par qeulque maniere que ce soit, ny contrefaire aucunes inventions trouvée et inventées par ledit Ballard, sur peine de confiscation desdits livres, despens dommages et interests, ainsi qu'il estplus amplement contenu et declaré esdites lettres.

L1607b:

Extraict du privilege

Par lettres patentes du Roy, données à Paris le vingt-cinquiesme iour de Mars, l'an de grace mil six cens sept, et de nostre regne le dix-huictiesme: Signées HENRY, et plus bas par le Roy, de Lomenie. Scellées du grand scel en cire jaune sur simple queuë: Il est permis à Pierre Ballard Imprimeur de Musique de sa Majesté, d'imprimer, vendre et distribuer toute sorte de Musique tant vocalle qu'instrumentalle, de quelque autheur que ce soit: faisant deffences à toutes autres d'imprimer vendre ny distribuer, extraire aucune partie par qeulque maniere que ce soit, ny contrefaire aucunes inventions trouvée et inventées par ledit Ballard, sur peine de confiscation desdits livres, despens dommages et interests, ainsi qu'il est plus amplement contenu et declaré esdites lettres.

L1608a:

Extraict du privilege

Par lettres patentes du Roy, données à Paris le vingt-cinquiesme iour de Mars, l'an de grace mil six cens sept, et de nostre regne le dix-huictiesme: Signées HENRY, et plus bas par le Roy, de Lomenie. Scellées du grand scel en cire jaune sur simple queuë: Il est permis à Pierre Ballard Imprimeur de Musique de sa Majesté, d'imprimer, vendre et distribuer toute sorte de Musique tant vocale qu'instrumentale, de quelque autheur que ce soit: faisant deffences à toutes autres d'imprimer vendre ny distribuer, extraire aucune partie par quelque maniere que ce soit, ny contrefaire aucunes inventions trouvée et inventées par ledit Ballard, sur peine de confiscation desdits livres, despens dommages et interests, ainsi qu'il est plus amplement contenu et declaré esdites lettres.

L1613:

Extraict du privilege

Par lettres patentes du Roy données à Fontainebleau le sixiesme jour d'octobre, l'An de grace mil six cens unze, et de nostre reigne le deuxiesme. Signées par le Roy en son conseil, Lardy: et scellées du grand sceau en cire jaune sur simple queuë, conformatives à d'autres precedentes. Il est permis à Pierre Ballard Imprimeur de Musique de sa Majesté, d'imprimer, faire imprimer, vendre et distribuer toute sorte de Musique tant vocale qu'instrumentale, de quelque Autheur que ce soit, nommément d'Orlande de Lassus: Faisant deffences à tous autres Libraires et Imprimeurs de quelque condition et qualité qu'ils soyent, d'imprimer, faire imprimer, extraire partie d'icelle par quelque maniere que ce soit, ny mesme vendre ny distribuer en general ne particulier, les livres de Musique imprimés et à imprimer par ledit Ballard, sans son congé et permission, sur peine de confiscation desdits livres, despens, dommages, interets et d'amende arbitraire: ainsi qu'il est plus amplement declaré esdites lettres: et ce pour le terme di dix années, à commancer du jour que les livres seront achevés d'imprimer, nonobstant toutes lettre impetrées ou à impertrer à ce contraires. Sadite Majesté veut sans autre signification ne formalité, l'extrait d'icelles mis au commencement ou fin de chacun desdits livres estre tenues pour bien et devëment signifiées à tous qu'il appartiendra.

C. Books that contain an excerpt from Lasso's Special Authorial Privilege

RISM-A Number	Title of Print	Indication of Privilege	Location in Print
L1573c	*Tertius liber modolurum quinis vocibus constantium, Orlando Lassusio auctore.*	Authorial privilege of 1571 (see below for full text). Cum privilegio Regis ad decennium.	Verso of title page: Q Title page: S, C, T, B, Q
L1577a	*Missae variis concentibus ornatae, ab Orlando de Lassus. Cum cantico beatae Mariae. Octo Modis Musicisi variato*	Authorial privilege of 1571 as confirmed in 1575.	Last page of each Mass in the set
L1578g	*Octo cantica divae mariae virginis, quorum initium est Magnificat, secundum octo modos, sev tonos in templis decantari solitos singula quinis vocibus constantia: Auctore Orlando Lassusio*	Authorial privilege of 1571 as confirmed in 1575.	Last page of choirbook
L1586e	*Ieremiae. Prophetae devotissimae lamentationes, una cum passione domini dominicae palmarum, quinque vocum. Auctore Orlando Lasso.*	Authorial privilege of 1571 as confirmed in 1575 and again in 1582. Cum privilegio Regis ad decennium.	Title page:: T, B, CT, S

Texts of the Authorial Privileges:

L1573c

Extrait du privilege.

Il a pleu au Roy ottroyer à ORLANDE DE LASSUS, Maistre Compositeur de Musique Privilege et permission de faire imprimer par tel imprimeur de ce Royaume que bon luy semblera la Musique de son invention estant par luy reveuë et remise en tel ordre qu'il adviseroit et aussi de faire imprimer celle qui n'a encores esté par cy devant mise en lumiere sans que pendant le temps de dix ans aucun autre imprimeur que celuy auquell ledit de lassus auroit baillé ses copies et permission se puisse ingerer d'en imprimer ne mettre en vente ne porcion d'icelle si ce n'estoit du consentement de l'un ou de l'autre soubz les peines contenues esdittes lettres, et qu'en mettant ledit privilege ou extraict d'icelluy au commencement ou à la fin desditz livres imprimez il soit tenu pour bien et devëment signifié à toutes personnes que besoin seroit et tout ainsi que si la notification leur en avoit esté particulierement faitte. Donné à Fontainebleau le XXV. jour de Iuillet lan de grace mil cinq cens LXXI. et de son regne l'unzième. Par le Roy Signé de Neufville soub le contrescel de la Chancellerie en cire Iaune.

L1577a, L1578g:

Extraict du Privilege.

Par lettres patentes du Roy données à Fontainebleau le vingtcinquiesme jour de Julliet, M.D.LXXI. Signées par le Roy, De Neufville: et scellées du grand seau en cire jaune sur simple queuë. Et par autres lettres patentes de confirmation du Roy Henry, données à Paris le vingtcinquiesme jour d'Aoust M.D.LXXV. aussi signées, De Neufville: Il est permis au sieur Orlande: de faire imprimer par tel Imprimeur ou Libraire que bon luy semblera, toutes et chacunes les Oeuvres qu'il a faictes et composées, et pourra cy aprez faire et composer, jusques au temps et terme de dix ans, à compter du jour qu'elles seront achevées d'imprimer. Avec defenses tresexpresses à toutes personnes de quelque qualité qu'elles soyent, de les imprimer, faire imprimer, ou mettre en vente, sans le congé et consentement dudict Orlande, ou de celuy auquel il aura baillé ledict congé: Sur peine d'amende arbitraire contre les contrevenans, confiscation des livres, despens, dommages et interests. En outre veut ledict Seigneur que mettant au commencement ou à la fin desdictes livres un extrait sommaire desdictes presentes, elles soyent tenues pour suffisamment notifées et venues à la cognoissance particuliere de tous Libraires, Imprimeurs, ou autres, sans qu'ils en puissent pretendre cause d'ignorance.

L1586e

Extraict du Privilege.

Par lettres patentes du Roy données à Fontainebleau le vingtcinquiesme iour de Iuillet, M.D. LXXI. Signées par le Roy, De Neufville: et scellées du grand seau en cire iaune sur simple queuë. Et par autres lettres patentes de confirmation du Roy Henry, données à Paris le vingtcinquiesme iour d'Aoust M.D. LXXV. aussi signées, De Neufville. Et par autres lettres données à Fontainebleau le deuxiesme iour de Iuing, M.D. LXXXII. Signées par le Roy, en son conseil, Gaudet. Il est permis au sieur Orlande: de faire imprimer par tel Imprimeur ou Libraire que bon luy semblera, toutes et chacunes les Oeuvres qu'il à faictes et composées, et pourra cy apres faire et composer, iusques au temps et terme de dix ans, à compter du iour qu'elles seront achevées d'imprimer. Avec deffenses trexexpresses à toutes personnes de quelque qualité qu'elle soyent, de les imprimer, faire imprimer, ou mettre en vente, sans le congé et consentement dudict Orlande, ou de celuy auquel il aura baillé ledict congé: Sur peine d'amende arbitrere contre les contrevenans, confiscation des livres, despens, dommages et interests. En outre veut ledict Seigneur que mettant au commencement ou à la fin desdicts livres un extraict sommaire de desdictes presentes, elles soyent tenues pour suffisamment notifées et venues à la congnoissance particuliere de tous Libraires, Imprimeurs, ou autres, sans qu'ils en puissent pretendre cause d'ignorance.

Notes

Preface

1. Quoted from a recent translation: Jean de Léry, *History of a Voyage to the Land of Brazil, Otherwise Called America*, trans. Janet Whatley (Berkeley: University of California Press, 1990), 144. The account appeared in no less than five different editions printed in La Rochelle and in Geneva between 1578 and 1611. For a facsimile of the second of these, see Jean de Léry, *Histoire d'un voyage fait en la terre du Brésil*, edited by Jean-Claude Morisot, Les classiques de la pensée politique, 9 (Geneva, 1580; reprint, Geneva: Droz, 1975). Important observations on the ideological implications of Léry's account in the context of historical thought (both sixteenth-century and modern) appear in Michel de Certeau, *The Writing of History*, trans. by T. Conley (New York: Columbia University Press, 1988), 209–43; and Frank Lestringant, "Millénarisme et âge d'or: Réformation et expériences coloniales au Brésil et en Floride (1555–1565)," in *Les réformes, enracinement socio-culturel. XXVe Colloque international d'études humanistes. Tours. 1–13 juillet, 1982*, ed. C. Chevalier (Paris: Éditions de la Maisnie, 1985), 25–42. On the musical examples that were included in the 1585 edition of Léry's story, see Luiz Heitor Corrêa de Azevedo, " 'Tupynamba' Melodies in Jean de Léry's *Histoire d'un voyage faict en la terre du Brésil*," in *Papers of the American Musicological Society. Annual Meeting. 1941. Minneapolis, Minnesota*, edited by Gustave Reese (1946): 85–96.

2. For the full titles of these books, see the Bibliography of Primary Sources. Throughout the body of this study I refer to these prints by short titles. For a bibliographical description and index of the great Lasso collections, see François Lesure and Geneviève Thibault, *Bibliographie des éditions d'Adrian Le Roy et Robert Ballard, 1551–1598* (Paris: Heugel, 1955), 139–41, 179–80.

3. For the full titles of these books, see the Bibliography of Primary Sources. Throughout the body of this study I refer to these prints by short titles. See the list of abbreviations on pp. xxiii–xxiv.

4. On the prefaces and their views on music, see chapter 1, below, and Appendix A.

5. Quoted in Orlando di Lasso, *The "Seven Penitential Psalms" and "Laudate Dominum de caelis,"* ed. Peter Bergquist, 2 vols., Recent Researches in the Music of the Renaissance, 86–87 (Madison, Wis.: A–R Editions, 1990), ix. Quickelberg's writings on Lasso from the *Prosopographia heroum* (Basel, 1566) and its German translation *Teutscher Nation Heldenbuch* (Basel, 1578) are reproduced in facsimile in Horst Leuchtmann, *Orlando di Lasso*, 2 vols. (Wiesbaden: Breitkopf und Härtel, 1976), 1:298–301.

6. "He presents to the eyes the thing signified so that it appears to the eyes as if it were alive." From the author's introduction to the *Musica autoschediastike* (Rostock, 1601), quoted in Joachim Burmeister, *Musical Poetics*, trans. by Benito V. Rivera, Music Theory Translation Series (New Haven and London: Yale University Press, 1993), 235.

7. The discussion of Lasso's motet appeared in the *Musica poetica* (Rostock, 1606), and can be found in English translation in his *Musical Poetics,* 205ff. For a facsimile edition of the treatise in question, see Joachim Burmeister, *Musica Poetica. Rostock: Stephan Myliander, 1606,* edited by Martin Ruhnke, Documenta musicologica, 1, Reihe: Druckschriften–Faksimiles, 10 (Kassel and Basel: Bärenreiter, 1955). Further on the rhetorical tradition of reading Lasso, see Claude Palisca, "*Ut Oratorica Musica*: The Rhetorical Basis of Musical Mannerism," in *The Meaning of Mannerism,* edited by Franklin W. Robinson and Stephen G. Nichols (Hanover, N.H.: University Press of New England, 1972), 37–65.

8. In Crook's words, "Magnificats on worldly chansons served to elevate the spirit and sublimate the original musical material. . . . [I]n Munich the prevailing attitude seems to have been somewhat different. Whereas Trent sought to banish secular music from church, Munich strove to elevate and purify it through its association with a more holy text." See David Crook, *Orlando di Lasso's Imitation Magnificats for Counter-Reformation Munich* (Princeton, N.J.: Princeton University Press, 1994), 81–82. For Crook's account of Canisius's ideas and their reception in Munich, see ibid., 65–79.

9. From one of Eco's now classic essays on texts and their meanings, Umberto Eco, "The Poetics of the Open Work," in *The Role of the Reader: Explorations in the Semiotics of Texts* (Bloomington, Ind.: Indiana University Press, 1979), 63. For a recent collection of essays (by Eco, Jonathan Culler, and Richard Rorty, among others) situating Eco's thought in the context of Continental and Anglo-American critical thought, see Eco, *Interpretation and Overinterpretation,* ed. Stefani Collini (Cambridge: Cambridge University Press, 1992).

10. Charles Keil sees an inherent bias towards what he calls "embodied meaning" in much formalist writing on music, and proposes a critical vocabulary for writing about performance and musical process that stresses what he terms "engendered feeling." The set of contrasts provided by his model informs much of what follows, and would serve well as a preface to any attempt to understand *how* (as distinct from *what*) any particular group of listeners heard in music. See Charles Keil, "Motion and Feeling through Music," in Charles Keil and Steven Feld, *Music Grooves: Essays and Dialogues* (Chicago: University of Chicago Press, 1994), 53–76. Tessa Watt's recent exploration of the successive revision, adaptation, and reprinting of broadside ballads in the popular English press of the years around 1600 likewise demonstrates how the efforts of printers could both reflect and help to engender changing ideas of religious belief and popular opinion. See her *Cheap Print and Popular Piety, 1550–1640,* Cambridge Studies in Early Modern British History (Cambridge: Cambridge University Press, 1991).

Chapter 1

1. For a recent chronicle and discussion of this period of French history, see Mack P. Holt, *The French Wars of Religion, 1562–1629,* New Approaches to European History, 8 (Cambridge: Cambridge University Press, 1995). Much of our image of the period was shaped by French historians of the nineteenth century, through the work of journals like the *Bulletin de la Société de l'histoire du protestantisme*

français and Eugene Haag's *La France protestante*, 2nd ed., 6 vols. (Paris: Sandoz et Fischbacher, 1877–88). On the influence of these projects and their editors, see David Nicholls, "The Social History of the French Reformation: Ideology, Confession, and Culture," *Social History* 9 (1984): 25–43.

2. For further information on the printers, Protestantism, and the French provinces, see Natalie Zemon Davis, "Strikes and Salvation at Lyon," in *Society and Culture in Early Modern France* (Stanford: Stanford University Press, 1975), 1–16.

3. Vautrollier settled in London during the 1560s, where he was active as a printer and bookseller. His 1575 edition of *Cantiones sacrae* by Tallis and Byrd was the first work published under the provisions of a printing privilege granted those composers by Elizabeth I. Vautrollier's publishing activities are considered in Donald W. Krummel, *English Music Printing, 1553–1700* (London: The Bibliographical Society, 1975), and John Cudworth Whitebrook, *Calvin's Institute of Christian Religion in the Imprints of Thomas Vautrollier* (London: A. W. Cannon, 1935). For recent discussion of Vautrollier's typesetting practices, see John Milsom, "Tallis, Byrd, and the 'Incorrected' Copy: Some Cautionary Notes for Editors of Early Music Printed from Type," *Music and Letters* 67 (1996): 348–67. On Vautrollier's Lasso book, see Joseph Kerman, "An Elizabethan Edition of Lasso," *Acta Musicologica* 27 (1955): 71–76; and Frederick William Sternfeld, "Vautrollier's Printing of Lasso's *Recueil du Mellange* (London, 1570)," *Annales musicologiques* 5 (1957): 199–227.

4. The *Premier* [and *Second*] *livre du Meslange des pseaumes et cantiques à trois parties, recueillis de la musique d'Orlande de Lassus et autres excellents musiciens de nostre temps* (Geneva, 1577) offer some of Lasso's three-voice motets (along with works by other mid-century masters) with French psalms and spiritual chansons standing in for the original Latin lyrics. Goulart also brought out two volumes of a *Theatrum musicum Orlandi de Lassus aliorumque praestissimorum musicorum selectissimas cantiones sacras, quatuor, quinque et plurium vocum, representas* (Geneva, 1580) that contain some of Lasso's Latin motets (again, along with works by composers from the middle years of the sixteenth century) without editorial additions or changes. Bibliographical descriptions of Goulart's books of motets by Lasso appear in Laurent Guillo, *Les éditions musicales de la Renaissance lyonnaise (1525–1615)*, Domaine musicologique (Paris: Klincksieck, 1991), 455–57. Further on the connections between the Goulart and Le Roy motet imprints, see *Boetticher Lasso*, 1:445–47.

5. Goulart's other sets of *contrafacta* are: the *Premier et Second livres du Meslange des pseaumes et cantiques* (Geneva, 1577), two volumes of *Sonets chrestiens* based on chansons by Guillaume Boni (1578), and two volumes of *Sonets chrestiens* based on chansons by Antoine de Bertrand (1580). Goulart also oversaw the publication of music by Jean Servin (1578 and 1579, with false place of imprint: Lyon), and of Psalm settings by the late Claude Goudimel (1580). For bibliographical descriptions of these prints, see Guillo, *Les éditions musicales,* 455–57

6. Goulart's poetry figures centrally in a new literary trend of the 1570s and 1580s wherein Protestant writers sought to appropriate the language of pulpit oratory and of the devotional tradition as a means of spiritual expression in art. On Goulart's work as editor and author, see Leonard Chester Jones, *Simon Goulart, sa vie et son oeuvre, 1543–1628* (Geneva: A. Kundig, 1916); Jones, *Simon Goulart, 1543–1628: Étude biographique et bibliographique* (Geneva: Georg et Cie, 1917);

Courtney S. Adams, "Simon Goulart (1543–1628), Editor of Music, Scholar and Moralist," in *Studies in Musicology in Honor of Otto E. Albrecht: A Collection of Essays by His Colleagues and Former Students at the University of Pennsylvania,* ed. J. W. Hill (Kassel: Bärenreiter, 1980), 125–41, and Jacques Pineaux, "Simon Goulart et les voies du sacré," *Bulletin de la Société de l'histoire du protestantisme français* 135 (1989): 161–76.

7. Concerning the family and the firm, see Louis Desgraves, *Les Haultin, 1571–1623,* Imprimerie à La Rochelle, 2, Travaux d'humanisme et renaissance, 34 (Geneva: E. Droz, 1960).; Desgraves, "Les relations entre les imprimeurs de Genève et de La Rochelle à la fin du xvie siècle," in *Cinq siècles d'imprimerie genevoise. Actes du Colloque international sur l'histoire de l'imprimerie et du livre à Genève. 27–30 avril 1978,* ed. Jean-Daniel Candaux and Bernard Lescaze (Geneva: Société d'histoire et d'archéologie, 1980–81), 199–207; and Eugénie Droz, "Pierre Haultin à Genève, ou la lutte pour la liberté," in *Chemins de l'hérésie: Textes et documents,* (Geneva: Droz, 1970–76), 373–78. For a bibliographical description of Goulart's editions of the writings of du Bartas, see Desgraves, *Les Haultin,* 60–68; on the Haultin editions of Goulart's *Premier* and *Second volume du Recueil contenant les choses memorables advenues soubs la Ligue,* (La Rochelle, 1587 and 1589), see ibid., 41–44 and 51. Concerning du Bartas, see his *La sepmaine,* 2 vols., ed. Yvonne Bellenger (Paris: Klincksieck, 1981).

The Haultins, it should also be noted, had a long association with music publishing. A member of the firm supplied Nicolas Du Chemin with his first music type during the late 1540s. See Desgraves, *Les Haultins,* viii, citing a document in the Minutier central of the Archives nationales in Paris. Further on the intellectual and religious climate of La Rochelle, see Kevin C. Robbins, "The Social Mechanisms of Urban Rebellion: A Case Study of Leadership in the 1614 Revolt at La Rochelle," *French Historical Studies* 19 (1995): 559–90; Judith Pugh Meyer, *Reformation in La Rochelle: Tradition and Change in Early Modern Europe, 1500–1568,* Travaux d'humanism et renaissance, 298 (Geneva: Droz, 1996); and Étienne Trocmé and Marcel Delafosse, *Le commerce rochelais de la fin du XVe siècle au début du XVIIe* (Paris: Armand Colin, 1952).

8. The connections between Haultin's *Premier* and *Second livre des cantiques et chansons sprituelles* of 1577 and 1578 and Lyonnaise prints of the 1540s and 1560s are mentioned in note 36, below.

9. Haultin's four books of motets by Lasso (all issued in 1576) apparently borrow their contents from books of motets issued by Le Roy et Ballard during the 1560s and early 1570s. The *Moduli quinque vocum* and *Moduli quinque et decem vocum* draw variously upon Le Roy's *Primus liber concentuum sacrorum* of 1564 (reprinted 1573), the *Modulorum Orlandi de Lassus . . . . Secundum volumen* of 1565 (reprinted 1571), and the *Moduli quinis vocibus* of 1571. Haultin's *Moduli quatuor et octo vocum* draws upon Le Roy's *Novem quiritationes divi Iob.* of 1565 (reprinted 1572), while Haultin's *Moduli sex septem, et duodecim vocum,* is based upon Le Roy's *Moduli sex, septem et duodecim vocum, Orlando Lassosio Auctore* of 1573. On the Le Roy–Lasso motet volumes of the 1560s and 1570s, see Orlando di Lasso, *Motets for Six Voices from "Primus liber concentuum sacrorum" (Paris, 1564) Motets for Four to Ten Voices from "Modulorum secundum volumen" (Paris, 1565),* ed. Peter Bergquist, The Complete Motets, 4, Recent Researches in the Music of the Renaissance, 105 (Madison, Wis.: A–R Editions, 1996). Concerning the

relationships among the Haultin books and the Le Roy volumes likely to have been their models, see Lasso, *Motets for Six Voices* and *Boetticher Lasso,* 1:124, 172–73, and 456.

10. The history of French book privileges and Protestant efforts to circumvent them are considered in Francis Higman, "Genevan Printing and French Censorship," in *Cinq siècles d'imprimerie genevoise. Actes du Colloque international sur l'histoire de l'imprimerie et du livre à Genève. 27–30 avril 1978,* ed. Jean-Daniel Candaux and Bernard Lescaze (Geneva: Société d'histoire et d'archéologie, 1980–81), 31–54; and in Michel Simonin, "Les contrefaçons lyonnaises de Montaigne et de Ronsard au temps de la Ligue," in *Les presses grises: La contrefaçon du livre (XVIe–XIXe siècles),* ed. François Moureau (Paris: Aux Amateurs de livres, 1988), 139–53. On the origins of the royal and parliamentary privileges in France, see Elizabeth Armstrong, *Before Copyright: The French Book-Privilege System, 1498–1526* (Cambridge: Cambridge University Press, 1990).

11. Among the Lasso books, only the last two carry any indication of the place of publication–both false or misleading. One copy (intended for export to France?) of the 1594 edition of *Le thrésor de musique d'Orlande* is stamped "À Coligny" (a town in the environs of Geneva, but too obscure a location to have been recognized by French censors). Goulart's 1597 *Cinquante pseaumes,* in which Lasso chansons were troped with texts of the Psalms in French translation, carries an imprint "Heidelberg. Jerome Commelin." Goulart signed the preface of this book with an anagram of his name: "Louis Mognard." In the *Thrésor de musique d'Orlande* and his other musical editions, Goulart identified himself simply as "S.G.S." (Simon Goulart Senlis [the latter for his native region]).

With the exception of the Servin books, none of Goulart's other music books bear any place of imprint. For bibliographical descriptions of each of these publications, along with notes (based on identification of type fonts) on the printer (then working in Geneva) who is likely to have produced them, see Guillo, *Les éditions musicales,* 100–101 and 457–59. Guillo tentatively identifies Goulart's printer as a certain Jean Le Royer, who in the winter of 1576 sought and was granted permission by the Genevan Council to print books of edited versions of the Lasso chansons and an edition of Goudimel's Psalm harmonizations. One of a number of expert typographers active in Geneva during the late sixteenth century, Le Royer had arrived in the city not long before this time, having previously been a royal printer of mathematical figures in Paris, where during the 1560s he also took part in publication by syndicate of the monophonic Psalter in French. In Geneva, Le Royer also worked with or for Pierre de St. André—the various editions bearing the name of the latter printer also share borders, music type, and decorative *lettrines* with those of Le Royer's production.

12. See Appendix A for the complete original text and translation of this preface.

13. See Appendix A for the complete original text and translation of this preface.

14. That Pasquier was originally from Sézanne (near Épernay in the Champagne) is noted in the prefaces to the Lasso books, but I have been unable to trace his career beyond La Rochelle with much confidence. A "Monsieur Pasquier, ancien de l'église de Troye en Champagne" is mentioned among a list of deputies to a synod of the Calvinist church held at La Rochelle in June of 1581. This must certainly be the

same man who prepared the Lasso *contrafacta* books. See J. Aymon, *Tous les synodes nationaux des églises reformées de France,* 2 vols. (La Haye, 1710), 1:147. A "Jehan Pasquier, notaire" is mentioned in a document compiled at Orleans in 1568 listing inhabitants of that town—many of them Protestants—who were obliged to sign an oath of loyalty to King Charles IX (for a partial transcription of this list, see E. Haag, *La France protestante,* 2nd ed., 6 vols. (Paris: Sandoz et Fischbacher, 1877–88), 4:568). And a certain "Pasquier" who had been serving as a Calvinist minister at Mâcon apparently needed help with his duties in 1561, when Olivier Dagoneau, an important resident of that town, wrote to some Genevan elders of the Calvinist church to ask for assistance (see *La France protestante,* 5:15).

Judith Pugh Meyer of the University of Connecticut reports that the surname Pasquier appears several times among the sixteenth-century notarial archives of La Rochelle. Several of the individuals in question were active in the Protestant church. None, however, is identifiable with our Jean. My thanks to Professor Pugh Meyer for having shared the results of her work with me (Personal correspondence, November 15, 1996). For a reference to her recent work on La Rochelle, see note 7, above.

15. Pasquier's dedication of the *Mellange d'Orlande 1575* appears in Appendix A. Catherine de Parthenay (1554–1631) was the daughter of Jean de Parthenay-Larchevêque, siegneur de Soubise, and Antoinette d'Aubeterre. Her grandmother, Anne de Parthenay, had been among the handmaidens of Renée de France during her years in Ferrara, itself an important haven for French Protestants and Protestant sympathizers, including Calvin and Clément Marot. See, on the Protestant leanings of the Ferrarese court of Renée, Emmanuel P. Rodocanachi, *Une protectrice de la réforme en Italie et en France: Renée de France duchesse de Ferrare* (Paris, 1896; reprint, Geneva: Slatkine, 1970). Catherine retired to La Rochelle following the death of her first husband during the St. Bartholomew's Day massacre, and married René II, vicomte de Rohan, in 1575. Her experiences are recounted in her *Holoferne* (now lost) and in her *Ballets allégoriques en vers* of 1592–93. Further on Catherine, see Haag, *La France protestante,* 2:958 and H. Imbert, "Lettres de Catherine de Parthenay, dame de Rohan-Soubise et de ses deux filles Henriette et Anne à Charlotte-Brabantine de Nassau, Duchesse de la Trémöille," *Mémoires de la Société de statistque des Deux-Sevres,* 12 (1874): 43–161.

Enquiries to libraries in La Rochelle and the region have yielded no further information on Catherine. Judith Pugh Meyer reports that she has seen nothing in the notarial records there alluding to Catherine's presence in the town.

16. Pasquier's dedication to the *Mellange d'Orlande 1576* appears in Appendix A. Pasquier's dedicatee for his second book of Lasso *contrafacta* was François de La Noüe, (called "bras de fer"), for a time governor of La Rochelle, and an important Protestant sympathizer. See Henri Hauser, *François de La Noüe (1531–1591)* (Paris, 1882; reprint, Geneva: Slatkine, 1970). François wrote a two-volume philosophical tract, *Discours politiques et militaires,* that was actively promoted by the Protestant press in Basel, La Rochelle, Lyons, and even in English translation. The La Rochelle edition (1590) was brought out by Jerome Haultin, who also published a collection of religious poetry, *L'Uranie ou nouveau recueil de chansons spirituelles et chrestiennes, comprinses en cinq livres et accomodées pour la pluspart au chant des Pseaumes de David* (1597), edited by François's son Odet (see Desgraves, *Les Haultin,* 54 and 103). Odet himself was the dedicatee of the Protestant composer Claude Le

Jeune's cyclical collection of Psalm settings, *Dodecacorde,* first issued in La Rochelle by Haultin in 1598 (see Desgraves, *Les Haultin,* 105–7). For a modern edition of this work, commentary on its genesis, and transcription of liminary materials, see Claude Le Jeune, *Dodecacorde: Comprising Twelve Psalms of David Set to Music according to the Twelve Modes,* ed. Anne Harrington Heider, 3 vols., Recent Researches in the Music of the Renaissance, 74–76 (Madison, Wis.: A-R Editions, 1988).

17. The original passage, from the preface to Pasquier's *Mellange d'Orlande 1576,* reads: "me faisiez cest honneur, me commander d'aller faire la musicque en vostre maison, pour (par ce moyens) vous aider à tromper aucunement l'ennuy, et la tristesse, que ces guerres civiles vous apportoient." For the full text and translation of the preface, see Appendix A.

18. Here (and in the remarks that follow) I am again indebted to Judith Pugh Meyer (see note 14 above), who reports that a Marie Le Blanc was baptized in the Reformed Church in December 1566.

19. Pugh Meyer (see note 14 above) was able to offer no other information on Judith Mage. But two poems by André Mage are among the prefatory material to Jerome Haultin's 1591 edition of Du Bartas's *La second sepmaine* (see Desgraves, *Les Haultin,* 68). Mage's collected poetic writings, *Oeuvres de Sieur de Fiefmelin, divisées en deux parties* (Poitiers, 1601), were dedicated to the grandmother of Catherine de Parthenay, Anne de Pons, then wife of Antoine de Pons. See P. Menanteau, *Images d'André Mage de Fiefmelin, poète baroque* (Limoges: Rougerie, 1965).

20. Pugh Meyer (see note 14 above) reports the existence of a baptismal record for Ester Rolland from 1563. Perhaps Jaquette was one of her siblings.

21. Pugh Meyer (see note 14 above) reports that Suzanne was baptized in the Reformed Church in January 1566.

22. Pugh Meyer (see note 14 above) notes that the surname in question (or some variant of it) makes frequent appearances in notarial records from La Rochelle. But Elizabeth de la Forest is not among the persons mentioned in these documents.

23. Pugh Meyer reports that Esther was baptized in 1562, daughter of René Bouisseau and Catherine DesChamps. The father belonged to an important family of merchants and minor officials in mid-century La Rochelle. Members of the family may also have served, she notes, as godparents to children born into the Poussart family mentioned above.

24. There were a number of Protestant academies created at La Rochelle during the last quarter of the sixteenth century, but I have not seen any references to one established exclusively for women. To judge from the baptismal records of those women mentioned in Pasquier's books, his students were in their early teens at the time the books were published. On the La Rochelle academies, see Leopold Chatenay, *La vie intellectuale en Aunis et en Saintonge de 1550 à 1610,* 2 vols. (La Rochelle: Librairie Quartier latin, 1959). Could Pasquier's "pupils" have been a literary circle organized around a private household, perhaps even that of Catherine de Parthenay? See the remarks on Catherine's La Rochelle court in note 15, above.

25. For a recent study of this body of thought, see John Lee Thompson, *John Calvin and the Daughters of Sarah: Women in Regular and Exceptional Roles in the Exegesis of Calvin, His Predecessors, and His Contemporaries,* Travaux d'humanisme et renaissance, 259 (Geneva: Droz, 1992). Natalie Davis reminds us

that women in Protestant households had educational opportunities not normally afforded those in Catholic households. See Natalie Zemon Davis, "City Women and Religious Change," in *Society and Culture in Early Modern France* (Stanford: Stanford University Press, 1975), 65–98.

26. The original text of the quoted passage from Vautrollier's preface reads "conjoincte avec une lettre grave, et eslongée de toute impurité."

27. Among the chansons considered in this study, six of the eleven that were printed in the *Recueil du mellange d'Orlande* appear there with the original texts unchanged.

28. Perhaps, too, we should note that Vautrollier's other important musical imprint, his edition of Thomas Tallis's and William Byrd's *Cantiones quae ab argumento sacrae vocantur* of 1575, similary moves on the margins of the presumed Protestant-Catholic divide. It was the first book printed under the new patent granted Tallis and the secretly-Catholic Byrd by the Protestant English Queen, with a title that pointedly avoids the questions of for whom such Latin motets might be sacred. Joseph Kerman translates the title as "Songs which are called sacred on account of their texts." See his "William Bryd," *The New Grove Dictionary of Music and Musicians,* 6th ed., ed. Stanley Sadie et al., 20 vols. (London: Macmillan, 1980), 3:539, which includes a facsimile of the title page of Vautrollier's *Cantiones* (the border was reused from the *Recueil du mellange d'Orlande* of 1570). For a facsimile of the official privilege granted Tallis and Byrd, see Paul Doe, "Thomas Tallis," *New Grove,* 18: 542. For a recent study of the history of the Cantiones in press, see John Milsom, "Tallis, Byrd, and the 'Incorrected' Copy: Some Cautionary Notes for Editors of Early Music Printed from Type," *Music and Letters* 67 (1996): 348–67.

29. From Goulart's *Thrésor de musique d'Orlande de Lassus* (Geneva, 1576): The original passages read "Comme de ma part j'ai trouvé en la Musique, d'Orlande specialement, des remedes souverains contre diverses blessures de l'ame. . . . qui n'ait l'ame picquée et comme tirée doucement du corps par les accords melodieux d'une si belle Musique que celle d'Orlande?" (For the complete text of the preface see Appendix A).

30. Further on the place of Neoplatonic thought about music and its effects upon the soul, see Kate van Orden, "Vernacular Culture and the Chanson in Paris, 1570–1580" (Ph. D. diss., University of Chicago, 1996), 338–41; and Gary Tomlinson, *Music in Renaissance Magic: Toward a Historiography of Others* (Chicago: University of Chicago Press, 1993), Chapter 5.

31. Vautrollier's original text reads: "aussi se represente-elle au vif dans un motet musical, au quel sous la conduite d'une partie, toutes les autres tiennent tellement mesure, qu'estant toutes diverses entres-elles, elles ne discordent en rien." For the complete text and translation of the preface, see Appendix A.

32. The translation is by Oliver Strunk, cited in *Strunk's Source Readings in Music History,* rev. ed., edited by Leo Treitler (New York: Norton, 1998), 366. The original text reads: "Et de fait, nous experimentons qu'elle ha une vertu secrete et quasi incredible à emouvoir les cueurs en une sorte, ou en l'autre." Quoted from Calvin's preface as it appears in a Genevan book issued in 1551, Thédore de Bèze and Clément Marot, *Pseaumes octantetrois de David mis en rime françoise* (Geneva, 1551; reprint, New Brunswick, N.J.: Friends of the Rutgers University Libraries, 1973). For a survey of the sources and contexts of Calvinist thought on music, see

H. P. Clive, "The Calvinist Attitude to Music, and its Literary Aspects and Sources," *Bibliothèque d'humanisme et de renaissance,* 19 (1957): 80–102, 294–319; and 20 (1958): 79–107. The classic studies of the French Psalter are Orentin Douen, *Clément Marot et le Psautier: Étude historique, littéraire, musicale, et bibliographique,* 2 vols. (Paris, 1878; reprint, Amsterdam: B. de Graaf, 1967), and Pierre Pidoux, *Le Psautier huguenot du XVIe siècle: Mélodies et documents,* 2 vols. (Basel: Bärenreiter, 1962). More recently, see L. Guillo, "Le Psautier de Paris et le Psautier de Lyon: À propos de deux corpus contemporains du Psautier de Genève (1549–1561)," *Bulletin de la Société de l'histoire du protestantisme français,* 136 (1990): 361–420.

33. Translation from Strunk's *Source Readings,* 366. The original text (cited in Bèze, *Pseaumes octantetrois de David*) reads: "Si nous doit elle bien emouvoir à moderer l'usage de la musique, pour la faire servir à toute honesté."

34. The original passage, from Goulart's *Thrésor de musique d'Orlande de Lassus* (Geneva, 1576): "Orlande l'avoit appropriée à la lettre, en quoy il est excellent (comme en tout ce qui est de ceste science liberale) pardessus tous les Musiciens de nostre temps." For the complete text of the preface see Appendix A.

35. From Pasquier's *Mellange d'Orlande 1575:* "J'ay pensé que je ferois devoir de Chrestien, si repurgeant ces tresgracieux et plaisans accords de tant de villenies et ordures, dont ilz estoient tous souillez, Je les remettois sur leur vray et naturel suject, qui est de chanter la puissance, sagesse et bonté de L'éternel. Ayant donc solicité aucuns de mes amis et emprunté d'eux quelques Cantiques de tel argument, au lieu de ces lascivetez et vaines resveries, Je les ay accommodez à la musique: voire tellement que l'harmonie de la voix respond à l'affection de la parolle, autant que faire se peut." For the complete text and a translation of the preface, see Appendix A.

36. The original passage, from another of Pasquier's musical prints, the *Premier livre des cantiques et chansons spirituelles à quatre parties en quatre volumes, recueillies de plusieurs excellens musiciens* (La Rochelle, 1578), reads: "Je m'estudie tant que je puis (Ami lecteur) à ramener la Musique à son vray but, qui est de glorifier ce grand Dieu, qui l'a créée, et nous l'a donnée avec les autres arts et sciences liberales pour le soulagement de ceste vie. Ainsi t'ay donné premierement, un recueil des divins accords d'Orlande, les retirant de la poësie profane, comme pierres precieuses d'un vilain bourbier" For the complete text of this preface, see Appendix A.

Pasquier's *Premier* and *Second livres* closely derive from two editions of *chansons spirituelles:* Didier Lupi Second's *Premier livre de chansons spirituelles* (Lyons, 1548) and Louis Des Masures *Vingt-six cantiques* (Lyons, 1564; musical settings here by Claude Goudimel). The contents of the Pasquier books are listed in Marc Honegger, "Les chansons spirituelles de Didier Lupi et les débuts de la musique protestante en France au xvie siècle," 2 vols. (Ph.D. diss., Université de Lille III, 1970), 2:248–54. On the Lyonnais models, see Guillo, *Les éditions musicales,* 253–55 and 320–22; and Honegger, "Les Chansons spirituelles," 1: 59–115; and 2: 41–43 and 143–49.

37. From Goulart's *Thrésor de musique d'Orlande de Lassus* (Geneva, 1576): The original passages read "En ostant quelques mots ou plusieurs et les accommodant (au moins mal qu'il m'a esté possible) à la Musique, j'ai rendu ces chansons honnestes et Chrestiennes pour la plupart. . . . " (For the complete text of the preface see Appendix A.)

38. For modern editions of Goudimel's three cycles of harmonizations, see his *Premier, second, tiers fasicules des 150 Pseaumes,* ed. Henri Expert, 3 vols., Maîtres musiciens de la renaissance française, 2, 4, 6 (Paris, 1895–97; reprint, New York: Broude Brothers, 1963); and his *Oeuvres complètes,* ed. Henri Gagnebin et al., 14 vols. (New York: Institute of Medieval Music, 1967). For a modern edition of some of Bourgeois's polyphonic settings of the Psalms, see his *Le premier livre des pseaumes,* ed. Pierre André Gaillard, Monuments de la musique suisse, 3 (Basel: Bärenreiter, 1960). See also note 39, below.

39. For a facsimile and facing translation of Bourgeois's treatise, see Loys Bourgeois, *The Direct Road to Music (Le droict chemin de musique, 1550),* trans. Bernarr Rainbow (Kilkenny: Boethius Press, 1982). See also Bourgeois, *Le droict chemin de musique,* edited by P. André Gaillard, Documenta musicologica, 1:6 (Geneva, 1550; reprint, Kassel: Bärenreiter, 1954).

40. For the story of the first Genevan editions of the monophonic Psalter, see Pidoux "Les origines de l'impression de musique à Genève," in *Cinq siècles d'imprimerie genevoise. Actes du Colloque international sur l'histoire de l'imprimerie et du livre à Genève. 27–30 avril 1978,* ed. Jean-Daniel Candaux and Bernard Lescaze (Geneva: Société d'histoire et d'archéologie, 1980–81), 97–108. Transcriptions of the official discussions of Bourgeois's "errors" appear on page 104 this study. (For a facsimile of the 1551 Psalter, see Bèze, *Pseaumes octantetrois de David.*) Further on Bourgeois, the Beringens, and music printing in Lyons, see Frank Dobbins, *Music in Renaissance Lyons* (Oxford: Clarendon Press, 1992), 259–64 and Guillo, *Les éditions musicales,* 67–73. Concerning Bourgeois's career as a composer and teacher, see Pierre André Gaillard, *Loys Bourgeois, sa vie, son oeuvre comme pédagogue et compositeur: Essai biographique et critique, suivi d'une bibliographie et d'un appendice* (Lausanne: Imprimeries réunies, 1948).

Simon Goulart apparently took no such chances with his books of *contrafacta*: Guillo (*Les éditions musicales,* 100 and 455) has uncovered references in the register of the Genevan council showing that in 1576 the Parisian emigré printer Jean Le Royer sought permission from this body to to issue "quelques chansons spirituelles sur la musique d'Orlande"—doubtless these included Goulart's *Thrésor.* Further on Le Royer and the *contrafacta* books, see above, note 11.

41. On the place of sacred Psalmody in the formation of Huguenot identity, see Barbara B. Diefendorf, "The Huguenot Psalter and the Faith of French Protestants in the Sixteenth Century," in *Culture and Identity in Early Modern Europe (1500–1800): Essays in Honor of Natalie Zemon Davis,* ed. Barbara B. Diefendorf and C. Hesse (Ann Arbor: University of Michigan Press, 1993), 41–63.

42. Henri Bordier's selection of material for his important modern edition of Protestant chanson texts dwells rather disproportionately upon the political and inflammatory segments of that repertory of texts and tunes. See his *Le chansonnier protestant,* 2 vols. (Paris: Tross, 1870); and Honegger, "Les chansons spirituelles," 1:5–7.

43. On the *Noël,* see Adrienne F. Block, *The Early French Parody Noël,* 2 vols. Studies in Musicology, 36 (Ann Arbor: UMI Research Press, 1983). For a recent study of lay piety and music in Italy, see Patrick Macey, "The *Lauda* and the Cult of Savonarola," *Renaissance Quarterly,* 45 (Autumn 1992): 439–83. Further on the phenomenon of the literary *contrafacta,* see Bruce W. Wardropper, "The Religious

Conversion of Profane Poetry," in *Studies in the Continental Background of Renaissance English Literature: Essays Presented to John L. Lievsan,* ed. D. Randall and G. W. Williams (Durham, N.C.: Duke University Press, 1977), 203–21.

44. For a bibliographical description and inventory of this print, see Guillo, *Les éditions musicales,* 253–55. See pp. 405–6 (Document 7) of the same study for a transcription of liminary poems in that print by Guéroult and Lupi.

45. On the musical legacy of Lupi's chanson see Kenneth Jay Levy, "'Suzanne un jour': The History of a 16th-Century Chanson," *Annales musicologiques,* 1 (1953): 375–408.

46. On the Lyonnais and Parisian reprints of the *Premier livre,* see Guillo, *Les éditions musicales,* 77–78 and 254.

47. Concerning the *Tiers livre,* which in addition to music by Lupi contains *contrafacta* of chansons by Pierre Certon, Pierre Sandrin, Claudin de Sermisy, and Nicolas Le Gendre, among others, see Honegger, "Les chansons spirituelles," 2:91–94, and Guillo, *Les éditions musicales,* 445–46. On the book issued by Pasquier in 1578 (not to be confused with his *Mellange d'Orlande* volumes) see Desgraves, *Les Haultin,* 20; and Appendix A, below. An inventory of the book can be found in Honegger, "Les chansons spirituelles," 2:248–51.

48. On the modes and mentalities of religious poetry among French Protestants of the sixteenth century, see Jacques Pineaux, *La poésie des protestants de langue françoise, du premier synode national jusqu'à la proclamation de l'édit de Nantes (1559–1598)* (Paris: Klincksieck, 1971); Pineaux, "La poésie religieuse," *Précis de littérature française du XVIe siècle: La Renaissance,* ed. Robert Aulotte (Paris: Presses universitaires de France, 1992), 214–28; and Michel Jeanneret, *Poésie et tradition biblique au XVIe siècle: Récherches stylistiques sur les paraphrases des "Psaumes" de Marot à Malherbe* (Paris: J. Corti, 1969). See also the works cited in the notes that follow.

49. Concerning this literature, see Terence Cave, *Devotional Poetry in France, c. 1570–1613* (Cambridge: Cambridge University Press, 1969); and Jeanneret, *Poésie et tradition biblique.*

50. Cave, *Devotional Poetry in France,* 40.

51. Cave, *Devotional Poetry in France,* 20–23.

52. On Du Plessis-Mornay and Bèze see Mario Richter, *Il "Discours de la vie et de la mort" di Philippe du Plessis-Mornay* (Milan: Editrice vita et pensiero, 1964); and Théodore de Bèze, *Chrestiennes méditations,* ed. Mario Richter (Geneva: Droz, 1964). Mornay's book, it should be added, was reprinted by Haultin at La Rochelle. See Desgraves, *Les Haultin,* 27 and 31.

53. Cave, *Devotional Poetry in France,* 40.

54. See Cave, "The Protestant Devotional Tradition: Simon Goulart's *Trente tableaux de la mort,*" *French Studies,* 21 (1967): 1–15.

55. Catharine Randall, *Building Codes: The Aesthetics of Calvinism in Early Modern Europe,* New Cultural Studies (Philadelphia: University of Pennsylvania Press, 1999), 31.

56. Ibid.

57. Palissy, *Recepte véritable,* 46. Quoted and translated in Randall, *Building Codes,* 56, 219 note 47. For a modern edition of Palissy's book, see *Recepte véritable,* edited by Keith Cameron, Textes littéraires français (Geneva: Droz, 1988).

58. Randall, *Building Codes,* 69.

Chapter 2

1. On Lasso's poetic choices in the context of the printed record of his chansons, see *Lasso Werke,* 12:lxii–lxxv; *Boetticher Lasso,* 1:111–13 and 277ff; and Kate van Orden, "Vernacular Culture and the Chanson in Paris, 1570–1580" (Ph.D. diss., University of Chicago, 1996), 182–98. We should note that the Lasso chansons that use these poems are sometimes surprisingly independent of those printed sources (the readings of his texts frequently differ in important ways).

2. On Marot's verse in the context of the early sixteenth-century chanson, see François Lesure, "Autour de Clément Marot et de ses musiciens," *Revue de musicologie* 33 (1951): 109–119 and Brian Jeffrey, "Thématique de la chanson entre 1480 et 1525," *La chanson à la Renaissance. Actes du XXe colloque d'études humanistes du Centre d'études supérieures de la renaissance de l'Université de Tours. Juillet 1977,* ed. Jean-Michel Vaccaro (Tours: Éditions Van de Welde, 1981), 51–60.

3. On the currency of the *formes fixes* in the middle years of the sixteenth century, see Jean-Pierre Ouvrard, "Pour le rondeau en forme mettre . . . : Mon confesseur, rondeau de Clément Janequin," *Revue de Musicologie* 64 (1978): 203–28.

4. Lasso's individual chansons were themselves widely imitated, both by his contemporaries and by the composer himself, who frequently turned to his own chansons as models for imitation Masses. See Frank Dobbins, "Lassus—Borrower or Lender: The Chansons," *Revue belge de musicologie,* 39–40 (1985–86): 101–57; David Crook, *Orlando di Lasso's Imitation Magnificats for Counter-Reformation Munich* (Princeton, N.J.: Princeton University Press, 1994), esp. 80–82; van Orden, "Vernacular Culture and the Chanson in Paris," 199–200; and Ignace Bossuyt, "Jean de Castro and His Three-Part Chansons Modelled on Four- and Five-part Chansons by Orlando di Lasso: A Comparison," in *Orlando di Lasso in der Musikgeschichte. Bericht über das Symposium der Bayerischen Akademie der Wissenschaften. München, 4–6. Juli 1994,* ed. Bernhold Schmid (Munich: Bayerischen Akademie der Wissenschaften, 1996), 25–67.

5. On this chanson, see Kenneth Jay Levy, " 'Susanne un jour': The History of a 16th-Century Chanson," *Annales musicologiques* 1 (1953): 375–408.

6. On the musical sensibilities of mid-century composers for sonnets and their formal hallmarks, see Ouvrard, "Le sonnet ronsardien en musique: Du Supplément de 1552 à 1580," *Revue de musicologie* 74 (1988): 149–64; Jeanice Brooks, "'Ses amours et les miennes tout ensemble': La structure cyclique du Premier livre d'Antoine de Bertrand (Paris 1576)," *Revue de musicologie* 74 (1988): 201–20; and Brooks, "Italy, the Ancient World and the French Musical Inheritance in the Sixteenth Century: Arcadelt and Clereau in the Service of the Guises," *Journal of the Royal Musical Association* 121 (1996): 147–90.

For recent discussions of the Pléiade and its other influences on musical thought and practice, see the special issue of *Early Music History* (volume 13, 1994): Howard Mayer Brown, "*Ut musica poesis*: Music and Poetry in France in the Late Sixteenth Century," 1–64; Jeanice Brooks, "Ronsard, the Lyric Sonnet and the Late Sixteenth-Century Chanson," 65–84; and John O'Brien, "Ronsard, Belleau and Renvoisy," 199–216.

7. van Orden, "Vernacular Culture and the Chanson in Paris," 200.

8. On the themes of retrospection and historicizing in the chanson, see van Orden, "Imitation and 'La musique des anciens': Le Roy et Ballard's 1572 *Mellange de chansons*," *Revue de musicologie* 80 (1994): 5–37, and chapter 8, below.

9. In the printer's words: "Item parmi celles à cinq il y en a deux de Philippes de Monté, lesquelles se sont glissées sans que celui qui a corrigé la lettre, s'en soit apperceu qu'incontinent apres qu'elles ont este imprimées. Ces deux sont, "L'homme inconstant ne peut vaincre le monde," et "Las! Je n'ai point victoire sur le monde." (For the complete text and a translation of the preface, see Appendix A. These two works do not appear in the 1582 and 1594 editions of Goulart's *Le thrésor de musique d'Orlande*.)

10. For a modern edition of Lasso's chanson, see Dobbins, ed., *The Oxford Book of French Chansons* (Oxford: Oxford University Press, 1987), 238–40; *Lasso Chansons,* 12:119–21; and *Lasso Werke,* 12:34–35. Further on the Evening/Morning meditation sequence in the context of devotional practice, see Terence Cave, *Devotional Poetry in France, c. 1570–1613* (Cambridge: Cambridge University Press, 1969), 38–57, and chapter 1, above.

Another of du Bellay's poems, "O foible esprit," which appeared in a similarly rich setting for five voices in Lasso's *Chansons nouvelles* of 1571, was subject to only minor correction in Goulart's *Le thrésor de musique d'Orlande*. The *contrafactum* preserves the aphoristic calls and rhetorical questions found here, but redirects them in the service of self-examination and a plea for divine clemency, replacing the allusion in verse 9 to the "jeune archer" (Cupid) with one to "Dieu tout puissant." For the texts in question, see *Lasso Werke,* 16:xx. A modern edition of the chanson can be found in ibid., 34–39 and *Lasso Chansons,* 13:52–62.

11. In Goulart's edition of this piece the text here reads "luisant" in place of "suivant."

12. Here Goulart's text reads "tient."

13. The orthography of Lasso's text differs slightly from that given in the earliest printed sources of Marot's poem, which was written before 1537. The "valet" mentioned in the poem was probably François Sagon, one of the poet's adversaries. For sources and variants of the text, see Clément Marot, *Oeuvres poétiques complètes,* ed. Gérard Defaux, 2 vols., Classiques Garnier (Paris: Bordas, 1996) 2:225. While they do not change the overall sense of Marot's poem, the texts printed in Pasquier's and Goulart's editions of Lasso's chansons also depart in minor ways from text offered by Le Roy et Ballard.

14. For modern editions of this chanson, see *Lasso Chansons,* 13:20–23; and *Lasso Werke,* 12:16–18. It is, in fact, the only time that Pasquier's book departs significantly from the sequence of chansons offered in the Le Roy et Ballard *Mellange d'Orlande* of 1570. On the organization of Pasquier's *Mellange d'Orlande,* see chapter 7, below.

Pasquier's *contrafactum* of the similarly scandalous and anticlerical poem "Il estoit une religieuse" takes a somewhat different approach. Whereas the original poem narrated the sexual escapades of a nun and a priest, Pasquier's revised text offers the relieved prayers of a former nun newly released from the convent. Pasquier, in short, censors erotic elements he deems unsuitable for his readers, but in so doing still makes what is ultimately a point critical of Catholic institutions and their inability to address the needs of individual believers. For the text and *contrafacta* of

"Il estoit une religeuse," see *Lasso Werke,* 12:cix. A modern edition of the chanson appears in ibid., 12:74–76; and in *Lasso Chansons,* 12:60–62.

15. For the contents of the 1570 print that contains "Maistre Robbin," see Henri Vanhulst, *Catalogue des éditions de musique publiées à Louvain par Pierre Phalèse et ses fils, 1545–1578* (Bruxelles: Palais des Académies, 1984), 156–57.

16. See Leuchtmann's remarks on this subject in the notes to the reprint edition of *Lasso Werke,* 12:lxxvi. Henri Bordier's selection of material for his important modern edition of Protestant chanson texts (*Le Chansonnier Huguenot du xvie siècle,* 2 vols. [Paris: Tross, 1870]) dwells rather disproportionately on the political and inflammatory segments of that repertory of texts and tunes. For a more balanced view of these lyrics, see Jacques Pineaux, *La poésie des protestants de langue française, du premier synode national jusqu'à la proclamation de l'édit de Nantes (1559–1598),* Bibliothèque française et romaine (Paris: Klincksieck, 1971).

17. See Bernhard Meier, *The Modes of Classical Vocal Polyphony,* trans. Ellen Beebe, (New York: Broude, 1988) and Meier, "Rhetorical Aspects of the Renaissance Modes," *Journal of the Royal Musical Association* 115 (1990): 183–90.

18. See Lasso, *The "Seven Penitential Psalms" and "Laudate Dominum de caelis",* ed. Peter Bergquist, 2 vols., Recent Researches in the Music of the Renaissance, 86–87 (Madison, Wis.: A-R Editions, 1990), x–xi for a detailed listing of such moments in the *Penitential Psalms.* For a complete exposition of Meier's case for this sort of representation, see Meier, *The Modes of Classical Vocal Polyphony,* 250–59.

19. On the ethos of the Phrygian mode in the context of the French chanson, see Ouvrard, "Modality and Text Expression in 16th-Century French Chansons: Remarks Concerning the E Mode," *Basler Jahrbuch für historische Musikpraxis,* 16 (1992): 89–104, and Brooks, " 'Ses amours et les miennes tout ensemble'; La structure cyclique du *Premier livre* d'Antoine de Bertrand (Paris 1576)."

20. For my commentary on "Quand me souvient" and its *contrafacta* see chapter 5, below.

21. For my commentary on "Si du malheur" and its *contrafacta* see chapter 5, below.

Chapter 3

1. From a translation by Frank Dobbins, from *The Oxford Book of French Chansons* (Oxford: Oxford University Press, 1987), 330. A modern edition of Claudin's chanson appears on pp. 38–39 of the same book.

2. The original text, which seems to be the refrain from a *rondeau,* reads: "Je l'ayme bien et l'aymeray,/En ce propos suis et seray/Et demourray toute ma vie/Et quoy que l'on me porte envie/Je l'ayme bien et l'aymeray." *Translation:* "I love her well and will love her, in this notion I am and will remain; And will remain all my life, and although others regard me with envy, I love her well and will love her." First published in 1555, Lasso's four-voice chanson shares a good deal stylistically with the chansons of Gombert and Clemens non Papa: it opens with a highly imitative texture, which also returns at the end of the chanson to support the refrain. The middle verses are treated with somewhat more animation than the opening and closing line, but here too, an imitative fabric prevails. For a modern edition of this

chanson, see *Lasso Chansons,* 12:77–79; and *Lasso Werke,* 12:41–42. Leuchtmann's commentary and notes on the poetic and musical sources appear in ibid., 12:ci-cii.

3. Boetticher also notes how the *contrafacta* for this poem (like those crafted for "Ardant amour"), transfer secular longing into a spiritual register. See *Boetticher Lasso,* 1:85. The original poem is an anonymous *quatrain* from *La Fleur de poésie françoyse recueil joyeulx* of 1543, and thus once again reflects the conservatism of Lasso's poetic choices. For a modern edition of this chanson, see *Lasso Chansons,* 11:164–66; and *Lasso Werke,* 12:55–56. Leuchtmann's commentary and notes on the poetic and musical sources appear in ibid., 12:cv. A poetic conceit similar to the one heard in "Du corps absent" is also at work in "Avecques vous," which pledges a kind of spiritual love that lives on even after death. For modern editions of this work, see *Lasso Chansons,* 11:54–56; *Lasso Werke,* 12:37–39.

4. Indeed, Janequin himself published a setting of this text in 1556, one that seems to have served as a model for the one by Lasso, which was issued only six years later. Dobbins observes that the Superius of Lasso's chanson reworks the Tenor from Janequin's piece. See Dobbins, "Textual Sources and Compositional Techniques in the French Chansons of Orlandus Lassus," in *Orlandus Lassus and his Time. Colloquium Proceedings. Antwerpen 24–26.08.1994,* ed. Ignace Bossuyt, Eugeen Schreurs, and Annelies Wouters, Yearbook of the Alamire Foundation, 1 (Peer, Belgium: Alamire Foundation, 1996), 151. For a modern edition of Janequin's setting, see his *Chansons polyphoniques,* ed. Tillman Merritt and François Lesure, 6 vols. (Monaco: L'Oiseau-lyre, 1967–71), 6: No. 245. For a modern edition of Lasso's chanson, see *Lasso Chansons,* 11:70–73; and *Lasso Werke,* 12:103–5. Leuchtmann's commentary and notes on the poetic and musical sources appear in ibid., 12:cxvi-cxvii.

5. Vautrollier's text begins: "Ce faux Sathan de toutes pieces s'arme, Et sans cesser me veut livrer l'assaut." Pasquier's offers a similar conceit: "Ce faux Sathan quand il s'equippe et arme, Et par agnetz me veut livrer l'assaut." For the full texts of these *contrafacta,* see *Lasso Werke,* 12:cxvi-cxvii. Boetticher notes how the *contrafacta* of this chanson (like those for "J'endure un tourment" and "Au feu, au feu") imitate the affective force of the original succession of syllables, in this case through the repetitions of "alarme," "las," and "au feu." See *Boetticher Lasso,* 1:489 n. 74.

6. This discussion of the two settings of "Ardant amour" and their various *contrafacta* draws heavily on an essay by one of my students, Michelle Mazzocco: "Saving Tunes from the Devil: Comparisons of Two Protestant *contrafacta* of Lasso's Four- and Five-voice Settings for 'Ardant amour,'" unpublished seminar paper, Haverford College, April, 1997. I am grateful to her for sharing this work with me. For information on the text and the musical sources, see *Lasso Werke,* 12:xcix and *Lasso Werke,* 14:xxv.

7. For modern editions of Lasso's chanson, see *Lasso Chansons,* 11:20–26; and *Lasso Werke,* 14:84–88.

8. In Pasquier's adaptation of the setting for five voices the last word of line 5 is spelled "torment."

9. For modern editions of Lasso's chanson, see *Lasso Chansons,* 11:15–19; and *Lasso Werke,* 12:25–27.

Chapter 4

1. Further on Renée's household and Marot's soujourn in Ferrara, Emmanuel Rodocanachi, *Une protectrice de la réforme en Italie et en France: Renée de France duchesse de Ferrare* (Paris: P. Ollendorff, 1896).

2. Lasso set only the first strophe of Marot's poem, which was the last in his *Adolescence clémentine* of 1532–33. See Clément Marot, *Œuvres poétiques complètes,* ed. Gérard Defaux, 2 vols., Classiques Garnier (Paris: Bordas, 1990), 1:200. The orthography used by Lasso and his printer Le Roy departs slightly from that found in the earliest edition of the poet's works.

3. For modern editions of this chanson, see *Lasso Chansons,* 13:15–19; and *Lasso Werke,* 14:15–17. Lasso's setting of this text inspired a number of musical emulations in the late sixteenth century. See Frank Dobbins, "Textual Sources and Compositional Techniques in the French Chansons of Orlandus Lassus," in *Orlandus Lassus and His Time. Colloquium Proceedings. Antwerpen 24–26.08.1994,* ed. Ignace Bossuyt, Eugeen Schreurs, and Annelies Wouters, Yearbook of the Alamire Foundation, 1 (Peer, Belgium: Alamire Foundation, 1996), 150. First issued in Le Roy et Ballard's *Livre de meslanges* of 1560, this piece was suppressed from the 1572 edition of that print.

4. Vautrollier's text here reads "fabuleux" in place of "vicieux."

5. On the polemical aspects of poems such as "Monsieur l'Abbé" and their "uncorrected" status in the Protestant chansonniers devoted to Lasso's music, see chapter 2, above. Bakhtin's seminal study appears in English as *Rabelais and His World,* trans. Hélène Iswolsky (Bloomington: Indiana University Press, 1984).

6. Kate van Orden, "Vernacular Culture and the Chanson in Paris, 1570–1580" (Ph. D. diss., University of Chicago, 1996), 317–18.

7. For a modern edition of Claudin's chanson and an English translation of Marot's verse, see Dobbins, ed., *The Oxford Book of French Chansons* (Oxford: Oxford University Press, 1987), 38–39, 330.

8. The chanson was first issued 1564, in a chansonnier brought out by Lasso's early collaborator, Tielman Susato of Antwerp. The work is one of a number of similar "non-courtly" compositions found in that print that share a similar emphasis on homorhythmic textures. On this little collection, see Dobbins, "Textual Sources and Compositional Techniques," 151–52. For modern editions of the chanson, see *Lasso Chansons,* 12:7–9; and *Lasso Werke,* 12:43–44. Leuchtmann's commentary and notes on the poetic and musical sources appear in ibid., 12:cii. Boetticher notes that the *contrafacta* of "Fleur de quinze ans" imitate the meter and end rhyme of the original poetry. See *Boetticher Lasso,* 1:77.

9. For transcriptions of the poems issued by Goulart and Phalèse see Leuchtmann's commentary, in *Lasso Werke,* 12:cii.

10. It is worth noting that the version of the text set by Lasso (and printed by Le Roy's typesetter) differs slightly from the one preferred by Marot himself: in line 5 the poets offers "le baiser suyt" (not "suit le baiser"); while line 7 reads "Qui est, et quoy" (not "Qui est—qui est"). First published in 1538, the poem carries the rubric "Des cinq points en Amours." See Marot, *Œuvres poétiques complètes,* 2:228–29.

11. Further on the dedicatees and the original audience of Pasquier's books, see chapter 1.

12. Note that line 7 has only 8 syllables, and thus must involve word repetition—doubtless "d'amour" is the likely choice, which supports the idea that the *contrafacta* makers saw this as an opportunity to question love through the agency of Lasso's music. In all the *contrafacta* (except Bavent's), a moral progress replaces the moral degeneration suggested in the previous poem.

Lasso's setting of "Je ne veux rien," with its long litany of sensual pleasures, was subjected to similar transformation by the Protestant editors. A translation of the original text reads: "I want only to kiss her mouth, and to look into her two languishing eyes. I also want her brow to touch mine, I want then her scattered hair to fly between us everywhere. I really want to see her neck a little closer. I want arms to make an embrace, and that her hand will entwine with mine: If she doesn't I don't know what I'll do." Bavent, like the editors of "Fleur de quinze ans," directly repudiates "lascivious thoughts" and "impudent glances," recanting the arts of Cupid in order to direct the poetic voice to divine goodness. Goulart, in contrast, retains much of the original rhyme scheme of "Je ne veux rien," and with it much of the original concern for physical intimacy, albeit transferred to a spiritual congress rather than a bodily one. Goulart's poem in particular aligns nicely with aspects of Lasso's setting, a chanson in which the additive rhetoric of the poem prompted a series ca. 1500," *Journal of the Royal Musical Association* 116 (1991): 161–200. My translation of the poetic text borrows heavily from the one given in a recent recording of Lasso's chansons by Ensemble Clément Janequin (Harmonia Mundi 901391).

14. Lasso's setting first appeared in the *Chansons nouvelles* of 1571 and thus was adapted as a *contrafactum* only in the second and third editions of Goulart's *Le thrésor de musique d'Orlande*. For modern editions of the Lasso chanson, see *Lasso Chansons*, 11:100–4; and *Lasso Werke*, 16:58–60. Leuchtmann's notes on the textual and musical sources appear in ibid, 16:xxi.

No significant variants distinguish Lasso's reading of the poem from the one given in Marot's *Adolescence clémentine* of 1532–33. Le Roy's typesetter, however, gives "amour" in place of "amours" in lines 1 and 6. See Marot's *Œuvres poétiques complètes*, 1:131–32, 193.

15. Frank Dobbins ("Textual Sources and Compositional Techniques," p. 155) notes that Lasso, with characteristic autonomy from the published chanson tradition, makes no musical acknowledgment of earlier settings of the same poem by Manchicourt (issued in 1545) and Waelrant (published in 1559). As Dobbins notes, there seems no direct musical connection between Manchicourt's setting and the one by Lasso. But Manchicourt nevertheless attempts to represent the "inversion" mentioned in the poem through an inversion of musical space: the last couplet of his setting repeats the music of the first line, a long ascending melodic gesture (repeated through imitative counterpoint), and then an inversion of that motive as a descending one. All of this, in short, mirrors the syntactic *chiasmus* found in the final pair of poetic lines. For a modern edition of Manchicourt's piece, see Pierre de Manchicourt, *Twenty-nine Chansons*, ed. Margery Anthea Baird, Recent Researches in the Music of the Renaissance, 11 (Madison, Wis.: A–R Editions, 1972), 14–17.

16. The text as set by Lasso and printed by Le Roy et Ballard differs slightly in orthography—but not wording—from the one that appears in Marot's record of publication. For a critical edition of the poem, see Marot, *Œuvres poétiques complètes*, 2:219.

17. The composition first appeared in 1564, and was frequently reprinted during the next decades. For a modern edition, see *Lasso Chansons*, 13:166–68; and *Lasso Werke*, 12:19–20. For references to the modern editions of Marot's poem, see ibid., xcviii. Lasso's setting of "En un chasteau," a poetic contemplation of a statue of Hercules, is in many respects reminiscent of the treatment afforded "Qui dort icy?" For a modern edition of this work, see *Lasso Chansons*, 11:180–82; and *Lasso Werke*, 12:14–16. The *contrafacta* for this poem are printed in ibid., 12:xcvii..

18. See Terence Cave, *Devotional Poetry in France, c. 1570–1613* (Cambridge: Cambridge University Press, 1969), 147ff. On allusions to classical civilization as an archaizing element in the Lasso chansons and in the aesthetic program of the late sixteenth-century chanson, see van Orden, "Vernacular Culture and the Chanson in Paris, 1570–1580," 198–200; and van Orden, "Imitation and 'La musique des anciens': Le Roy et Ballard's 1572 *Mellange de chansons*," *Revue de musicologie* 80 (1994): 5–37.

19. See Cave, *Devotional Poetry*, 45, 164–65.

20. Wolfgang Boetticher proposed Octavien de Saint-Gelais as author of this poem, but he offers nothing to substantiate the claim. See *Boetticher Lasso*, 1:277. Frank Dobbins ("Textual Sources and Compositional Techniques," 152), characterizes this text as one of a series of "non-courtly" poems selected for a collection of chansons by Lasso issued by Susato in 1564. Further on the poem and its sources, see Leuchtmann's commentary in *Lasso Werke*, 12:cxii.

21. For a modern edition of this chanson, see *Lasso Chansons*, 11:183–86; and *Lasso Werke*, 12:83–85. Leuchtmann's commentary and notes on the poetic and musical sources appear in ibid., 12:cxii.

22. Dobbins ("Textual Sources and Compositional Techniques," 152), surmises that Lasso's text was carved out of a longer *rondeau*. Boetticher (*Boetticher Lasso*, 1:111), notes the existence of an old *rondeau* by Guillaume Crétin that begins with a similar incipit, although there seems little reason to link Lasso's poetic choice with that earlier text. Boetticher's claim (*Boetticher Lasso*, 1:190) that "De tout mon coeur" was Lasso's earliest published chanson (1556) is mistaken, having been based on the erroneous date on the title page (1556 instead of 1565) from Le Roy et Ballard's *15e livre*. For a modern edition of this chanson, see *Lasso Chansons*, 11:119–25; and *Lasso Werke*, 14:33–37. Leuchtmann's commentary and notes on the poetic and musical sources appear in ibid., 14:xx.

23. Bernhard Meier, *The Modes of Classical Vocal Polyphony*, trans. Ellen S. Beebe (New York: Broude, 1988), 365. Meier's remarks on "De tout mon coeur" appear in the context of his discussion of similar sorts of "normative" representations of verbal texts.

24. Vautrollier's text reads "escritte" in place of "escrite," but is otherwise the same as the one printed by Pasquier.

Chapter 5

1. Terence Cave, *Devotional Poetry in France, c. 1570–1613* (Cambridge: Cambridge University Press, 1969), 40.

2. Vautrollier prints the chanson without change. According to Frank Dobbins, Lasso seems to have based his setting of this text, with its characteristic half-line refrain, or *rentrement*, on Thomas Crequillon's setting of the same poem. See Dobbins, "Textual Sources and Compositional Techniques in the French Chansons of Orlandus Lassus," in *Orlandus Lassus and His Time. Colloquium Proceedings. Antwerpen 24–26.08.1994*, ed. Ignace Bossuyt, Eugeen Schreurs, and Annelies Wouters, Yearbook of the Alamire Foundation, 1 (Peer, Belgium: Alamire Foundation, 1996), 151. For a modern edition of Crequillon's setting, see his *Fourteen Chansons for Four Voices or Instruments ATTB*, ed. Bernard Thomas (London: Pro Musica Editions, 1978). Boetticher's claim (*Boetticher Lasso*, 1:276) that the poem was penned by Clement Marot, is dubious—see Leuchtmann's commentary, in *Lasso Werke*, 14:xxx. The Lasso setting first appeared in print in 1563. A *rentrement* also figures in "Sur tous regretz" (and in Pasquier's *contrafactum* of this poem), where it prompts a similar reprise of musical material from the opening of the chanson. Both pieces thus present the special challenge of devising music that will work well as opening and closing alike. For modern editions of this chanson, see *Lasso Chansons*, 14:46–51; and *Lasso Werke*, 14:26–28.

3. For modern editions of this work, *Lasso Chansons*, 14:73–77; and *Lasso Werke*, 14:130–32.

4. The sixth stanza of Marot's translation of Psalm 6 reads: "Toute nuict tant travaille, Que lict, chalit, et paille, En pleurs je fays noyer, Et en eau goutte à goutte, S'en va ma couche toute, Par si fort larmoyer." This was evidently Marot's first completed translation. For a modern edition of this text, see Marot, *Œuvres poétiques complètes*, ed. G. Defaux, 2 vols. (Paris: Classiques Garnier, 1996), 2:572–74, 1225–26. Further on the Psalm paraphrase in the context of devotional literatures, see Cave, *Devotional Poetry*, 94–97.

5. See Dobbins, "Textual Sources and Compositional Techniques," 153. Leuchtmann's commentary on the poetic and musical sources of this work appears in *Lasso Werke*, 14:xxx.

6. For modern editions of this chanson, see *Lasso Chansons*, 13:132–35; and *Lasso Werke*, 14:128–29.

7. See Bernhard Meier, *The Modes of Classical Vocal Polyphony*, trans. Ellen S. Beebe (New York: Broude, 1988), 271.

8. Lasso's chanson was first issued by the Munich printer Adam Berg in his famous "four language" print of 1573, the *Sex cantiones latinae . . . Sechs Teutsche Lieder . . . Six chansons francoises . . . Sei Madrigali nuouvi*, dedicated by the composer to members of the Fugger family of Augsburg. Further on this print, see Lasso, *The Four-Language Print for Four and Eight Voices (Munich, 1573)*, ed. Peter Bergquist, Recent Researches in the Music of the Renaissance, 102 (Madison, Wis.: A-R Editions, 1995). For modern editions of this chanson, see *Lasso Chansons*, 13:192–94; and *Lasso Werke*, 12:50–52. Lasso seems to have been the only composer to have set this anonymous text; see ibid., civ.

9. For Boetticher, the chanson and its *contrafacta* are examples of madrigalesque "Weltschmerz" [!] as appropriated in the service of religious sensibility, and especially, the condemnation of the everyday world. See *Boetticher Lasso*, 1:82.

10. Meier, *The Modes of Classical Vocal Polyphony*, 262, Further on Meier's view of the "mi" cadence as representation of fear, see ibid., 274.

11. For modern editions of this chanson, see *Lasso Chansons,* 13:5–7; and *Lasso Werke,* 12:87–89. For Leuchtmann's commentary on the poetic and musical sources of this work, see ibid., cxii–cxiii.

12. Pasquier's typesetter mistakenly put "& lez" here.

13. For Leuchtmann's commentary on the poetic and musical sources of this work, see *Lasso Werke,* 14:xxii.

14. For modern editions of this chanson, see *Lasso Chansons,* 11:80–86; and *Lasso Werke,* 14:50–54.

15. See Barbara B. Diefendorf, "The Huguenot Psalter and the Faith of French Protestants in the Sixteenth Century," in *Culture and Identity in Early Modern Europe (1500–1800): Essays in Honor of Natalie Zemon Davis,* ed. Barbara B. Diefendorf and C. Hesse (Ann Arbor: University of Michigan Press, 1993), 41–63.

16. Goulart's Psalm project, the *Cinquante pseaumes de David, avec la musique à cinq parties d'Orlande de Lasso, vinqt autres pseaumes à cinq et six parties, par divers excellents musiciens de nostre temps,* was issued in 1597. See *Lasso Werke,* 14:xxii for the complete Psalm text found in this print. Concerning the Protestant Psalm tradition, see chapter 1, above.

17. The chanson first appeared in print in 1564. For modern editions of this chanson, see *Lasso Chansons,* 14:43–45; and *Lasso Werke,* 12:20–26.

18. For modern editions of this chanson, *Lasso Chansons,* 13:87–88; *Lasso Werke,* 12:36–37. For Leuchtmann's commentary on the poetic and musical sources of this work, see ibid., c. Pasquier's *contrafactum* of this same chanson likewise takes the original incipit as an invitation to praise "Grace divine, qui la mort nous extermine." In some respects this song anticipates the language of the Protestant reception of some of Ronsard's Anacreontic verse (see chapter 6, below).

Chapter 6

1. Further on Ronsard in the context of late sixteenth-century musical practice, see Jeanice Brooks, "French Chanson Collections on the Texts of Pierre de Ronsard, 1570–1580" (Ph.D. diss., The Catholic University of America, 1990), and Brooks, "Ronsard, the Lyric Sonnet and the Late Sixteenth-Century Chanson," *Early Music History* 13 (1994): 65–84. The basic bibliographical guides to this repertory are Geneviève Thibault and L. Perceau, *Bibliographie des poésies de P. de Ronsard mises en musique au XVIe siècle* (Paris: Droz, 1941) and Jean-Pierre Ouvrard, "Le sonnet ronsardien en musique: Du Supplément de 1552 à 1580," *Revue de musicologie* 74 (1988): 149–64.

For excerpts from Goulart's editions of Boni's sonnets, see Guillaume Boni, *Sonetz de Pierre de Ronsard mis en musique à quatre parties,* ed. Frank Dobbins (Paris: Salabert, 1987), 20–21. The books by Boni and Bertrand were carefully organized according to idiosyncratic modal schemes, ones that may well have stimulated Goulart's increasing sensibility to the modal organization of his *Thrésor de musique d'Orlande.* See chapter 7, below.

2. On the Protestant reception of Ronsard, see Jacques Pineaux, *La polémique protestante contre Ronsard* (Paris: M. Didier, 1973), 178–86; and Pineaux, *La poésie des protestants de langue française, du premier synode national jusqu'à la procla-*

mation de l'édit de Nantes (1559–1598), Bibliothèque française et romaine (Paris: Klincksieck, 1971).

3. For a modern edition of this chanson, see *Lasso Chansons,* 11:68–69; and *Lasso Werke,* 12:101. Lasso's setting of "Bon jour mon coeur" first appeared in Phalèse's *Quatriesme livre des chansons à quatre et cincq parties nouvellement composées par Orlando di Lassus.* See Henri Vanhulst, *Catalogue des éditions de musique publiées à Louvain par Pierre Phalèse et ses fils, 1545–1578* (Bruxelles: Palais des Académies, 1984), 112. The other printed sources of Lasso's setting of this text are listed in *Lasso Werke,* 12:cxv-cxvi. A facsimile of the superius part of "Bon jour mon coeur" as it appears in the Gdansk chansonnier (Ms. 4030, long thought to have been a Lasso autograph) can be seen in Sandberger's critical notes to *Lasso Werke,* 12:li. The same poem was also set by Philippe de Monte (à 6, issued in his *Sonetz de P. de Ronsard* of 1575), by Jean de Castro (à 3, issued in his *Livre de chansons,* also of 1575) and by Claude Goudimel (à 4, first issued in Le Roy and Ballard's *Neufiesme livre de chansons* of 1559). For a modern edition of the de Monte setting, see Brooks, "French Chanson Collections on the Texts of Pierre de Ronsard," 468–91. A modern edition of Goudimel's piece appears in his *Œuvres complètes,* ed. Pierre Pidoux, et al., 14 vols. (New York: Institute of Medieval Music, 1974), 13:35–36. These settings bear no apparent musical resemblance to the one by Lasso. For a modern edition of Castro's three-voice arrangement of Lasso's setting, see Jean de Castro, *Il primo libro di madrigali, canzoni et motetti a tre voci (1569),* ed. Ignace Bossuyt, *Jean de Castro Opera Omnia,* 3 (Leuven: Leuven University Press, 1995).

Ronsard's poem was issued in two versions during the sixteenth century. Both share the same first strophe (the one set by Lasso), but the second stanza as issued in the *Nouvelle continuation des amours* of 1556 and in the *Continuation des amours* of 1557 was apparently revised in the *Œuvres* issued between 1560 and 1587. See Ronsard, *Œuvres complètes,* ed. P. Laumonier, 18 vols. (Paris: Hachette, 1934), 7:247. It is impossible to tell which of these editions Lasso might have had at hand when he set "Bon jour mon coeur." In any event the text set by Lasso differs slightly in orthography and wording from the one given by Laumonnier (see notes 4 and 7, below, for the most important of these differences).

4. In Laumonnier's edition (Ronsard, *Oeuvres complètes,* 7:247) read "toute belle" in place of Lasso's "tourterelle." The spellings used by Lasso at times differ from those found in Ronsard's published texts. See also notes 3 and 7.

5. Translation adapted from the one by Frank Dobbins, from Dobbins, ed., *The Oxford Book of French Chansons* (Oxford: Oxford University Press, 1987), 336.

6. My thanks to Lawrence Bernstein for noting this last correspondence of text and tone in Goulart's *contrafactum.*

7. The spellings used by Lasso and his printer Le Roy differ slightly from Ronsard's published text, notably in the use of "rendz" rather than "ren" throughout. Other variant readings printed in this musical setting suggest that Lasso used an edition of Ronsard's *Amours* that appeared before 1560, for starting in that year line 6 of the poem reads "en aimant" rather than "au cours de." We should also note that starting in the collected *Oeuvres* of 1584, Ronsard used "mignarde" ("pretty one") in place of "pillarde" ("thief") at the end of line 1. After 1584 line 10 ends "meurtrierement" instead of "cruellement." For a critical report on Ronsard's poem,

see his *Œuvres complètes,* 4:156. Recall, in this respect, the variants also encountered between Lasso's version of "Bon jour mon coeur" and the one published in Ronsard's own collected poetry. See notes 3 and 4, above.

8. See Ouvrard, "Le Sonnet ronsardien en musique: Du Supplément de 1552 à 1580." Lasso's setting, with its idiosyncratic truncation of Ronsard's poem, provided the model for a four-voice setting by Nicholas Millot that appeared in print in 1570. For a modern edition of this piece, which alludes to many of the important moments in Lasso's chanson, see Millot, *Unpublished Chansons issued by Le Roy and Ballard,* ed. Jane Bernstein, The Sixteenth Century Chanson, 18 (New York: Garland Publishing, 1991), 87–90. Lasso's setting was first published in 1561. For more on the connection between the two pieces, see Dobbins, "Textual Sources and Compositional Techniques in the French Chansons of Orlandus Lassus," in *Orlandus Lassus and His Time. Colloquium Proceedings. Antwerpen 24–26.08.1994,* ed. Ignace Bossuyt, Eugeen Schreurs, and Annelies Wouters, Yearbook of the Alamire Foundation, 1 (Peer, Belgium: Alamire Foundation, 1996), 150–51. For a modern edition of Lasso's piece, see *Lasso Chansons,* 13:174–80; and *Lasso Werke,* 14:18–21. On the text and sources, see ibid., 14:xviii.

9. See Bernhard Meier, *The Modes of Classical Vocal Polyphony,* trans. Ellen S. Beebe (New York: Broude, 1988), 277. Further on the construction of the "mi" cadence, see ibid., 96–99. The association of B flat, E flat, etc. with "softness" in Renaissance musical theory depends on the ancient contrast of "mi" (B natural) as "hard" (hence B *durum*) and "fa" (B flat) as "soft" (B *mollum*).

10. Vautrollier prints "rends" or "ren" in place of "rendz" as found in Pasquier. All other readings for the poem are the same.

11. According to Dobbins ("Textual Sources and Compositional Techniques," 152) the text is a strophe of an *odelette* by Ronsard. Further on Ronsard's odes and their musical implications in sixteenth-century France, see Brooks, "Italy, the Ancient World and the French Musical Inheritance in the Sixteenth Century: Arcadelt and Clereau in the Service of the Guises," *Journal of the Royal Musical Association* 121 (1996): 147–90. The Lasso setting bears no musical resemblance to one by the royal musician Guillaume Costeley. For a modern edition of this work, see his *Musique,* ed. Henry Expert, 3 vols., *Les Maîtres musiciens de la Renaissance Française,* 3, 18, 19 (New York: Broude, 1963), 1:23–26.

12. For the story of Ronsard's encounter with this Anacreontic poetry, see John O'Brien, "Ronsard, Belleau and Renvoisy," *Early Music History* 13 (1994): 199–216.

13. On the connection between the Anacreontic material and the carnivalesque see Kate van Orden, "Vernacular Culture and the Chanson in Paris, 1570–1580" (Ph. D diss., University of Chicago, 1996), 42–45.

14. In line 2 Le Roy mistakenly prints "les bois" in place of "la boit." In line 5 he mistakenly prints "est beau" in place of "es beu." Neither of these readings makes grammatical sense.

15. For modern editions of this chanson, see *Lasso Chansons,* 12:146–51; and *Lasso Werke,* 14:7–10. The poem was first published in Ronsard's own *Meslanges* of 1555, and thereafter appeared in his collected *Œuvres* of 1560. In line 3, the reading "La mer esparse" (the one used by Lasso) appears only in editions of the *Oeuvres* printed before 1578. See Ronsard, *Œuvres complètes,* 6:256.

Chapter 7

1. The original text reads: "reveuz par luy, et augmentez."

2. Concerning the symmetrical musical organization of the *Musica nova,* in which not only the succession of vocal forces, but also tonal types are mirrored by the two large generic divisions, see Martha Feldman, *City Culture and the Madrigal at Venice* (Berkeley: University of California Press, 1995), 224–26.

3. This changing distinction among language and genre is also manifest in the *contrafacta* books prepared by Pasquier and Goulart, which edit, omit, and include pieces in part according to generic distinctions of this kind. Pasquier omits all of the motets. The second and third editions of Goulart's *Le Thrésor de musique d'Orlande* follow the general strategy set out in the 1576 edition of *Les meslanges d'Orlande* of 1576, putting the motets (the secular ones with substitute or altered texts) in a special section of the print. But Goulart was highly selective in this respect, replacing the original secular Latin texts of some pieces with ones of his own pen, and substituting motets of his own choosing for some of those printed by Le Roy.

4. For a recent study of the intellectual contexts of theories of modality, see Sarah Fuller, "Defending the *Dodecachordon*: Ideological Currents in Glarean's Modal Theory," *Journal of the American Musicological Society* 49 (1996): 191–224.

5. Quoted in Adrian Le Roy, *Les instructions pour le luth (1574),* ed. Jean Jacquot, Pierre-Yves Sordes, and Jean-Michel Vaccaro, 2 vols. (Paris: Éditions du Centre national de la recherche scientifique, 1977), 5, as it appeared in *A brief and plaine Instruction to set all Musicke of eight divers tunes in Tablature for the lute. With a briefe instruction how to play on the Lute by Tablature, to conduct and dispose thy hand unto the Lute, with certaine easie lessons for that purpose . . . All first written in French by Adrian Le Roy* (London: James Rowbothome, 1574). Concerning the lost original, see François Lesure and Geneviève Thibault, *Bibliographie des éditions d'Adrian Le Roy et Robert Ballard, 1551–1598* (Paris: Heugel, 1955), 132–33 (No. 130); and Lionel de La Laurencie, *Chansons au luth et airs de cour français du xvie siècle* (Paris: Heugel, 1934), lvi–lviii. In this treatise and in his music prints Le Roy (like Lasso) was clearly an advocate for the octenary system, although in the *Traicté de musique* of 1583, Le Roy seems to have at least provisionally embraced the system of 12 modes proposed by Zarlino. See the recent modern edition of this treatise: *Traicté de musique,* ed. Máire Egan-Buffet, Musicological Studies, 66 (Paris, 1583; reprint, Ottawa, Canada: Institute of Mediaeval Music, 1996). It is perhaps worth noting in this connection that manuscript copies of Zarlino's writings in French translations survive in Paris libraries, although they seem to have been generally overlooked by modern scholars of tonal thought in France (these sources are cited by Egan-Buffet). In any event Zarlino's (and not Glarean's) disposition of the twelve modes was the one used by the French Protestant composer Claude Le Jeune in his *Dodécacorde selon les douse modes* (Paris, 1618). See Le Jeune, *Dodécacorde: Comprising Twelve Psalms of David Set to Music According to the Twelve Modes,* ed. Anne Harrington Heider, 3 vols., Recent Researches in the Music of the Renaissance, 74–76 (Madison, Wis.: A-R Editions, 1988), 1:xiii–xvi. On Zarlino's modal thought, see Gioseffo Zarlino, *On the Modes: Part Four of "Le istitutioni harmoniche," 1558,* ed. Claude V. Palisca, trans. Vered Cohen (New Haven: Yale University Press, 1983).

6. Harold Powers, "Tonal Types and Modal Categories in Renaissance Polyphony," *Journal of the American Musicological Society* 34 (1981): 440.

7. Quoted in Le Roy, *Les instructions pour le luth (1574)*, 45.

8. Lechner's letter is transcribed in Georg Reichert, "Martin Crusius und die Musik in Tübingen um 1590," *Archiv für Musikwissenschaft* 10 (1953): 185–212, and has been explored in relation to the organization of the 1562 print in Bernhard Meier, *The Modes of Classical Vocal Polyphony*, trans. Ellen S. Beebe (New York: Broude, 1988), 30–31; in Jessie Ann Owens's review of that book (in *Rivista Italiana di musicologia* 14 [1979]: 449), and in Harold Powers, "Anomalous Modalities," *Orlando di Lasso in der Musikgeschichte. Bericht über das Symposium der Bayerischen Akademie der Wissenschaften. München, 4–6. Juli 1994*, ed. Bernhold Schmid (Munich: Bayerischen Akademie der Wissenschaften, 1996), 239. Lechner had been a pupil of Lasso's starting in 1570. By 1576 he had joined the Protestant church. An autograph letter of recommendation from Lasso on Lechner's behalf from 1585 is transcribed in Horst Leuchtmann, *Orlando di Lasso*, 2 vols. (Wiesbaden: Breitkopf und Härtel, 1976), 2:244–45. Further on Lechner's emulation of Lasso's construction of the octenary system, see Meier, "Bemerkungen zu Lechners *Motectae sacrae* von 1575," *Archiv für Musikwissenschaft* 14 (1957): 83–101.

9. The print in question is the *Novae aliquot et ante hac non ita usitate ad duas voces cantiones suavissimae omnibus musicis summe utiles*. See Powers, "Tonal Types," 451–52, and "Anomalous Modalities," 241 for a summary of the contents of this print.

10. It is worth nothing that the *Penitential Psalms* were originally composed by Lasso in the late 1550s as a set of seven works only (that is how the pieces are preserved in a famous illuminated and glossed manuscript compiled around that time for the Munich court chapel). The *Laudate Dominum* (representing the eighth mode) was added only for the subsequent publication of the set by Adam Berg. Further on the history of the set, see Lasso, *The "Seven Penitential Psalms" and "Laudate Dominum de caelis"*, ed. Peter Bergquist, 2 vols., Recent Researches in the Music of the Renaissance, 86–87 (Madison, Wis.: A-R Editions, 1990).

11. Powers, "Anomalous Modalities," 228–29. Further on the *Lagrime* and its literary sources, see Fritz Jensch, "Orlando di Lassos *Lagrime di San Pietro* und ihr Text," *Musik in Bayern* 32 (1986): 43–62.

12. For a survey of the Lasso books issued by Le Roy et Ballard, see Peter Bergquist, "Modal Ordering within Orlando di Lasso's Publications," *Orlando di Lasso Studies*, ed. Peter Bergquist (Cambridge: Cambridge University Press, 1999), 210–18.

13. Peter Bergquist, "The Modality of Orlando di Lasso's Compositions in 'A Minor,'" in *Orlando di Lasso in der Musikgeschichte. Bericht über das Symposium der Bayerischen Akademie der Wissenschaften. München, 4–6. Juli 1994,* ed. Bernhold Schmid (Munich: Bayerische Akademie der Wissenschaften, 1996), 8–10. Harold Powers, "Anomalous Modalities," 221–42.

14. Powers, "Modal Representation in Polyphonic Offertories," *Early Music History* 2 (1982): 52–58 discusses the Le Roy print in relation to its models.

15. On the modality of "Je suis quasi prest d'enrager," see Bergquist, "The Modality of Orlando di Lasso's Compositions in 'A Minor.'" Le Roy allows that Mode 3 is at times transposed (as "flat/G2/A") in just this way. In "Anomalous Modali-

ties," 232, Powers notes that Lasso also used the tonal type "natural/G2/D" as a representation of Mode 2 in the didactic duos printed by Berg in 1577.

16. Quoted in Le Roy, *Les instructions pour le luth (1574)*, 33. Further on the expressive connotations of the *Deuterus* modes, see Jean-Pierre Ouvrard, "Modality and Text Expression in 16th-Century French Chansons: Remarks Concerning the E Mode," *Basler Jahrbuch für historische Musikpraxis* 16 (1992): 89–104.

17. On the place of the exceptional tonal type "natural/G2/A" in Lasso's production, see Powers, "Anomalous Modalities."

18. In the book of 1576 Pasquier also inexplicably omitted chanson No. 57 from his model, "Et d'ou venez vous."

19. In Pasquier's volume as in Le Roy's *Mellange d'Orlande* of 1570 a rubric connects the latter chanson with the former. In Le Roy's *Les meslanges d'Orlande* of 1576, the two pieces appear together (among the Mode 2 group, as they should be). See Nos. 69 and 69.2 in Table 7.1.

20. This seems particularly significant in light of what was said above about the *Chansons nouvelles*, which were otherwise never assimilated to *Les meslanges d'Orlande* or its companion volumes. Only three pieces found in the 1576 edition of Goulart's *Thrésor de musique d'Orlande* derived from sources *other* than *Les meslanges d'Orlande* of 1576: "Que gaignez vous" (printed in the Le Roy *Mellange d'Orlande* of 1570 but *omitted* from the 1576 edition of that print); "O foible esprit" (from the *Chansons nouvelles* of 1571); and "Du fonds de ma pensée" (Lasso's setting of a French Psalm translation). On the latter work, see Frank Dobbins, "Textual Sources and Compositional Techniques in the French Chansons of Orlandus Lassus," in *Orlandus Lassus and His Time. Colloquium Proceedings. Antwerpen 24–26.08.1994*, ed. Ignace Bossuyt, Eugeen Schreurs, and Annelies Wouters, Yearbook of the Alamire Foundation, 1 (Peer, Belgium: Alamire Foundation, 1996), 151. "Celebrons sans cesse," a four-voice perpetual canon, is unique to the Goulart *Thrésor de musique d'Orlande*. It is doubtful that this piece was really composed by Lasso. For a modern edition of this work see *Lasso Chansons*, 14:164 and *Lasso Werke*, 16:162–63.

21. Goulart's placement of "Je ne veux plus chanter" (à 5; No. 91) with the very unusual "flat/G2/A" tonal disposition, likewise confirms Le Roy's understanding, for here in the *Thrésor de musique d'Orlande* as in the 1576 edition of *Les meslanges d'Orlande*, the work is poised between the Mode 3/4 ensemble with which it shares a final sonority and the Mode 5 pieces, with which it shares system and cleffing.

22. On the other hand, another work from this small group of compositions à 5, "Qui veult d'amour" (No. 104; tonal type "natural/G2/A") was displaced to the section of the 1582 and 1594 books nominally representing Mode 7, presumably on the basis of the system and cleffing this work shares with those now surrounding it.

23. "O foible esprit," the only piece from the *Chansons nouvelles* to have appeared in the 1576 edition of the *Thrésor de musique d'Orlande*, is apparently out of place in this process of assimilation. It is worth noting that the first half of "O foible esprit" has D as the lowest tone of its final sonority, which might conceivably have prompted the confused modal assignment at hand here.

24. For a modern edition of "Comme une qui prend une couppe" and "Ton nom que mon vers dira," see *Lasso Chansons*, 11:95–99 and 14:62–67; and *Lasso Werke*, 16:3–5 and 6–11. Leuchtmann details the textual sources of the lyrics for the original chansons, which juxtapose poems and parts of poems in ways that must have

surprised even Ronsard; see Lasso Werke, 16:xvii–xviii. Further on the Protestant polemic against Ronsard and on the *contrafacta* of Lasso chansons based on his poetry, see chapter 6, above.

25. On the modal background of Boni's cycle and its relationship to the themes of the texts it embraces, see Kate van Orden, "Vernacular Culture and the Chanson in Paris, 1570–1580" (Ph.D. diss., University of Chicago, 1996), 134–37. Goulart's *Sonets chrestiens mis en musique à quatre parties par Boni de S. Flour en Auvergne. Premier [-Second] livre* ([Geneva: Le Royer], 1578) is described in Laurent Guillo, *Les éditions musicales de la Renaissance lyonnaise (1525–1615)*, Domaine musicologique (Paris: Klincksieck, 1991), 455. For a modern edition of Boni's sonnets, along with excerpts from the liminary materials from Goulart's print, see Boni, *Sonetz de Pierre de Ronsard mis en musique à quatre parties*, ed. Frank Dobbins (Paris: Salabert, 1987), 20–21.

Boni's sonnet settings were not his first attempt at modal representation, as Jeanice Brooks has recently demonstrated, for in his *Primus liber modulorum quinis, senis et septenis vocibus* Boni's chosen texts "are linked together to form a quasi-narrative sequence dealing with the Lenten themes of penitence and Christ's promise of redemption. Their musical settings follow a pre-determined musical organization according to tonal structure and number of voices." See Brooks, "Music and Devotion in Renaissance Toulouse: The Motets of Guillaume Boni," in *"La musique de tous les passetemps le plus beau": Hommage à Jean-Michel Vaccaro*, ed. V. Coelho, F. Lesure, and H. Vanhulst (Paris: Klincksieck, 1998), 24. I am grateful to Jeanice Brooks for sharing a copy of this article with me in advance of its publication. For a modern edition of the volume in question, see Guillaume Boni, *Motets de 1573*, ed. J. Brooks (Paris and Tours: Centre de musique ancienne, 1997).

26. See Brooks, " 'Ses amours et les miennes tout ensemble': La structure cyclique du *Premier livre* d'Anthoine de Bertrand (Paris, 1576)," *Revue de musicologie* 74 (1988): 201–20. Goulart's books of *contrafacta* based on this print and its companion volumes, the *Second livre des Amours de P. de Ronsard. Mis en musique à IIII parties par Anthoine de Bertrand* (Paris: Le Roy et Ballard, 1578, 1587) and the *Tiers livre de chansons* (Paris, 1578) were issued in Geneva as *Premier [-Second] livre de Sonets chrestiens mis en musique à quatre parties* ([Geneva: Le Royer], 1580). These prints are described in Guillo, *Les éditions musicales de la Renaissance lyonnaise*, 455. On Goulart's reform of Lasso's settings of texts by Ronsard, see chapter 6, above.

27. In reproducing these final remarks Goulart carefully suppresses Bertrand's authorial allusions to "mes livres," even as he repeats (with irony for the modern reader) the composer's admonitions to respect "l'intention de l'auteur" where chromatic notation was concerned. For a facsimile of Bertrand's preface, see Henri Expert's modern edition of the *Premier livre des Amours de Pierre de Ronsard*, Monuments de la musique française au temps de la Renaissance, 4 (Paris, 1926–27; reprint, New York, 1960), vi–vii. The contents of the prefaces are considered in Brooks, " 'Ses amours et les miennes tout ensemble,'" 201–20; and Vaccaro, "Les préfaces d'Anthoine de Bertrand," *Revue de musicologie* 74 (1988): 221–36.

28. In Vautrollier's words: "Voila pourquoy je les ay voulu imprimer, et communiquer principallement à ceux qui aiment la perfection de cest art, conjoincte avec une lettre grave, et eslongée de toute impurité." For a complete transcription and translation of the preface to this print, see Appendix A.

29. See Joseph Kerman, "An Elizabethan Edition of Lassus," *Acta Musicologica* 27 (1955): 74.

30. Terence Cave, *Devotional Poetry in France, c. 1570–1613* (Cambridge: Cambridge University Press, 1969) provides the single best introduction to devotional practices in sixteenth-century France and their relationship to contemporaneous poetry. On penitence and the life of Jesus in the Evening and Morning meditations, see pp. 38–57 of his study.

31. Concerning Chandieu's cyclic poem and its place in literary representation of the *vanitas* theme, see Cave, *Devotional Poetry,* 150–56. A modern edition of the poem appears in Antoine de Chandieu, *Octonaires sur la vanité et inconstance du monde,* ed. Françoise Bonali-Fiquet (Geneva: Droz, 1979). For a modern edition of Le Jeune's cycle, which was posthumously published in 1606, see his *Octonaires de la vanité et inconstance du monde,* ed. Henry Expert, Monuments de la musique française au temps de la Renaissance, 1 and 8 (Paris, 1924; reprint, New York: Broude, 1960). Pascal de L'Estocart also published settings of these poems in 1582. See his *Premier livre des Octonaires de la vanité du monde,* ed. Henry Expert, Monuments de la musique française au temps de la Renaissance, 10 (Paris, 1929; reprint, New York: Broude, 1960).

32. Quoted in his *Dodecacorde: Comprising Twelve Psalms of David Set to Music according to the Twelves Modes,* 1:xvi–xvii.

33. On this print and the poetics of its contributors, see Cave, *Devotional Poetry,* 76–77. For Cave's discussion of Goulart's cyclic sonnets, see pp. 149ff of the same study.

34. For a modern edition of du Bartas's famous poem, see Guillaume Saluste du Bartas, *La sepmaine,* ed. Yvonne Bellenger (Paris: Klincksieck, 1981). Goulart's redaction of *La sepmaine* was also printed by Haultin. See Louis Desgraves, *Les Haultin, 1571–1623,* Imprimerie à La Rochelle, 2, Travaux de humanisme et de Renaissance, 34(Geneva: Droz, 1960), 60–64. According to Cave, among Goulart's independent poetry are texts that freely imitate some of the Creation themes explored by du Bartas. See *Devotional Poetry,* pp. 78–79.

35. On the overall plan of Goulart's *Quarante tableaux* of 1607 as well as the various editions of the *Trente tableaux,* see Cave, *Devotional Poetry,* 21–22 and Cave, "The Protestant Devotional Tradition: Simon Goulart's *Trente tableaux de la mort,*" *French Studies* 21 (1967): 1–15. See *Devotional Poetry,* 27–28 for quotations from Goulart's descriptions of death and the corruption of physical form.

36. Powers, "Tonal Types and Modal Categories," 446.

37. For a modern reprint of this book, see Jean Nicot, ed., *Thrésor de la langue françoise, tant ancienne que moderne* (Paris, 1606; reprint, Paris : Picard, 1960).

Chapter 8

1. See Appendix A for the full text of the preface.

2. See Appendix A for the full text of the preface. The same comments reappear in the 1582 and 1594 editions of the *Le Thrésor de musique d'Orlande.*

3. We might note as further confirmation of Goulart's debt to Vautrollier's print the fact that he included Vautrollier's *contrafactum* of "Que gaignez vous" ("D'où

vient cela"), a work that was otherwise omitted from Le Roy et Ballard's *Les meslanges d'Orlande* of 1576.

4. See Appendix A for the full text of the printer's note. Further on the "unchanged" texts in the *contrafacta* books, see chapter 2, above.

5. Concerning the *Tiers livre* and its borrowings, see Marc Honegger, "Les chansons spirituelles de Didier Lupi et les débuts de la musique protestante en France au xvie siècle" (Ph.D. diss., Université de Lille III, 1970), 2:91–94, and Laurent Guillo, *Les éditions musicales de la Renaissance lyonnaise (1525–1615),* Domaine musicologique (Paris: Klincksieck, 1991), 445–46. Pasquier's *Premier* and *Second livre* (not to be confused with the books of Lasso *contrafacta*) are closely based on two editions of *chansons spirituelles*: Didier Lupi Second's *Premier livre de chansons spirituelles* (Lyons, 1548) and Louis Des Masures *Vingt-six cantiques* (Lyons, 1564; musical settings here by Claude Goudimel). The contents of the Pasquier books are listed in Honegger, "Les chansons spirituelles," 2:248–54. On the Lyonnais models for his prints, see Guillo, *Les éditions musicales,* 235–55 and 320–22; and Honegger, "Les chansons spirituelles," 1:59–115 and 2:41–43 and 143–49.

6. Lasso, *Motets for Six Voices from "Primus liber concentuum sacrorum" (Paris, 1564) Motets for Four to Ten Voices from "Modulorum secundum volumen" (Paris, 1565),* ed. Peter Bergquist, The Complete Motets, 4, Recent Researches in the Music of the Renaissance, 105 (Madison, Wis.: A-R Editions, 1996), xi. See *Motets for Six Voices,* xvi for a facsimile and translation of this preface.

7. Concerning the now lost book, see François Lesure and Geneviève Thibault, *Bibliographie des éditions d'Adrian Le Roy et Robert Ballard, 1551–1598* (Paris: Heugel, 1955), 132–33 (No. 130). The English translation, printed by James Rowbothome, is contained in *A brief and plaine Instruction to set all Musicke of eight divers tunes in Tablature for the lute. With a briefe instruction how to play on the Lute by Tablature, to conduct and dispose thy hand unto the Lute, with certaine easie lessons for that purpose . . . All first written in French by Adrian Le Roy.* Further on this volume, see Geneviève Thibault and Lionel de La Laurencie, *Chansons au luth et Airs de Cour français du xvie siècle* (Paris: Heugel, 1934), lvi–lviii. For a modern edition of Le Roy's manuals, see Adrian Le Roy, *Les instructions pour le luth (1574),* ed. Jean Jacquot, Pierre-Yves Sordes, and Jean-Michel Vaccaro, 2 vols. (Paris: Éditions du Centre national de la recherche scientifique, 1977).

According to Lesure, Le Roy's *Livre d'airs de cour* (1571), addressed to Catherine de Clermont, the contesse de Retz, mentions a forthcoming book for lute, based mainly on Lasso. Whether this was to have been a reprint of the lost volume or a new book remains uncertain. See Lesure, *Bibliographie des éditions,* 150 (No. 154). A modern edition of the 1571 preface appears in La Laurencie, *Chansons au luth,* xxv–xxvi. Further on French lute traditions, see Jean-Michel Vaccaro, *La musique de Luth en France au xvie siècle* (Paris: Éditions du Centre national de la recherche scientifique, 1981).

8. Emphasis added. Quoted from the last page of the Bassus partbook of *Primus liber modulorum quinis vocibus constantium, Orlando Lassusio auctore* (Paris: Le Roy et Ballard, 1571). A Latin epistle to King Charles IX, extolling the special virtues of Lasso's music appears in each of the five partbooks of this set. The general privilege of 1567 also appears in a number of other Le Roy et Ballard publications devoted exclusively to the music of Lasso, including, *Secundus liber modulorum Quinis vocibus constantium Orlando Lassusio auctore* (1571), *Novem quiritationes*

divi Iob. Quaternis vocibus ab Orlando de Lassus (1572), *Moduli nondum prius editi monachii Boioarie ternis vocibus* (1576). Further on the general privilege of 1567, see *Boetticher Lasso,* 2:481 and Lesure, *Bibliographie des éditions,* 12. A different general privilege, conferred by Henry IV upon Pierre Ballard, appears in Ballard's choirbook editions of some Masses by Lasso, *Missa ad imitationem* (1607) and *Missa ad imitationem moduli "Credidi" auctore Orlando de Lassus, cum quinque vocibus* (1608). This privilege makes no special mention of individual composers. See Appendix B for a listing of the Le Roy–Lasso books and the privileges they contain.

9. The *Chansons nouvelles* was also reprinted almost simultaneously (but without the dedicatory materials) by Phalèse and Bellère in Louvain and Antwerp as the *Livre cinquiesme de chansons nouvelles . . . d'Orlande de Lassus.* Further on the relationship between the *Livre cinquiesme* and the *Chansons nouvelles,* see Henri Vanhulst, *Catalogue des éditions de musique publiées à Louvain par Pierre Phalèse et ses fils, 1545–1578* (Bruxelles: Palais des Académies, 1984), 177–79. Phalèse's *Moduli quinis vocibus* of 1571 is similarly a republication, minus the dedication and liminary poem, of Le Roy et Ballard's work with the same name (also 1571). Phalèse's *Primus liber modulorum* of 1571 and the *Secundus liber modulorum* of 1572 also depend very closely on publications offered by the Paris firm. See ibid., 174–92.

10. Circumstantial evidence suggests that Lasso visited the French capital and the royal court in April and May of 1571. In a letter King Charles IX wrote to Lasso's principal patron, Duke Albrecht V of Bavaria on 10 May 1571, he noted Lasso's "great and extraordinary skill" ("grand et rare science"). Lasso had apparently served as something of a courier during the trip from Munich to Paris, for he is mentioned in two letters written by Charles' young spouse, Elizabeth (she was also Albrecht's neice) as having delivered correspondence to her in Paris during April and May. The contents and dating of all of these documents as they relate to the timing of Lasso's brief visit to Paris in 1571 are discussed in Horst Leuchtmann, *Orlando di Lasso,* 2 vols. (Wiesbaden: Breitkopf und Härtel, 1976), 1:155–57; and Wolfgang Boetticher, *Aus Orlando di Lassos Wirkingskreis: Neue archivalische Studien zur Münchener Musikgeschichte* (Kassel: Bärenreiter, 1963), 29.

11. The privilege of 1571 given here is quoted from Le Roy et Ballard's *Tertius liber modolurum quinis vocibus constantium, Orlando Lassusio auctore* of 1573, which is the earliest publication known to include the special authorial privilege. Later versions of this authorial privilege appeared in only a very few other prints brought out by Le Roy et Ballard. It appears, for instance, in each of a series of imitation Masses issued in 1577, prints collected together under the general title *Missae variis concentibus ornatae, ab Orlando de Lassus. Cum cantico beatae Mariae. Octo Modis Musicisi variato.* The original privilege of 1571, we read in this document, had apparently been confirmed in 1575 by Henry III. This same 1575 confirmation of the 1571 privilege also appears in *Octo cantica divae mariae virginis, quorum initium est Magnificat, secundum octo modos, seu tonos in templis decantari solitos singula quinis vocibus constantia: Auctore Orlando Lassusio* of 1578. The confirmation of 1575 was itself confirmed again in 1582 (apparently on the anniversary of the original 1571 privilege). An excerpt from this document appears in *Ieremiae. Prophetae devotissimae lamentationes, una cum passione domini dominicae palmarum, quinque vocum. Auctore Orlando Lasso* of 1586. For a full listing of the Le Roy–Lasso books and the privileges they mention, see Appendix B. We should

also note that the 1571 *Tertius liber* seems to have been the first of the Le Roy–Lasso collaborations wholly organized according to a scheme of modal representation. Further on the practice, see chapter 7.

Curiously, the other volumes brought out by Le Roy et Ballard and devoted exclusively to works by Lasso nevertheless print either Le Roy's old general privilege of 1567 (see above), or make very brief allusion (on the title pages) to a royal privilege ("avec privilege du Roy pour dix ans" or "Cum privilegio Regis ad decennium") without further explanation. The two privileges—the one for the author, the other for the printer—never appear together in the same print, but they do seem to have coexisted, even among the Lasso–Le Roy collaborations. Some, but not all of the privilege documents are cited and quoted in Leuchtmann, *Orlando di Lasso*, 1:53, 158; Hansjorg Pohlmann, *Frühgeschichte des musikalischen Urheberrechts* (Basel: Bärenreiter, 1962), 270; and *Boetticher Lasso*, 1:481. Lesure makes only passing reference to the general and special authorial privileges.

12. See Haar's "Orlando di Lasso, Composer and Print Entrepeneur," in *Music and the Cultures of Print*, edited by Kate van Orden (New York: Garland Publishing, 2000), 134–35.

13. The *Moduli quinis vocibus nunquam hactenus editi Monachii Boioariae compositi* bears a dedication to Wilhelm of Bavaria, dated 26 May 1571. Leuchtmann (*Orlando di Lasso*, 1:156) tries to clear up Boetticher's confusion about the dedicatee and dating of this print. See 1:278–79 of his book for a transcription of the liminary poem. For the poem from the *Livre de chansons nouvelles*, see Leuchtmann, *Orlando di Lasso*, 1:279. The first two chansons from this collection are settings of Ronsard poems in praise of royal patrons. The *Chansons nouvelles* was reprinted by Le Roy et Ballard, but its contents were never assimilated to the great *Les meslanges d'Orlande* issued and reissued with additions by that firm. The *Primus liber modulorum, quinis vocibus constantium, Orlando Lassusio auctore*, appeared with a dedication to Charles IX of 1 August 1571. All three books were quickly reprinted—some without the dedications to their respective patrons—by the Louvain music printer Pierre Phalèse. For bibliographical descriptions of these prints, see Vanhulst, *Catalogue des éditions*, 174–79.

14. The imperial decree and its effect is considered in Pohlmann, *Frühgeschichte des musikalischen Urheberrechts*, 164–65 and 203–5 and in Leuchtmann, *Orlando di Lasso*, 1:194–96. Further on the relations of the Berg and Gerlach firms, see Susan Jackson, "Berg and Neuber: Music Printers in Sixteenth-Century Nuremberg," (Ph.D. diss., City University of New York, 1998).

15. For a subtle assessment of the French privilege system and its economic incentives for authorial revision and renewal, see George Hoffmann, "The Montaigne Monopoly: Revising the 'Essais' under the French Privilege System," *Publications of the Modern Language Association of America*, 108 (1993): 308–19.

16. On the Phalèse-Lasso books and their relationship to the Le Roy publications upon which they were modeled, see Vanhulst, *Catalogue des éditions*, 174–79. On the general history of Lasso's changing relationship to his printers, see Vanhulst, "Lassus et ses éditeurs: Remarques à propos de deux lettres peu connues," *Revue belge de musicologie*, 39–40 (1985–1986): 80–100.

17. See van Orden, "Vernacular Culture and the Chanson in Paris, 1570–80," (Ph.D. diss., University of Chicago, 1996), 178ff, and van Orden, "Imitation and 'La musique des anciens': Le Roy et Ballard's 1572 *Mellange de chansons*," *Revue de musicologie* 80 (1994):

5–37. For a complete edition and further commentary on the expanded edition of the *Mellange,* see Charles Jacobs, ed., *Le Roy & Ballard's 1572 "Mellange de Chansons"* (University Park, Pa: Pennsylvania State University Press, 1982).

18. For an introduction to the Du Chemin chanson series, see Freedman, "Du Chemin's *Second livre* of 1549 and the Commerce of the French Chanson," in *Second livre de chansons à quatre. Nicolas Du Chemin, 1549* (Paris, 1549; reprint, Tours: Centre de musique ancienne, 1993), v–xv.

19. On the historical consciousness articulated in this book, see van Orden, "Imitation and 'La musique des anciens.' "

20. Castro's title page announces the organizing principle in so many words: "mis en ordre convenable suyvant leurs tons," in this case the system of twelve modal categories proposed by Zarlino, with the modes on C coming first. Castro also served as musical editor for a number of the prints issued by Phalèse during the 1570's and 1580's, including a modally reorganized 1576 issue of the famous *Livre septieme.* See Isabelle His, "Les *Mélanges musicaux* au XVIe et au début du XVIIe siècle [avec une liste des ouvrages parus entre 1560 et ca. 1754," *Nouvelle revue du XVIe siècle* 8 (1990): 102ff; Rudolf Rasch, "The 'Livre septième,' " in *Atti del XIV Congresso della Società Internazionale di Musicologia, Bologna, 27 aug.–1 sept. 1987,* ed. Angelo Pompilio et al. (Turin, 1990), 1:306–418; and Vanhulst, "Un succès de l'édition musicale: *le Septième livre des chansons à quatre parties* (1560–1661/3)," *Revue belge de musicologie* 32–33 (1978–79): 97–120. Castro's work as editor of his own music is considered in Jeanice Brooks, "Jean de Castro, the Pense Partbooks and Musical Culture in Sixteenth-Century Lyons," *Early Music History* 11 (1992): 91–150.

21. Edward Kovarik, "The Parody Chansons of Certon's *Meslanges,*" in *Music and Context, Essays for John M. Ward,* ed. Anne D. Shapiro (Cambridge, Mass.: Harvard University Press, 1985), 317–51.

22. See Guillaume Costeley, *Musique,* ed. Henry Expert, 3 vols., Les maîtres musiciens de la Renaissance française, 3, 18, 19 (Paris, 1896; reprint, New York: Broude, 1963); and the preface to Guillaume Costeley, *Selected Chansons,* ed. Jane Bernstein, The Sixteenth-Century Chanson, 8 (New York and London: Garland Publishing, 1989).

23. See His, "*Les Mélanges* de Claude Le Jeune (Anvers: Plantin, 1585): transcription et étude critique" (Ph.D. diss., Université de Tours, 1990).

24. Elizabeth L. Eisenstein's work appears in her two important studies, *The Printing Press as an Agent of Change: Communications and Cultural Transformations in Early-Modern Europe,* 2 vols. (Cambridge: Cambridge University Press, 1979), and *The Printing Revolution in Early Modern Europe* (Cambridge: Cambridge University Press, 1983). For an important review of Eisenstein's book, see Anthony Grafton, "The Importance of Being Printed," *Journal of Interdisciplinary History* 2 (1980): 265–86.

25. Hoffmann, "The Montaigne Monopoly," 308–19.

26. On Goulart's work as an editor of Montaigne and others, see Leonard Chester Jones, *Simon Goulart, sa vie et son oeuvre, 1543–1628* (Geneva: A. Kundig, 1916), and his *Simon Goulart, 1543–1628: Étude biographique et bibliographique* (Geneva: Georg et Cie, 1917).

27. See Tessa Watt, *Cheap Print and Popular Piety, 1550–1640,* Cambridge Studies in Early Modern British History (New York and Cambridge: Cambridge University Press, 1991).

28. See Chartier's many recent writings on the subject: Chartier, "Laborers and Voyagers: From the Text to the Reader," *Diacritics* 22 (1992): 26–37; Chartier, ed., *The Culture of Print: Power and the Uses of Print in Early Modern Europe* (Princeton, N.J.: Princeton University Press, 1989); Chartier, *Cultural History: Between Practices and Representations* (Ithaca, N.Y.: Cornell University Press, 1988); and Chartier, *The Cultural Uses of Print in Early Modern France,* trans. Lydia G. Cochrane (Princeton, N.J.: Princeton University Press, 1987).

Bibliography

Early Printed Sources

Arcadelt, Jacques. *L'excellence des chansons musicales composees par M. Iacques Arcadet, tant propres à la voix, qu'aux instruments. Recueillies et reueuës par Claude Goudimel natif de Besançon.* Lyon [Geneva]: Jean II de Tournes, 1586.

Bertrand, Anthoine de. *Premier [-Second] livre des Amours de P. de Ronsard. Mis en musique à IIII parties par Antoine de Bertrand.* Paris: Le Roy et Ballard, 1576, 1578.

———. *Premier [-Second] livre de Sonets chrestiens mis en musique à quatre parties.* [Geneva]: [Jean Le Royer], 1580.

———. *Tiers livre de chansons.* Paris: Le Roy et Ballard, 1578.

Boni, Guillaume. *Sonets chrestiens mis en musique à quatre parties par G. Boni de S. Flour en Auvergne. Premier [-Second] livre.* [Geneva]: [Jean Le Royer], 1578.

———. *Sonetz de P. de Ronsard. Mis en musique à IIII parties par G. Bni, de S. Flour en Auvergne. Premier [-Second] livre.* Paris: Le Roy et Ballard, 1576.

Bosc, Simon Du, and Guillaume Guéroult, eds. *Tiers ivre où sont contenues plusieurs chansons . . . desquelles avons changé la verbe lubrique en lettre spirituelle et chrestienne.* Geneva: Simon Du Bosc and Guillaume Guéroult, 1555.

La fleur de poésie françoyse recueil joyeulx contenant plusieurs huictains, dixains, quatrains, chansons et autres dictez de diverses matières, mis en nottes musicalles par plusieurs autheurs, et réduictz en ce petit livre. Paris: Lotrain, 1543.

La fleur des chansons. Des deux plus excellents musiciens de nostre temps, a sçavoir, de M. Orlande de Lassus, et de M. Claude Goudimel. Celles de M. Claude Goudimel n'ont iamais esté mises en lumiere. . . premier [-second] livre, à quatre parties. Lyon: Jean Bavent [Jean II de Tournes], 1574.

Goudimel, Claude. *Les cent cinquante Pseaumes de David nouvellement mis en musique à quatre parties . . ..* [Geneva]: Pierre de Saint-André, 1580.

Lasso, Orlando di. *Cinquante pseaumes de David, avec la musique à cinq parties d'Orlande de Lasso, vingt autres pseaumes à cinq et six parties, par divers excellents musiciens de nostre temps.* [Heidelberg]: Jerome Commelin and Louis Mongard, 1597

———. *Continuation du Mellange d'Orlande de Lassus, à 3, 4, 5, 6, et dix parties.* Paris: Adrian Le Roy et Robert Ballard, 1584.

————. *Livre de chansons nouvelles à cinq parties, avec deux dialogues: à huict.* Paris: Adrian Le Roy et Robert Ballard, 1571.

————. *Mellange d'Orlande de Lassus, contenant plusieurs chansons, à cinq, et huit parties, desquelles la lettre profane a esté changée en spirituelle.* La Rochelle: P. Haultin, 1576.

————. *Mellange d'Orlande de Lassus, contenant plusieurs chansons, à quatre parties, desquelles la lettre profane a esté changée en spirituelle.* La Rochelle: Haultin, 1575.

————. *Mellange d'Orlande de Lassus, contenant plusieurs chansons, tant en vers latin qu'en ryme francoyse, à quatre, cinq, six, huit, dix parties.* Paris: Adrian Le Roy et Robert Ballard, 1570.

————. *Les meslanges d'Orlande de Lassus, contenantz plusieurs chansons à III, V, VI, VIII, X parties: revuez par luy, et augmentez.* Paris: Adrian Le Roy et Robert Ballard, 1576.

————. *Moduli, quatuor, et octo vocum, partim e quiritationibus Iobi, partim e psalmis Davidis, et aliis scripturae locis desumpti.* La Rochelle: P. Haultin, 1576.

————. *Moduli, quinque et decem vocum.* La Rochelle: P. Haultin, 1576.

————. *Moduli, quinque vocum.* La Rochelle: P. Haultin, 1576.

————. *Moduli, sex septem et duodecim vocum.* La Rochelle: P. Haultin, 1576.

————. *Premier livre du Meslange des pseaumes et cantiques à trois parties, recueillis de la musique d'Orlande de Lassus et autres excellents musiciens de nostre temps.* [Geneva], [Jean Le Royer], 1577.

————. *Recueil du mellange d'Orlande de Lassus, contenant plusieurs chansons tant en vers latins qu'en ryme francoyse, à quatre, et cinq parties.* London: Thomas Vautrollier, 1570.

————. *Second livre du Meslange des pseaumes et cantiques à trois parties, recueillis de la musique d'Orlande de Lassus et autres excellents musiciens de nostre temps.* [Geneva], [Jean Le Royer], 1577.

————. *Theatrum musicum Orlandi de Lassus aliorumque praestissimorum musicorum selectissimas cantiones sacras, quatuor, quinque et plurium vocum, representas. Liber primus.* [Geneva]: [Le Royer], 1580.

————. *Theatrum musicum Orlandi de Lassus aliorumque praestissimorum musicorum selectissimas cantiones sacras, quatuor, quinque et plurium vocum, representas. Liber secundus.* [Geneva]: [Le Royer], 1580.

————. *Thrésor de musique d'Orlande de Lassus, contenant ses chansons à quatre, cinq, et six parties.* [Geneva]: [S. Goulart], 1576.

————. *Le thrésor de musique d'Orlande de Lassus . . . contenant ses chansons françoises, italiennes et latines, à quatre, cinq et six parties: augmenté de plus de la moitié en ceste seconde edition.* [Geneva]: [S. Goulart], 1582.

————. *Le thrésor de musique d'Orlande de Lassus . . . contenant ses chansons françoises, italiennes, et latines, à quatre, cinq, et six parties: reveu et corrigé diligemment en ceste troisieme edition.* [Cologny]: [Paul Marceau] [really Geneva: S. Goulart], 1594.

Pasquier, Jean, ed. *Premier [-Second] livre des cantiques et chansons spirituelles à quatre parties.* La Rochelle: Haultin, 1578.

Servin, Jean. *Meslange de chansons nouvelles à quatre parties.* Lyon: Charles Pesnot, 1578.

———. *Premier [-second] livre de Chansons nouvelles à quatre, cinq, six, et huit parties.* Lyon: Charles Pesnot, 1578.

———. *Psalmi Davidis a G. Buchanano versibus expressi: nunc primum modulis III. V. VI. VII et VIII vocum.* Lyon: Charles Pesnot, 1579.

Secondary Sources and Modern Editions

Adams, Courtney S. "Simon Goulart (1543–1628), Editor of Music, Scholar and Moralist." In *Studies in Musicology in Honor of Otto E. Albrecht: A Collection of Essays by His Colleagues and Former Students at the University of Pennsylvania,* edited by J. W. Hill, 125–41. Kassel: Bärenreiter, 1980.

Armstrong, Elizabeth. *Before Copyright: The French Book-Privilege System 1498–1526.* Cambridge: Cambridge University Press, 1990.

Aymon, Jean. *Tous les synodes nationaux des églises reformées de France.* 2 vols. La Haye: Charles Delo, 1710.

Bakhtin, Mikhail. *Rabelais and His World.* Translated by Hélène Iswolsky. Bloomington: Indiana University Press, 1984.

Bergquist, Peter. "Modal Ordering within Orlando di Lasso's Publications." In *Orlando di Lasso Studies,* edited by Peter Bergquist, 203–26. Cambridge: Cambridge University Press, 1999.

———. "The Modality of Orlando di Lasso's Compositions in 'A Minor.' " In *Orlando di Lasso in der Musikgeschichte. Bericht über das Symposium der Bayerischen Akademie der Wissenschaften. München, 4–6. Juli 1994,* edited by Bernhold Schmid, 7–18. Munich: Bayerische Akademie der Wissenschaften, 1996.

Bertrand, Anthoine de. *Premier [-second] livre des Amours de Pierre de Ronsard.* 3 vols. Monuments de la musique française au temps de la Renaissance, 4–6. Paris, 1926–27; reprint, New York: Broude, 1960.

Bèze, Théodore de. *Chrestiennes méditations.* Edited by Mario Richter. Geneva: Droz, 1964.

———. *Pseaumes octantetrois de David, mis en rime françoise.* Geneva, 1551; reprint New Brunswick, N. J.: Friends of the Rutgers University Libraries, 1973.

Block, Adrienne Fried. *The Early French Parody Noel.* 2 vols. Studies in musicology, 36. Ann Arbor: UMI Research Press, 1983.

Boetticher, Wolfgang. *Aus Orlando di Lassos Wirkungskreis: Neue archivalische Studien zur Münchener Musikgeschichte.* Kassel: Bärenreiter, 1963.

———. *Orlando di Lasso und seine Zeit, 1532–1594.* Revised ed. 2 vols. Wilhelmshaven: Florian Noetzel, 1998.

Boni, Guillaume. *Motets de 1573.* Edited by Jeanice Brooks. Paris and Tours: Centre de musique ancienne, 1997.

———. *Sonetz de Pierre de Ronsard mis en musique à quatre parties.* Edited by Frank Dobbins. Paris: Salabert, 1987.

Bordier, Henri-Léonard. *Le chansonnier huguenot du xvie siècle.* 2 vols. Paris: Tross, 1870.

Bossuyt, Ignace. "Jean de Castro and His Three-Part Chansons Modelled on Four- and Five-part Chansons by Orlando di Lasso: A Comparison." In *Orlando di Lasso in der Musikgeschichte. Bericht über das Symposium der Bayerischen Akademie der Wissenschaften. München, 4–6. Juli 1994,* edited by Bernhold Schmid, 25–67. Munich: Bayerischen Akademie der Wissenschaften, 1996.

———, and Peter Michielsen. "Lassos erste Jahre in München (1556–1559): Eine "cosa non riuscita"? Neue Materialien aufgrund unveröffentlichter Briefe von Johann Jakob Fugger, Antoine Perrenot de Granvelle und Orlando di Lasso." In *Festschrift fur Horst Leuchtmann zum 65. Geburtstag,* edited by Stephan Horner and Bernhold Schmid, 55–67. Tutzing: Schneider, 1993.

Bourgeois, Loys. *The Direct Road to Music (Le droict chemin de musique, 1550).* Translated by Bernarr Rainbow. Kilkenny: Boethius Press, 1982.

———. *Le droict chemin de musique.* Edited by P. André Gaillard. Vol. 1:6, Documenta musicologica. Geneva, 1550; reprint, Kassel: Bärenreiter, 1954.

———. *Le premier livre des pseaumes.* Edited by Pierre André Gaillard. Monuments de musique suisse, 3. Basel: Bärenreiter, 1960.

Brooks, Jeanice. "French Chanson Collections on the Texts of Pierre de Ronsard, 1570–1580." Ph.D. diss., The Catholic University of America, 1990.

———. "Italy, the Ancient World and the French Musical Inheritance in the Sixteenth Century: Arcadelt and Clereau in the Service of the Guises." *Journal of the Royal Musical Association* 121 (1996): 147–90.

———. "Jean de Castro, the Pense Partbooks and Musical Culture in Sixteenth-Century Lyons." *Early Music History* 11 (1992): 91–150.

———. "Music and Devotion in Renaissance Toulouse: The Motets of Guillaume Boni." In *"La musique de tous les passetemps le plus beau": Hommage à Jean-Michel Vaccaro,* edited by V. Coelho, F. Lesure, and H. Vanhulst, 17–31. Paris: Klincksieck, 1998.

———. "Ronsard, the Lyric Sonnet and the Late Sixteenth-Century Chanson." *Early Music History* 13 (1994): 65–84.

———. " 'Ses amours et les miennes tout ensemble:' la structure cyclique du *Premier livre* d'Anthoine de Bertrand (Paris 1576)." *Revue de musicologie* 74 (1988): 201–20.

Brown, Howard Mayer. "Theory and Practice in the Sixteenth Century: Preliminary Notes on Attaingnant's Modally Ordered Chansonniers." In *Essays in Musicology: A Tribute to Alvin Johnson,* edited by Lewis Lockwood and Edward Roesner. Philadelphia: American Musicological Society, 1990.

———. "*Ut musica poesis*: Music and Poetry in France in the Late Sixteenth Century." *Early Music History* 13 (1994): 1–64.

Burmeister, Joachim. *Musica poetica.* Documenta musicologica, 1. Reihe: Druckschriften-Faksimiles, 10. Rostock, 1606; reprint Kassel: Bärenreiter, 1955.

———. *Musical Poetics.* Translated by Benito V. Rivera. Music Theory Translation Series. New Haven and London: Yale University Press, 1993.

Castro, Jean de. *Il primo libro di madrigali, canzoni et motetti a tre voci (1569).* Edited by Ignace Bossuyt, *Jean de Castro Opera Omnia,* 3. Leuven: Leuven University Press, 1995.

Cave, Terence. *Devotional Poetry in France, c. 1570–1613.* Cambridge: Cambridge University Press, 1969.

———. "The Protestant Devotional Tradition: Simon Goulart's *Trente tableaux de la mort.*" *French Studies* 21 (1967): 1–15.

Certeau, Michel de. *The Writing of History.* Translated by T. Conley. New York: Columbia University Press, 1988.

Chandieu, Antoine de. *Octonaires sur la vanité et inconstance du monde.* Edited by Françoise Bonali-Fiquet. Geneva: Droz, 1979.

Chartier, Roger. *Cultural History: Between Practices and Representations.* Ithaca, N.Y.: Cornell University Press, 1988.

———. *The Cultural Uses of Print in Early Modern France.* Translated by Lydia G. Cochrane. Princeton, N.J.: Princeton University Press, 1987.

———. "Laborers and Voyagers: From the Text to the Reader." *Diacritics* 22 (1992): 26–37.

———, ed. *The Culture of Print: Power and the Uses of Print in Early Modern Europe.* Princeton: Princeton University Press, 1989.

Chatenay, Leopold. *La vie intellectuale en Aunis et en Saintonge de 1550 à 1610.* 2 vols. La Rochelle: Librairie Quartier latin, 1959.

Clive, H. P. "The Calvinist Attitude to Music, and Its Literary Aspects and Sources." *Bibliothèque d'humanisme et de renaissance* 19 (1957): 80–102, 294–319 and 20 (1958): 79–107.

Corrêa de Azevedo, Luiz Heitor. " 'Tupynamba' Melodies in Jean de Léry's *Histoire d'un voyage faict en la terre du Brésil.*" In *Papers of the American Musicological Society, Annual Meeting, 1941, Minneapolis, Minnesota.* Edited by Gustave Reese, (1946): 85–96:

Costeley, Guillaume. *Musique.* Edited by Henry Expert. 3 vols. Les Maîtres musiciens de la Renaissance française, 3, 18, 19. Paris, 1896; reprint, New York: Broude, 1963.

———. *Selected Chansons.* Edited by Jane Bernstein, *The Sixteenth Century Chanson,* 8. New York and London: Garland Publishing, 1989.

Crecquillon, Thomas. *Fourteen Chansons for Four Voices or Instruments ATTB.* Edited by Bernard Thomas. London: Pro Musica Edition, 1978.

Crook, David. *Orlando di Lasso's Imitation Magnificats for Counter-Reformation Munich.* Princeton, N.J.: Princeton University Press, 1994.

Davis, Natalie Zemon. "City Women and Religious Change." In *Society and Culture in Early Modern France,* 65–98. Stanford, Calif.: Stanford University Press, 1975.,

———. "Strikes and Salvation at Lyon." In *Society and Culture in Early Modern France,* 1–16. Stanford, Calif.: Stanford University Press, 1975.

Desgraves, Louis. *Les Haultin, 1571–1623.* Imprimerie à La Rochelle, 2. Travaux d'humanisme et renaissance, 34. Geneva: E. Droz, 1960.

———. "Les rélations entre les imprimeurs de Genève et de La Rochelle à la fin du xvie siècle." In *Cinq siècles d'imprimerie genevoise. Actes du colloque internationale sur l'histoire de l'imprimerie et du livre à Genève. 27–30 avril 1978,* edited by Jean–Daniel Candaux and Bernard Lescaze, 199–207. Geneva: Société d'histoire et d'archéologie, 1980–81.

Diefendorf, Barbara B. "The Huguenot Psalter and the Faith of French Protestants in the Sixteenth Century." In *Culture and Identity in Early Modern Europe (1500–1800): Essays in Honor of Natalie Zemon Davis,* edited by Barbara B. Diefendorf and C. Hesse, 41–63. Ann Arbor: University of Michigan Press, 1993.

Dobbins, Frank. "Lassus—Borrower or Lender: The Chansons." *Revue belge de musicologie* 39–40 (1985–86): 101–57.

———. *Music in Renaissance Lyons.* Oxford: Clarendon Press, 1992.

———. "Textual Sources and Compositional Techniques in the French Chansons of Orlandus Lassus." In *Orlandus Lassus and His Time. Colloquium Proceedings. Antwerpen 24–26.08.1994,* edited by Ignace Bossuyt, Eugeen Schreurs, and Annelies Wouters, 139–62. Yearbook of the Alamire Foundation, 1. Peer, Belgium: Alamire Foundation, 1996.

———, ed. *The Oxford Book of French Chansons.* Oxford: Oxford University Press, 1987.

Douen, Orentin. *Clément Marot et le psautier: Étude historique, littéraire, musicale et bibliographique.* 2 vols. Paris, 1878; reprint, Nieuwkoop: B. de Graaf, 1967.

Droz, Eugenie. "Pierre Haultin à Genève, ou la lutte pour la liberté." In *Chemins de l'hérésie. Textes et documents,* 373–78. Geneva: Droz, 1970–76.

Du Bartas, Guillaume Saluste. *La sepmaine.* 2 vols. Edited by Yvonne Bellenger. Paris: Klincksieck, 1981.

Eco, Umberto. *Interpretation and Overinterpretation.* Edited by Stefani Collini. Cambridge: Cambridge University Press, 1992.

———. "The Poetics of the Open Work." In *The Role of the Reader: Explorations in the Semiotics of Texts,* 47–66. Bloomington, Ind.: Indiana University Press, 1979.

Eisenstein, Elizabeth L. *The Printing Press as an Agent of Change: Communications and Cultural Transformations in Early Modern Europe.* 2 vols. Cambridge: Cambridge University Press, 1979.

———. *The Printing Revolution in Early Modern Europe.* Cambridge: Cambridge University Press, 1983.

Feldman, Martha. *City Culture and the Madrigal at Venice.* Berkeley: University of California Press, 1995.

Freedman, Richard. "Du Chemin's *Second livre* of 1549 and the Commerce of the French Chanson." In *Second livre de chansons à quatre. Nicolas Du Chemin, 1549,* v–xv. Paris, 1549; reprint, Tours: Centre de musique ancienne, 1993.

———. "*Pastourelle jolie*: The Chanson at the Court of Lorraine, ca. 1500." *Journal of the Royal Musical Association* 116 (1991): 161–200.

Fuller, Sarah. "Defending the *Dodecachordon*: Ideological Currents in Glarean's Modal Theory." *Journal of the American Musicological Society* 49 (1996): 191–224.

Gaillard, Paul André. *Loys Bourgeois, sa vie, son oeuvre comme pédagogue et compositeur: Essai biographique et critique, suivi d'une bibliographie et d'un appendice.* Lausanne: Imprimeries réunies, 1948.

Goudimel, Claude. *Œuvres complètes.* Edited by Pierre Pidoux. 14 vols. New York: Institute of Medieval Music, 1967.

———. *Premier, second, tiers fasicules des 150 Pseaumes.* Edited by Henry Expert. 3 vols. Maîtres musiciens de la renaissance française, 2, 4, 6. Paris; 1895–97; reprint New York: Broude, 1963.

Grafton, Anthony. "The Importance of Being Printed." *Journal of Interdisciplinary History* 2 (1980): 265–86.

Guillo, Laurent. *Les éditions musicales de la renaissance lyonnaise (1525–1615).* Domaine musicologique. Paris: Klincksieck, 1991.

———. "Le Psautier de Paris et le Psautier de Lyon: À propos de deux corpus contemporains du Psautier de Genève (1549–1561)." *Bulletin de la Société de l'histoire du protestantisme français* 136 (1990): 361–420.

Haag, Eugene. *La France protestante.* 2nd ed. 6 vols. Paris: Sandoz et Fischbacher, 1877–88.

Haar, James. "Orlando di Lasso, Composer and Print Entrepeneur." In *Music and the Cultures of Print,* edited by Kate van Orden, 125–62. New York: Garland Publishing, 2000.

Hauser, Henri. *François de la Nouë (1531–1591).* Paris, 1892; repint ed. Geneva: Slatkine Reprints, 1970.

Higman, Francis. "Genevan Printing and French Censorship." In *Cinq siècles d'imprimerie genevoise. Actes du Colloque international sur l'histoire de l'imprimerie et du livre à Genève. 27–30 avril 1978,* edited by Jean-Daniel Candaux and Bernard Lescaze, 31–54. Geneva: Société d'histoire et d'archéologie, 1980–81.

His, Isabelle. "Les *mélanges musicaux* au XVIe et au début du XVIIe siècle [avec une liste des ouvrages parus entre 1560 et ca. 1754]." *Nouvelle revue du XVIe siècle* 8 (1990): 95–110.

———. "*Les mélanges* de Claude Le Jeune (Anvers: Plantin, 1585): Transcription et étude critique." Ph.D. diss.: Université de Tours, 1990.

———. "Les modèles italiens de Claude Le Jeune." *Revue de musicologie* 77 (1991): 25–58.

Hoffmann, George. "The Montaigne Monopoly: Revising the *Essais* under the French Privilege System." *Publications of the Modern Language Association of America* 108 (1993): 308–19.

Holt, Mack P. *The French Wars of Religion, 1562–1629.* New Approaches to European History, 8. Cambridge: Cambridge University Press, 1995.

Honegger, Marc. "Les Chansons spirituelles de Didier Lupi et les débuts de la musique protestante en France au xvie siècle." Ph.D. diss., Université de Lille III, 1970.

Imbert, Henri François. "Lettres de Catherine de Parthenay, dame de Rohan-Soubise et de ses deux filles Henriette et Anne à Charlotte-Brabantine de Nassau, Duchesse de la Trémoille." *Mémoires de la Société de statistique des Deux-Sévres* 12 (1874): 43–161.

Jackson, Susan. "Berg and Neuber: Music Printers in Sixteenth-Century Nuremberg." Ph.D. diss., City University of New York, 1998.

Jacobs, Charles, ed. *Le Roy & Ballard's 1572 "Mellange de chansons."* University Park, Pa.: Pennsylvania State University, 1982.

Janequin, Clément. *Chansons polyphoniques.* Edited by A. Tillman Merritt and François Lesure. 6 vols. Monaco: L'Oiseau-lyre, 1967–71.

Jeanneret, Michel. *Poésie et tradition biblique au XVIe siècle: Recherches stylistiques sur les paraphrases des "Psaumes," de Marot à Malherbe.* Paris: J. Corti, 1969.

Jeffrey, Brian. "Thématique de la chanson entre 1480 et 1525." In *La chanson à la Renaissance. Actes du XXe colloque d'études humanistes du Centre d'études supérieures de la Renaissance de l'Université de Tours. Juillet 1977,* edited by Jean-Michel Vaccaro, 51–60. Tours: Editions Van de Velde, 1981.

Jensch, Fritz. "Orlando di Lassos *Lagrime di San Pietro* und ihr Text." *Die Musik in Bayern* 32 (1986): 43–62.

Jones, Leonard Chester. *Simon Goulart, 1543–1628: Étude biographique et bibliographique.* Geneva: Georg et Cie, 1917.

———. *Simon Goulart, sa vie et son oeuvre, 1543–1628.* Geneva: A. Kundig, 1916.

Keil, Charles, and Steven Feld. *Music Grooves: Essays and Dialogues.* Chicago: University of Chicago Press, 1994.

Kerman, Joseph. "An Elizabethan Edition of Lassus." *Acta Musicologica* 27 (1955): 71–76.

Kovarik, Edward. "The Parody Chansons of Certon's *Meslanges.*" In *Music and Context, Essays for John M. Ward,* edited by Anne D. Shapiro, 317–51. Cambridge, Mass.: Harvard University Press, 1985.

Krummel, Donald W. *English Music Printing, 1553–1700.* London: The Bibliographical Society, 1975.

L'Estocart, Pascal. *Premier livre des Octonaires de la vanité du monde.* Edited by Henry Expert, Monuments de la musique française au temps de la Renaissance, 10. Paris, 1929; reprint New York: Broude, 1960.

La Laurencie, Lionel de. *Chansons au luth et airs de cour français du xvie siècle.* Paris: Heugel, 1934.

Lasso, Orlando di. *Chansons from the Atelier of Le Roy and Ballard.* Edited by Jane Bernstein. 4 vols. The Sixteenth–Century Chanson, 11–14. New York: Garland, 1987.

———. *The Four-Language Print for Four and Eight Voices (Munich, 1573).* Edited by Peter Bergquist, Recent Researches in the Music of the Renaissance, 102. Madison, Wis.: A-R Editions, 1995.

———. *Motets for Six Voices from "Primus liber concentuum sacrorum" (Paris, 1564); Motets for Four to Ten Voices from "Modulorum secundum volumen" (Paris, 1565).* Edited by Peter Bergquist, The Complete Motets, 4. Recent Researches in the Music of the Renaissance, 105. Madison, Wis.: A-R Editions, 1996.

Lasso, Orlando di. *Orlando di Lasso Sämtliche Werke,* ed. F. X. Haberl and A. Sandberger, rev. ed, edited by Hörst Leuchtmann, 21 vols. Leipzig, 1894; reprint, Leipzig and Wiesbaden, Breitkopf und Härtel, 1968–1990.

———. *The "Seven Penitential Psalms" and "Laudate Dominum de caelis".* Edited by Peter Bergquist. 2 vols. Recent Researches in the Music of the Renaissance, 86–87. Madison, Wisconsin: A-R Editions, 1990.

Le Jeune, Claude. *Dodecacorde: Comprising Twelve Psalms of David Set to Music According to the Twelve Modes.* Edited by Anne Harrington Heider. 3 vols. Recent Researches in the Music of the Renaissance, 74–76. Madison, Wis.: A-R Editions, 1988.

———. *Octonaires de la vanité et inconstance du monde.* Edited by Henry Expert. Maître musiciens français au temps de la Renaissance, 1, 8. Paris, 1924; reprint New York: Broude, 1960.

Le Roy, Adrian. *Traicté de musique.* Edited by Máire Egan-Buffet. Musicological Studies, 66. Paris, 1583; reprint Ottawa, Canada: Institute of Mediaeval Music, 1996.

———, ed. *Les instructions pour le luth (1574).* Edited by Jean–Michel Vaccaro, Jean Jacquot, and Pierre–Yves Sordes. 2 vols. Corpus des luthistes français. Paris: Éditions du Centre national du la recherche scientifique, 1977.

Léry, Jean de. *Histoire d'un voyage fait en la terre du Brésil.* Edited by Jean–Claude Morisot. Les Classiques de la pensée politique, 9. Geneva,

1580; reprint, Geneva: Droz, 1975.

———. *History of a Voyage to the Land of Brazil, Otherwise Called America*. Translated by Janet Whatley. Berkeley: University of California Press, 1990.

Lestringant, Frank. "Millénarisme et âge d'or: Réformation et expériences coloniales au Brésil et en Floride (1555–1565)." In *Les Réformes, enracinement socio-culturel. XXVième Colloque international d'études humanistes. Tours, 1–13 juilliet, 1982*. Edited by C. Chevalier, 25–42. Paris: Éditions de la maisnie, 1985.

Lesure, François. "Autour de Clément Marot et ses musiciens." *Revue de musicologie* 33 (1951): 109–19.

———, and Geneviève Thibault. *Bibliographie des éditions d'Adrian Le Roy et Robert Ballard, 1551–1598*. Paris: Heugel, 1955.

Leuchtmann, Horst. *Orlando di Lasso*. 2 vols. Wiesbaden: Breitkopf und Härtel, 1976.

Levy, Kenneth Jay. " 'Susanne un jour': The History of a 16th-Century Chanson." *Annales musicologiques* 1 (1953): 375–408.

Macey, Patrick. "The *Lauda* and the Cult of Savonarola." *Renaissance Quarterly* 45 (1992): 439–83.

Manchicourt, Pierre de. *Twenty-Nine Chansons*. Edited by Margery Anthea Baird. Recent Researches in the Music of the Renaissance, 11. Madison, Wis.: A-R Editions, 1972.

Marot, Clément. *Œuvres poétiques complètes*. Edited by Gérard Defaux. 2 vols. Classiques Garnier. Paris: Bordas, 1990.

Meier, Bernhard. "Bemerkungen zu Lechners *Motectae sacrae* von 1575." *Archiv für Musikwissenschaft* 14 (1957): 83–101.

———. *The Modes of Classical Vocal Polyphony*. Translated by Ellen S. Beebe. New York: Broude, 1988.

———. "Rhetorical Aspects of the Renaissance Modes." *Journal of the Royal Musical Association* 115 (1990): 183–90.

Menanteau, Pierre, ed. *Images d'André Mage de Fiefmelin, poète baroque*. Limoges: Rougerie, 1965.

Meyer, Judith Pugh. *Reformation in La Rochelle: Tradition and Change in Early Modern Europe, 1500–1568*. Travaux d'humanism et renaissance, 298. Geneva: Droz, 1996.

Millot, Nicholas. *Unpublished Chansons Issued by Le Roy and Ballard*. Edited by Jane Bernstein. The Sixteenth–Century Chanson, 18. New York: Garland Publishing, 1991.

Milsom, John. "Tallis, Byrd, and the 'Incorrected' Copy: Some Cautionary Notes for Editors of Early Music Printed from Type." *Music and Letters* 67 (1996): 348–67.

Nicholls, David. "The Social History of the French Reformation: Ideology, Confession, and Culture." *Social History* 9 (1984): 25–43.

Nicot, Jean, ed. *Thrésor de la langue françoise, tant ancienne que moderne*.

Paris, 1606; reprint, Paris: Picard, 1960.

O'Brien, John. "Ronsard, Belleau and Renvoisy." *Early Music History* 13 (1994): 199–216.

Ouvrard, Jean-Pierre. "Modality and Text Expression in 16th-Century French Chansons: Remarks Concerning the E Mode." *Basler Jahrbuch für historische Musikpraxis* 16 (1992): 89–104.

———. "Pour le rondeau en forme mettre. . . : Mon confesseur, rondeau de Clément Janequin." *Revue de Musicologie* 64 (1978): 203–28.

———. "Le sonnet ronsardien en musique: Du Supplément de 1552 à 1580." *Revue de musicologie* 74 (1988): 149–64.

Palisca, Claude. "*Ut Oratorica Musica*: The Rhetorical Basis of Musical Mannerism." In *The Meaning of Mannerism,* edited by Franklin.W. Robinson and Stephen G. Nichols, 37–65. Hanover, N.H.: University Press of New England, 1972.

Palissy, Bernard de. *Recepte véritable,* edited by Keith Cameron. Text littéraires français. Geneva: Droz, 1988.

Pidoux, Pierre. "Les Origines de l'impression de musique à Genève." In *Cinq siècles d'imprimerie genevoise. Actes du Colloque international sur l'histoire de l'imprimerie et du livre à Genève. 27–30 avril 1978,* edited by Jean-Daniel Candaux and Bernard Lescaze, 97–108. Geneva: Société d'histoire et d'archéologie, 1980–81.

Pidoux, Pierre, ed. *Le Psautier huguenot du XVIe siècle: Mélodies et documents.* 2 vols. Basel: Bärenreiter, 1962.

Pineaux, Jacques. *La poésie des protestants de langue française, du premier synode national jusqu'à la proclamation de l'édit de Nantes (1559–1598).* Bibliotheque française et romaine. Paris: Klincksieck, 1971.

———. "La poésie religieuse." In *Précis de littérature française du XVIe siècle: La Renaissance,* edited by Robert Aulotte, 214–228. Paris: Presses universitaires de France, 1992.

———. *La polémique protestante contre Ronsard.* Paris: M. Didier, 1973.

———. "Simon Goulart et les voies du sacré." *Bulletin de la Société de l'histoire du protestantisme français* 135 (1989): 161–76.

Pohlmann, Hansjorg. *Frühgeschichte des musikalischen Urheberrechts ca. 1400–1800 .* Basel: Bärenreiter, 1962.

Powers, Harold S. "Anomalous Modalities." In *Orlando di Lasso in der Musikgeschichte. Bericht über das Symposium der Bayerischen Akademie der Wissenschaften. München, 4–6. Juli 1994,* edited by Bernhold Schmid, 221–42. Munich: Bayerischen Akademie der Wissenschaften, 1996.

———. "Modal Representation in Polyphonic Offertories." *Early Music History* 2 (1982): 43–86.

———. "Tonal Types and Modal Categories in Renaissance Polyphony." *Journal of the American Musicological Society* 34 (1981): 428–70.

Randall, Catharine. *Building Codes: The Aesthetics of Calvinism in Early*

Modern Europe. New Cultural Studies. Philadelphia: University of Pennsylvania Press, 1999.

Rasch, Rudolf. "The *Livre septième.*" In *Atti del XIV Congresso della Società Internazionale di Musicologia, Bologna, 27 aug.–1 sept. 1987,* edited by Angelo Pompilio et al., 306–418. Turin: Edizioni di Torino, 1990.

Reichert, Georg. "Martin Crusius und die Musik in Tübingen um 1590." *Archiv für Musikwissenschaft* 10 (1953): 185–212.

Richter, Mario. *Il "Discours de la vie et de la mort" di Philippe du Plessis-Mornay.* Milan: Editrice vita et pensiero, 1964.

Robbins, Kevin C. "The Social Mechanisms of Urban Rebellion: A Case Study of Leadership in the 1614 Revolt at La Rochelle." *French Historical Studies* 19 (1995): 559–90.

Rodocanachi, Emmanuel. *Une protectrice de la réforme en Italie et en France: Renée de France duchesse de Ferrare.* Paris, 1896; reprint, Geneva: Slatkine, 1970.

Ronsard, Pierre de. *Œuvres complètes.* Edited by Paul Laumonnier. 18 vols. Paris: Hachette, 1921–67.

Simonin, Michel. "Les contrefaçons lyonnaises de Montaigne et de Ronsard au temps de la Ligue." In *Les presses grises: La contrefaçon du livre (XVIe–XIXe siècles),* edited by François Moureau, 139–53. Paris: Aux Amateurs de livres, 1988.

Sternfeld, Frederick William. "Vautrollier's Printing of Lasso's *Recueil du Mellange* (London, 1570)." *Annales musicologiques* 5 (1957): 199–227.

Strunk, Oliver, ed. *Source Readings in Music History,* rev. ed., edited by Leo Treitler. New York: W. W. Norton and Co., 1998.

Thibault, Geneviève, and L. Perceau. *Bibliographie des poésies de P. de Ronsard mises en musique au XVIe siècle.* Paris: Droz, 1941.

Thompson, John Lee. *John Calvin and the Daughters of Sarah: Women in Regular and Exceptional Roles in the Exegesis of Calvin, His Predecessors, and His Contemporaries.* Travaux d'humanisme et renaissance, 259. Geneva: Droz, 1992.

Tomlinson, Gary. *Music in Renaissance Magic: Towards a Historiography of Others.* Chicago: University of Chicago Press, 1993.

Trocmé, Étienne, and Marcel Delafosse. *Le commerce rochelais de la fin du XVe siècle au début du XVIIe.* Paris: Armand Colin, 1952.

Vaccaro, Jean-Michel. *La musique de luth en France au xvie siècle.* Paris: Éditions du Centre national du la recherche scientifique, 1981.

―――. "Les préfaces d'Anthoine de Bertrand." *Revue de musicologie* 74 (1988): 221–36.

van Orden, Kate. "Imitation and 'La musique des anciens': Le Roy et Ballard's 1572 *Mellange de chansons.*" *Revue de musicologie* 80 (1994): 5–37.

————. "Vernacular Culture and the Chanson in Paris, 1570–1580." Ph.D. diss., University of Chicago, 1996.

Vanhulst, Henri. *Catalogue des éditions de musique publiées à Louvain par Pierre Phalèse et ses fils, 1545–1578*. Bruxelles: Palais des Académies, 1984.

————. "Lassus et ses éditeurs: Remarques à propos de deux lettres peu connues." *Revue belge de musicologie* 39–40 (1985–1986): 80–100.

————. "Un succès de l'édition musicale: *Le septième livre des chansons à quatre parties* (1560–1661/3)." *Revue belge de musicologie* 32–33 (1978–79): 97–120.

Wardropper, Bruce W. "The Religious Conversion of Profane Poetry." In *Studies in the Continental Background of Renaissance English Literature: Essays Presented to John L. Lievsan*, edited by D. Randall and G. W. Williams, 203–21. Durham, N.C.: Duke University Press, 1977.

Watt, Tessa. *Cheap Print and Popular Piety, 1550–1640*, Cambridge Studies in Early Modern British History. Cambridge: Cambridge University Press, 1991.

Whitebrook, John Cudworth. *Calvin's Institute of Christian Religion in the Imprints of Thomas Vautrollier*. London: A. W. Cannon, 1935.

Zarlino, Gioseffo. *On the Modes: Part Four of "Le istitutioni harmoniche," 1558*. Translated by Vered Cohen. Edited by Claude V. Palisca. New Haven: Yale University Press, 1983.

Selective Discography of Lasso's Chansons

Chansons. Performed by the Ricercar Consort. Ricercar RIC 154149

Chansons and Madrigals. Performed by the Toronto Consort. Dorian Discovery DIS 80149

Deftige Lieder und Chansons. Performed by the Münchener Motettenchor. Christophorus CHE 009.2

Meslanges. Performed by the Ensemble polyphonique de France. Telefunken AW 41934 and AW 6.42281

Stabat Mater; In monte Oliveti; Cum natus esset Jesus; Chansons. Performed by the Hilliard Ensemble. Virgin CDM 5.61166.2

Index